The Management of Change in Universities

SRHE and Open University Press Imprint
General Editor: Heather Eggins

Current titles include:

Ronald Barnett: *Improving Higher Education*
Ronald Barnett: *Learning to Effect*
Ronald Barnett: *The Limits of Competence*
Ronald Barnett: *The Idea of Higher Education*
Tony Becher: *Governments and Professional Education*
Robert Bell and Malcolm Tight: *Open Universities: A British Tradition?*
Hazel Bines and David Watson: *Developing Professional Education*
Jean Bocock and David Watson: *Managing the Curriculum*
David Boud *et al.*: *Using Experience for Learning*
John Earwaker: *Helping and Supporting Students*
Roger Ellis: *Quality Assurance for University Teaching*
Gavin J. Fairbairn and Christopher Winch: *Reading, Writing and Reasoning: A Guide for Students*
Shirley Fisher: *Stress in Academic Life*
Diana Green: *What is Quality in Higher Education?*
Susanne Haselgrove: *The Student Experience*
Jill Johnes and Jim Taylor: *Performance Indicators in Higher Education*
Ian McNay: *Visions of Post-compulsory Education*
Robin Middlehurst: *Leading Academics*
Henry Miller: *The Management of Change in Universities*
Jennifer Nias: *The Human Nature of Learning: Selections from the Work of M.L.J. Abercrombie*
Keith Noble: *Changing Doctoral Degrees*
Gillian Pascall and Roger Cox: *Women Returning to Higher Education*
Graham Peeke: *Mission and Change*
Moira Peelo: *Helping Students with Study Problems*
Kjell Raaheim *et al.*: *Helping Students to Learn*
Tom Schuller: *The Future of Higher Education*
Michael Shattock: *The UGC and the Management of British Universities*
Geoffrey Squires: *First Degree*
Ted Tapper and Brian Salter: *Oxford, Cambridge and the Changing Idea of the University*
Kim Thomas: *Gender and Subject in Higher Education*
Malcolm Tight: *Higher Education: A Part-time Perspective*
David Warner and Gordon Kelly: *Managing Educational Property*
David Warner and Charles Leonard: *The Income Generation Handbook*
Sue Wheeler and Jan Birtle: *A Handbook for Personal Tutors*
Thomas G. Whiston and Roger L. Geiger: *Research and Higher Education*
Gareth Williams: *Changing Patterns of Finance in Higher Education*
John Wyatt: *Commitment to Higher Education*

The Management of Change in Universities

Universities, State and Economy in Australia, Canada and the United Kingdom

Henry D.R. Miller

The Society for Research into Higher Education
& Open University Press

To my parents Norah Miller and Henry W.L. Miller
and my children Alan and Kate

Published by SRHE and
Open University Press
Celtic Court
22 Ballmoor
Buckingham
MK18 1XW

and 1900 Frost Road, Suite 101
Bristol, PA 19007, USA

First published 1995

A catalogue record of this book is available from the British Library

ISBN 0-335-19089-8

Library of Congress Cataloging-in-Publication Data is available

Typeset by Graphicraft Typesetters Limited, Hong Kong
Printed in Great Britain by St Edmundsbury Press,
Bury St Edmunds, Suffolk

Contents

Acknowledgements

I have many acknowledgements to make to all the academics and academic managers, secretarial and administrative staff in twenty universities in Australia, Canada and the United Kingdom who gave me their time and attention, answered questions and provided material which provided the basis for this book. I would like to thank in particular:

In Australia:
For hospitality, help and stimulating discussion, Sue Robertson at Edith Cowan University and her husband Victor Socek, Don Smart and David Tripp at Murdoch University, Bob Meyenn at Charles Sturt University and his wife Val, and their children Natalie, John and David, Colin Hockley in Melbourne, John Smyth at Deakin and Roger Woock at Melbourne University, William and Jill Smith in Canberra and my uncle Dick Hedges, his wife Olive and son Michael.

In Canada:
Thanks to Jane and Bill Coombe in Victoria, Lawrence Pinfield of Simon Fraser University, and his wife Caroline in Vancouver. Raj Pannu of the University of Alberta and his family in Edmonton were particularly helpful as were Andy Hargreaves and Sandy Acker at OISE in Toronto and Jean-Pierre Réverèt at l'Université de Québec à Montrèal.

In the United Kingdom:
In England I appreciated help from ex-colleagues and Miriam David at South Bank University in London and Terry Mandrell and Christine Hardy at the University of Central England in Birmingham. In Scotland, thanks to Doug Carroll and his colleagues at Glasgow Caledonian University. In Northern Ireland, Merlyn and Desmond Bell and Penny Holloway and their colleagues at the University of Ulster gave invaluable help and hospitality.

Various people have read and commented on one or two chapters. These include John Bowen of Keele University, Alan Jones of University, Polytechnic of East Anglia, Fred Steward and Geoff Walford at Aston University and Jan Birtle and Sue Wheeler at Birmingham University, Sue contributed much to Chapter Five.

At the Aston University Business School I have benefited from the support and critical discussion of Peter Clark, Ian Glendon, Dian Hosking, Gloria Lee, Roger Lumley, Viv Shackleton and Dennis and Chris Smith. Fred Steward as Director of Business School Research encouraged and facilitated throughout. John Fletcher, Vice President and Mike Cooke, Secretary, and fellow members of the Aston Branch of the Association of University Teachers, together with Martin Machon, Regional Official and John Akker the then Deputy General Secretary gave insight and support in dealing with university management. Yvonne Greenop and Gillian Woolvern and the library at the Association of Commonwealth Universities provided much help and very useful material. Thanks to Denise Griffin who did most of the index.

For material support I am indebted to Edith Cowan University for a Research Fellowship for two months in 1991, to the Canadian Studies Research Program for a grant for research in Canada in the same year and to the University of Aston's Business School Professionalism Research Group.

Thanks and appreciation for secretarial and administrative support to Edna Bland, Jenny Green and Pat Newman of the Organization Studies and Applied Psychology Office and to Beryl Hodder, Jane Winder, Julie Ellen and Pat Clark in the Business School Research Office who word-processed various drafts and provided administrative and sometimes editorial expertise. In a university where many staff are on short term contracts they were models of professionalism and commitment.

At the Open University Press, John Skelton, Pat Lee and Sue Hadden provided the understanding and skill which ensured the book got to publication.

Papers given at conferences and in seminars at Edith Cowan, McQuarie and Murdoch universities in Australia, and Aston, Central England and Warwick universities and Coombe Lodge Staff College in England, and to the 8th Congress of World Council of Comparative Education Societies at Charles University, Prague, Czechoslovakia and the Comparative and International Education Society conference in Kingston, Jamaica, gave me the opportunity to present work in progress and to benefit from criticism and comment.

Thanks to family and friends for their tolerance of my time consuming concern to write about management and universities, in particular to Alan and Kate, Helen and Hugh and their families and to past and present inhabitants of 42 Grove Avenue, John and Sally, Christine, Fiona, Tess, Marie, Patries and Julie. They have all helped more than they perhaps realize. Greatest thanks for their patience and crucial support to Marvin, Caroline and Sue Wheeler.

Acknowledgement is due to the University of California Press for permission to use a diagram from Burton Clark's *The Higher Education System* (1983). I have adapted previously published work on *The Academic Labour Process* (1991) and *The State of the Academic Profession* (1993) for Chapters One, Five and Six.

1

Developments in Higher Education in Australia, Canada and the United Kingdom

'Management' and the 'market' became increasingly important concepts in the changing culture of higher education institutions during the 1980s. This book examines how these changes came about in Australia, Canada and the United Kingdom. It discusses ways in which managerialism and market forces have modified or came to dominate the governance and culture of universities, polytechnics and colleges, and how such changes relate to established forms of collegiality, professionalism and bureaucratic administrative cultures.

The varying meanings and impacts of management and market on higher education will be explored in interrelated ways. First, the book gives a brief historical account of the main characteristics of the higher education systems in Australia, Canada and the UK. It focuses on developments in governance since the Second World War, with particular reference to the last two decades. There follows a discussion in Chapters 2 and 3 of the relationships of state and economy to the management of universities. In Chapter 4 there is description and analysis at the institutional level of university management. As well as documentary sources, the book utilizes the perceptions and comments of senior academics, such as deputy vice-chancellors, deans and heads of department, who in the new climate have come to occupy managerial roles. In Chapter 5 a case study account is given of one university's management. In the final chapter, I draw together the various threads of the argument about the relationships between state, economy and the management of universities, and how these affect the situation and work of academics. There are continuing themes about the nature, purpose and control of academic work, particularly 'professionalism' and 'proletarianization' and the 'corporatist' character of the states, economies and management structures and styles. I comment on the various theoretical perspectives used and their applicability, and the prospects and choices for the future.

Theory and method

Why Australia, Canada and the UK? Comparative studies of higher education have included wide-ranging ambitious accounts spanning the world, the most prominent of which is probably Clark's *The Higher Education System* (1983), collections of essays on themes or countries, as well as conference papers detailing their authors' impressions of another country's system, sometimes making a comparison with the home country. There are at least two advantages to the comparative method. First, by studying more than one system, it may be possible to discuss some underlying patterns or dynamics which can transcend the specifics of a single culture, and in this case to show something more general about the nature of governance of academics in teaching and research institutions in relation to the states and economies of advanced industrialized societies. Second, the investigator, although apparently familiar with his or her own relationship to national, regional, class, professional, academic and institutional cultures finds, when confronted with another set of cultures and institutions, that the institutions in the home country are seen in a different light, thus revealing features not previously apparent.

In this case, the comparisons, although widely separated geographically, are in other respects quite close. The UK and its constituent countries – England, Wales, Scotland and Northern Ireland – the states and Commonwealth of Australia, and the provinces and federal state of Canada, were (in different relations of domination and subordination) all part of the British Empire and latterly the Commonwealth. In terms of contemporary political economy, all three nations are capitalist liberal democracies with advanced industrial economies, and each has had to deal with considerable unemployment, balance of trade and budget deficits. They now face stiff competition from the newly industrialized nations, in addition to the USA, Germany and Japan.

The dominant language in all three is English, although clearly French in Quebec and to a degree Welsh in Wales challenge that dominance. In all three nations there has been considerable population movement. The populations of Canada and Australia both before the Second World War and more recently grew significantly through immigration as well as by natural increase. In terms of the higher education systems, there is also considerable movement of staff between the three countries; initially, this was primarily composed of British academics moving to Australia and Canada.

The universities in the three countries share enough characteristics to make them recognizably the same sort of institution, engaging in research and teaching, largely supported from public funds, yet having a degree of autonomy. Higher education as a sector has been predominantly publicly funded and controlled in all three countries, there being few significant private higher education institutions, as in the USA and Japan.

The comparisons attempted are specific and focused. There is no attempt to come to grips with the complexities and size of the US higher education system, nor of the very different systems of the major countries of the European Union like France and Germany. Nevertheless, it is recognized that the US system has had an important influence not only in Canada, but also in Australia and the UK, in part as a model but also as a source of academic personnel and as a destination for faculty dissatisfied with their own systems. Also, the increasingly close political economic and social links within the European Union make the characteristics of the higher education institutions of mainland Europe of increasing relevance to developments in universities and colleges in the UK. Thus some reference will be made to US and European higher education and the role of the Organization for Economic Cooperation and Development (OECD) in terms of comparisons and agenda-setting.

Although there is much in common between the three countries, there are important differences, including the historical development of the various educational systems and the different nature of the states concerned – unitary (UK), and 'soft' (Canada) and 'hard' (Australia) federal systems. There are also differences in general economic structure, the way institutions are organized and the degree of differentiation within the three systems. These differences are sufficient to make for a range of useful comparisons of specific arrangements, which in the institutions of a single country might go unchallenged because they have become part of the unexamined common sense of the institutional culture.

While familiar with the higher education institutions of the UK, I came as a comparative stranger to those of Australia and Canada. There are advantages and disadvantages to both familiarity and strangeness: an understanding of the nuances of familiar institutional management on the one hand is balanced by a tendency to accept too readily the given order of things. On the other hand, coming new to a university in Canada or Australia, one could ask a naive question and receive a direct and maybe more illuminating answer than a native researcher. These strengths and weaknesses inherent in any comparative work are reflected in this account.

The research reported here involved visiting 20 universities in Australia, Canada and the UK, which led to an awareness of the physical location of each university, its place in the country, its distance from the next institution, its relationship to its city and community. I experienced each university in terms of coherence or dispersal, accessibility, clarity, its position on a hill, by the sea, in the bush, the beauty or otherwise of its buildings, the car parking facilities, its proximity to public transport and the degree of security. Inside the buildings, how easy it was to find one's way about, how helpful and friendly were people. There was the crucial negotiation of access to academics, often through secretaries – always female, usually friendly, efficient and courteous, sometimes motherly. The context and dynamics of the interview itself – degree of formality and informality, seating arrangements and the nature of the interaction with other members of the academic and secretarial staff – often gave clues to managerial style. And there was always the characteristics of the physical environment – landscape, buildings, spaces, rooms, chairs, decor, books, telephones, computers, insignia – and the social arrangements embodied in them. Descriptions and metaphors drawing from geography, landscape and perspective seemed attractive and natural, both substantively and symbolically.

The study focuses on various perspectives on the purposes of the university and the choices, initiatives and responses of academic management. It places these within the wider landscape of political, economic and institutional structures and processes. Within and at times pervading that analysis is the importance of language, its use and context, and the discourses within which academics are located and define themselves and their choices.

A discussion by Bowe *et al.* (1992) of the problems of methodology in researching parental choice may prove useful in understanding the approach taken. Bowe *et al.* refer to the distinction that Grace (1991) makes between policy research and policy scholarship: *policy research* can be seen as investigation of how institutions or governments meet the objectives of stated policy; *policy scholarship* is presented as a deeper analysis of the roots, assumptions and implications of the development of policies. In the case of university management, this means that it is possible to go beyond questions of how far government or institutional policy has been effective in policy research terms to the central matters of meaning, value orientation and power which lie behind the publicly presented definitions of the work of universities and university management.

In presenting pictures, or rather snapshots, of the institutional management of higher education in the three countries, official accounts and figures are inevitably presented in a positivistic mode. Even when using interview techniques, the search for factors and exploration of problems and answers is partly predefined by the participants in the interview. It could be argued that a large-scale survey, or statistical analysis, might give a more coherent, quantitative account. This latter approach was not adopted, in part because of resources but also because it was felt to be important to try to capture the personal perspectives of the academics who were managing the universities. Bowe *et al.* (1992) argue that all sociological methods use metaphors and advocate the metaphor 'landscape of choice' drawn from geography. 'Landscape, whether in the physical environment or in the form of a painting, does not exist without an observer although the land exists . . . Mentally or physically, we frame the view, and our appreciation depends upon our frame of mind' (Porteous 1990: 4; Bowe *et al.* 1992: 13).

Substituting academic managers for parents making choices, we arrive at the statement that:

> [Academic managers] are the active observers and participants in landscapes of choice. They are both *of* it and *in* it. However, this landscape is full of complex and contradictory 'messages', choice is 'framed' by location by material and social circumstances . . . the experience of choice [of management style, structure or objectives] is of a landscape that is neither flat nor unidimensional, nor linear nor ordered nor tidy.

> Decision making involves not merely inductive or deductive but also reductive moments. Information is rarely complete, decisions often seem only to be 'the best that can be done', provisional and fragile. From where one stands aspects of the landscape may be 'out of sight' and moving across a landscape changes the 'way things look'. Decisions are made about the possibilities available on the basis of look, feel and judgement, as well as rational reflection.
>
> (Bowe *et al.* 1992: 13)

It may be that academic managers are in possession of more rationally organized information than the average parent who chooses a school. Academics often subscribe to a rational model of decision making and usually will have been trained in a discipline and sometimes in managerial analysis. Whatever their situation, the institutional, social, economic and governmental constraints force a partial perspective on the landscape of managerial choice. Moreover, the language within which information, policy and decisions are presented to and by them is, within a set of particular discourses, the product and producer of specific power relations. Attention to viewpoint, perspective and mapping is important in the building of a picture of the structures and processes of managing universities.

In this chapter, the theoretical perspective is left largely implicit. However, the foregoing comments on method indicate a sympathy for a social action approach that takes seriously the intentions and actions of the *individuals* involved in university governance. At the same time, by taking into account the economic, political and institutional contexts, there is a recognition of the utility of Marxist, Weberian and functionalist approaches, which focus on particular problems in the relationship between universities and higher education as a system of the economy and state. This is implicit in the largely descriptive account which follows of the development of higher education in Australia, Canada and the UK.

Between March and December 1991, just over 100 interviews were conducted with senior academic managers – vice-chancellors, deans and heads of department – and union and staff association representatives in 15 universities, two of them at the time designated polytechnics. In Australia, senior staff and union representatives were interviewed in six universities in Western Australia and in New South Wales. In Canada, interviews were conducted in six universities in the provinces of British Columbia, Alberta, Ontario and Quebec. In the UK, the study included new universities, former polytechnics – one in England and one in Scotland – and a university in Northern Ireland. The account is also based on previous work by Miller (1991a) and Walford (1987) on Aston University's management, and by Samut (1986), Palfreyman (1988) and Sheffield (1990) on management and enterprise in six English universities.

The interviews usually lasted between 45 and 90 minutes and were conducted in the respondent's office and were in almost all cases tape-recorded. A checklist of questions was used which differed only slightly between the three countries (see the Appendix), but often the interview topics ranged well beyond this format. A degree of confidentiality and anonymity was negotiated. No-one is quoted by name, but reference to position and institution are given in order for the account to be meaningful. Quite often, 'off the record' comments were offered, which have been used so as to present the reader with a clearer picture. The term 'central administrator' is used to refer to vice-chancellors and directors and their deputies. An earlier paper of mine (Miller 1991b) was circulated to the interviewees in the three countries, with a request for comments, corrections and permission to quote. This account has benefited from the sometimes quite detailed replies.

My background and perspective is germane both to the way in which the study was conducted and also how the interview materials were interpreted. My background is in the sociology of education and industrial sociology, and my teaching experience was gained in a technical college and polytechnic in London, a college of education in Scotland and a technological university in Birmingham. Activity in trades unions – the Association of Teachers in Technical Institutions (ATTI) and the Association of University Teachers (AUT) – has certainly shaped my perspective, as has membership of my university's senate and council. Some or all of this background was revealed to the respondents, especially those who were union officials. I found that although I wasn't directly involved in senior academic management, I was able to establish some sort of rapport with most of the respondents. Indeed, I found myself becoming ever more sympathetic and appreciative of the pressures and problems they faced, while not always agreeing with the strategies or solutions they proposed.

One of the problems about writing a contemporary comparative account of the management of change in universities is one of nomenclature. This was reflected in a change in the proposed title of the book from 'The Management of Change in Higher Education' to 'The Management of Change in Universities'. This in part reflects a shift in focus from an examination of process and system to one of institutional management. It also represents an attempt to engage with the problem of what to call higher education institutions. In the period 1988–93, first in Australia and then in the UK, the funding and structure of the system changed from a binary to a unified one. Higher education institutions in Australia ('colleges of advanced education') and the UK ('polytechnics') have been designated 'universities'. Part of the purpose of this book is to examine the nature of that change and the different cultures and management styles of the different institutions, how they interact, and how they are developing and adapting to the pressures of a unified system. This has presented difficulties in naming institutions, particularly as many of the interviews in the UK in 1991 and 1992 were in institutions which were then polytechnics. I refer to 'old' and 'new' universities, and ex-colleges of advanced education and ex-polytechnics. In the UK, many of the polytechnics were teaching at degree level before universities like Warwick or redesignated colleges of advanced technology like Aston or Salford, which were established in the 1960s. London polytechnics like Regent Street and the Borough were established at the end of the nineteenth century and the University of the West of England, ex-Bristol Polytechnic, notes in its publicity that its origins can be traced to fifteenth-century institutions. An alternative designation would be to differentiate between 'private' universities and 'public' polytechnics or colleges. Certainly, the British polytechnics were publicly funded and administered by local education authorities until 1988, and thus contrasted with the 'private' universities incorporated by Royal Charter. However, by the 1940s, the predominance of public funds as well as increasing state control makes the designation 'private' inappropriate, particularly when contrasted with 'private' universities like Buckingham in England or Bond in Australia or the private as opposed to state universities in the USA.

The problem about naming represents a deeper difficulty about the description and analysis of the development of universities. A discussion of the nature and designation of towns by Bartlett (1993) in his study of *The Making of Europe* provides a useful analogy. Bartlett points out that settlements have been described as towns when they meet certain criteria – relative size, density of settlement, division of labour, the presence of commercial activity or a trading or market centre. In a similar way, one might see an educational institution as having the characteristics of a university, if it engaged in teaching at degree level, taught students of a certain age, employed academics who engaged in research, had a degree of self-governance or was of a certain minimum size. But there has been for both 'towns' and 'universities' a process of designation, often by the giving of a charter by some superior political authority, monarch, church, feudal lord or state. This process of designation as a 'town' or 'university' confirms its legal status, often giving it rights, duties and a system of governance. This often occurs because the settlement or institution has already acquired the characteristics of a 'town' or 'university', but the designation or giving of a charter – the renaming of 'polytechnics' as 'universities', for example – makes not just a legal difference to the cultural characteristics and activities of the institution. Just as the legal status of 'town' brought with it certain liberties and exemptions from taxation and control by feudal lords, which encouraged the development of trade and industry, so the title of university and concomitant change in methods of funding, governance and control may provide the opportunity for the development of research or higher degree work that was not possible previously.

Before turning to the perspectives, perceptions and account, which senior academics and union representatives provided, of the pressures from the state and the economy on universities and their strategies for dealing with those pressures, it is necessary to briefly sketch the factors that have affected the functioning of universities within the higher education systems in Australia, Canada and the UK. The background information used covers the post-war period, but focuses in particular on the last decade. In doing this, an outline is provided of the relationships between developments in the political economy and discourses relating to political and educational policy and decision making in each country. This is explored further in subsequent chapters on the state, the economy and institutional management.

There has been a substantial movement of academics between Australian universities and colleges of advanced education, Canadian universities and UK universities and polytechnics. The ideas that inform the dominant political discourse have flowed between the three countries and often found common ground. The influence of political and economic ideas developed in the USA by Milton Friedman, the Chicago School and Reagonomics have directly – or mediated by Thatcherism in the UK, or by home-grown New Right or corporate advocates in Australia or Canada – been significant. These educationally influential discourses are connected with the dynamics and problems that the economies of the USA, the UK, Canada and Australia experienced in the 1970s and 1980s – inflation, stagnation, budget and trade deficits and unemployment.

Higher education in Australia

Following the accounts and analyses given by Smart (1989) and by Robertson and Woock (1989), one can distinguish a number of stages of increasing involvement and control by the Australian Commonwealth Government in the shaping of the higher education system. There is a parallel development of a discourse increasingly marked by a market and managerialist perspective. Post-war reconstruction and the educational needs of demobilized soldiers enrolling in universities saw Commonwealth funding to universities in each state assume a significant proportion of total budgets. In the 1950s, a Commonwealth Universities Commission and a system of triennial grants was established. In the early 1960s, following the Martin Report (1963), the colleges of advanced education, geared to the need for a technological workforce, were established (Smart 1989). In the late 1960s, both the university and college of advanced education sectors were expanding, in the main funded by both the state and commonwealth authorities, but with some tuition fee income. In 1972, the Whitlam Labor government abolished tuition fees and by 1974 took financial control and support into the province of the federal government. Smart (1989) argues that it was the budgetary repercussions of the over-ambitious Whitlam commitments which led in part to the reforms introduced by the minister responsible for higher education in the late 1980s, John Dawkins.

Before looking at recent reforms, let us consider the following quote from the Hudson Committee set up by the Commonwealth Tertiary Education Commission shortly before its demise:

> The Committee is thus emphasizing the professional responsibility of academic staff as being fundamental to the successful maintenance and development of our higher education system. By making institutions and their staff the agents of reform standards can be increased

> and morale improved. The Committee is convinced that this approach is more conducive to high levels of efficiency and effectiveness than greater direction or influence through increased bureaucratic control or the free-reign of market forces.
>
> (Hudson *et al.* 1986: 27)

This marks a point where the language of efficiency and effectiveness had been adopted by influential advisers and officials but where there was still resistance to centralized bureaucratic control or untrammelled market forces operating in higher education. The notion of 'professional responsibility' referred to by the committee contains aspects of autonomy and independence, but says little about the exact forms of control to be used, and is open to incorporation into the delivery of rationales and objectives largely determined outside the institution, by the state or market, or indeed by the state purporting to act for the market. The ambiguities in the appeal to professionalism, as well as the effective abolition of any professional intermediary body between the central state and the universities and colleges of advanced education, allowed the development under Dawkins of a policy and practice that directed higher education towards the service of the economy. This was expressed in terms of promoting Australia as the 'clever country', where universities' prime responsibility is the provision of a skilled workforce and research that will increase the competitiveness of Australian corporations.

Between 1975 and 1989, Australia experienced a series of budgetary deficits, a faltering economy and consequent squeezing of public expenditure, within which the higher education cut of total federal budgetary outlay shrank from 4.5 per cent to less than 3 per cent. This was paralleled by similar phenomena in the UK and Canada. The cumulative effect of this trend brought 'Serious deterioration in: capital buildings and research equipment provision and maintenance; student staff ratios; current student demand; and academic morale' (Smart 1989: 3).

From 1987, with the third Hawke Labor government working against the background of an increasing trade deficit and the influence of New Right free market analysis, Australian higher education entered a phase of increased federal intervention which both rationalized the system and attempted to relate it to the needs of the economy. This was symbolized by the establishment of the new mega-Department of Employment, Education and Training (DEET), headed by John Dawkins. Dawkins, previously trade minister, had already had a substantial impact on universities and colleges through legislation that had encouraged the development of programmes to recruit full-fee paying overseas students.

Dawkins abolished the Commonwealth Tertiary Education Committee in October 1987. This independent buffer body was replaced by a small National Board of Employment, Education and Training, which was 'deliberately crafted by Dawkins and his bureaucracy DEET to be under-staffed, tokenistic and ineffectual' (Smart 1989: 5). Certainly, the publication by Dawkins of 'The challenge for higher education in Australia' (1987a) and the subsequent Green Paper (Dawkins 1987b) and ministerial White Paper (Dawkins 1988a) set out a vigorous analysis and programme for the restructuring of higher education.

The main points of the analysis in the Green Paper and the ministerial White Paper were that Australia's economy needed to increase the annual output of graduates from 88,000 in 1986 to 125,000 by 2001. Given that this would need substantial additional resources and that the Commonwealth of Australia was incapable of meeting the costs, supplementary means of funding would have to be found. Institutions would have to implement substantial economies and improve efficiency. It was against this background that tuition fees were effectively re-introduced through the mechanism of the Higher Education Contribution Scheme (HECS). This followed a recommendation of the Wrann Committee on Higher Education Funding in 1988. Under this scheme, practically all students had to pay about 20 per cent of the costs of their higher education, a tuition fee of (by 1991) A$1125 a semester which could be paid 'up front' with a 15 per cent discount or, after graduation, as a surcharge on income tax once the graduates' income reached average Australian earnings.

The main recommendations of the Green and White Papers and subsequent legislation were implementated and have been summarized by Smart (1989: 9–10) as follows:

1. The replacement of the university/college of advanced education (CAE) binary system by a 'Unified National System', with a marked reduction in the number of tertiary institutions through the amalgamation of smaller CAEs with each other or with universities. These amalgamations have been encouraged by financial and status incentives and sanctions against institutions which remain below specified sizes. The crude assumption was that 'bigger is better'.
2. The concentration of research and postgraduate research training.
3. Funding based on individual institutions negotiating directly with the ministry in terms of 'institutional teaching and research profiles'.
4. The reform of institutional management from a collegial to an efficient 'corporate' managerial model.

The ministerial White Paper established that government would determine national priorities in research and graduate production and that institutions would compete against each other for resources to meet these needs. Dawkins elaborated the funding and expansion strategies of the Canberra government in the statement *New Commitments to Higher Education in Australia* (Dawkins 1988b), and in a statement on triennial funding (Dawkins 1988c) for 1989–91 claimed the following:

> A major expansion of higher education opportunities, improved funding arrangements, a more equitable system, improving access and equity in student expansion, a more unified yet diverse system, greater institutional freedom and flexibility, more effective institutional management,

improvements in effectiveness and efficiency, greater staffing flexibility, the encouragement of alternative sources of funds and new advisory and consultative arrangements.

(Smart 1989: 9–10)

Smart points out that this was a formidable programme. Most of the institutional arrangements and processes to bring it about are now in place and certainly its language has become increasingly dominant.

There are paradoxes and tensions that Smart (1989: 17) identifies between advocacy of the deregulation of economic and academic activity on the one hand, and the establishment of institutional autonomy through a more centralist, regulated and federally controlled system on the other. The question remains whether institutional mergers, the establishment of a unified system of higher education, and new arrangements for the funding of research and teaching separately within the same institutions will yield the desired result. This can be summarized as the production of a higher education system in Australia more attuned to the needs of the economy.

Higher education in Canada

Canada is a federal state of ten provinces and two territories, whose constitution in Article 93 of the British North America Act and subsequently the Constitution Act of 1982 established and recognized education and particularly higher education as a matter of provincial jurisdiction and control. Canada's federal nature and geographical extent are similar to those of Australia and some formal legal provisions for the control of universities are similar, but the effective operation of political economy in terms of the balance of provincial/state influences versus federal/commonwealth ones is markedly different. This can in part be traced back to the differences between two distinct societies – French-speaking, catholic Quebec and English-speaking, protestant Ontario. As the federation grew, and with it the predominance of English-speaking protestants, the education system of Quebec was used to protect its language and culture and shape the identity of its French-speaking majority. More important than the formal legal control of universities by provincial governments is the way in which substantial federal funding is channelled and controlled by the provinces. In effect, Canada has a federal form which can be characterized as 'soft', with much less central control than the 'hard' form found in Australia.

Federal involvement in the funding of higher education became important after the Second World War, and direct financial aid to institutions served to enrol veterans. Higher education doubled in size in the 1950s, from 68,595 to 101,934 by 1959. By the end of the 1960s, it had risen to 294,000. Over the same period, the provincial governments almost doubled the number of universities in their jurisdiction, from 27 to 48. In 1967, the federal–provincial Fiscal Arrangements Act provided that federal funds for post-secondary education were to be administered by the provinces by tax transfers and cash payments and no longer directly allotted to institutions. In 1972, the federal government placed a 15 per cent annual limit on increases to its provision. In 1976, the federal–provincial Fiscal Arrangements and Established Programs Financing (EPF) Act – amended and renamed in 1984 the Federal Provincial Arrangements and Federal Post-Secondary Education and Health Contribution Act – introduced a new system (Gregor 1991). As the name of the Act suggests, federal money for post-secondary education became part of block funding, which included hospital insurance and medical care. The total transfer was related to gross national product (GNP), and although the federal government made specific calculations for post-secondary education, the provincial governments were allowed to distribute the grant as they wished.

Two important consequences have been that the demands of health care have often squeezed the higher education budget and federal funds appear as provincial grants. In 1986 the federal government limited the growth of these transfer payments to 2 per cent below the rate of growth of GNP, and in the April 1989 budget the federal government proposed that the rate of growth of the EPF be reduced by 1 per cent annually. Universities also receive direct support from national research councils (C$658.4 million in 1988–89), which is supplemented by research and consultancy for government departments: health and welfare C$16.6 million, agriculture C$6.1 million, energy, mines and resources C$7.2 million and national defence C$12.8 million. In total in 1988–89, federal funding of this sort constituted 12.5 per cent of universities' total income. Of all government funding, 70.7 per cent was provided by the provincial authorities. In addition, 12.5 per cent of income was received from fees and 7.8 per cent from other sources in 1988–89.

The largely provincial control of the budget means that there can be variation in the amount of resources allocated to higher education provision. In the mid-1980s, both British Columbia and Alberta universities suffered reductions in resources and in 1989–90 received increases below the rate of inflation. The organization of research funding has increasingly concentrated on competitive bidding for large projects, which has involved networking between institutions, partnerships with the private sector and a focus on topics considered of 'central importance to the country's development and well-being' and with a 'discernible prospect for innovation and commercial exploitation' (Gregor 1991: 1020). Half of federal research funds go to five large universities, which account for about half of the graduates and one-third of full-time faculty.

Pedersen (1991: 4), President of the University of Western Ontario, pointed out that:

> Recent trends in ministries of higher education across Canada are toward directing the universities' size, shape, and orientation through the mechanism of 'Targeted funding'. While enrolment accessibility

incentives are a general instance of this, specific manipulation is often used directly at the program level.

In several provinces, Alberta, British Columbia and Ontario in particular, financial steering of academic programmes is complemented by direct government involvement in programme review. Newly-proposed courses of study are evaluated not only on the bases of academic legitimacy, instructional and research support available within the institution, and compatibility with the academic aspirations of the particular university, but they are also scrutinized in terms of their likely immediate social impacts and potential for generating funding from business and industry. New programmes are required not only to address specific 'societal needs', but to offer at least the promise of entrepreneurial opportunities before they will be authorized for government funding support.

Some of the characteristics of the Canadian system are comparable to those of Australia and the UK. For example, the pressure to develop research related to the needs of the economy, increases in student numbers and the squeeze in government resources with the consequent pressure on universities to attempt to raise funds from alternative sources.

There are two noticeable differences, however: first, the degree of provincial control and differentiation, especially significant in the case of Quebec; and, second, the absence of a large polytechnic or college of advanced education sector as in the UK up until 1992 and in Australia up until 1989. There is a substantial community college network, and the full-time student body of the institutes of technology is about two-thirds that of the university student population, but with few exceptions these are not degree-conferring institutions, although they are increasingly providing the first one or two years of degree courses conferred by neighbouring universities. In practice, then, it is possible to compare the Canadian system with both the unified Australian system and the unified system in the UK, where previously separate college and polytechnic sectors and universities have become part of a unified system with common university titles and government funding arrangements.

Higher education in the UK

As in Australia and Canada, the immediate post-war period saw an expansion in student numbers due to demobilization. However, in 1946, the universities were still essentially elitist institutions with only 50,000 students. There were also teacher training colleges, technical colleges and polytechnics giving diplomas and London external degrees, but the universities were the dominant higher education institutions both in terms of prestige and numbers of students. While former university colleges of London University like Leicester and Exeter attained university status, between 1945 and 1960 only Keele was established as a completely new university in 1950.

In terms of the rationale for expansion, Simon (1991) points to the Barlow Committee's report on 'Scientific Manpower' in 1946 and to the Parliamentary and Scientific Committee (1946), which concluded that 'materials and manpower must secure that rapid and sustained increase in scientific manpower which is so vital to the well-being and prosperity of the British Commonwealth in the years that lie ahead' (Simon 1991: 2–3), and that 'the big issue in higher education was seen to be a radical expansion in science and technology to meet the needs of the economy' (Simon 1991: 95).

The 1950s and 1960s saw an overall increase in student numbers, from 85,000 in 1950 to 108,000 in 1960 in the universities and a further 61,000 in teacher training and technical colleges. By 1970, there were 443,000 students pursuing degree or equivalent courses in universities, colleges of education (as the teacher training colleges had been renamed) or polytechnics.

But the pace of expansion was uneven. Tapper and Salter (1992: 120) point out that although 'the 25 years following the end of the Second World War have been portrayed as a golden age for British universities, one of unparalleled growth and public esteem', this was 'no more than a nostalgic reflection on the past from the hard years of the 1970s and 1980s'. The Robbins Report (1963) showed that although there was an increase in full-time student numbers between 1944–45 and 1949–50, in the period 1950–54 numbers actually declined. It wasn't until 1956–57 that the numbers of full-time students in British universities exceeded those in 1949–50, increasing from just over 85,000 to just under 90,000 (Committee on Higher Education 1963, cited in Tapper and Salter 1992: 120).

However, by 1980 there had been a six-fold increase compared with 1946 to over 300,000 students. Nevertheless, when compared with the USA and many other industrialized nations, the higher education system in the UK was small and exclusive. In 1981, only 13.2 per cent of those eligible entered higher education (compared with 30, 26 and 20 per cent in the USA, Japan and France, respectively).

The Robbins Report (1963) was a key educational document that legitimized a pattern of expansion founded on the double grounds of student demand and the needs of the economy. Those very grounds (or rather a narrow and partial understanding of them), provided a rationale for the government cutbacks in the 1980s. Rothblatt (1993: 14), reflecting on the significance of the Robbins Report after 30 years, wrote that:

> The language of Robbins was also the language of the Thatcher period: efficiency, manpower, systems, global competition. But the greater continuity is special, a gift from Robbins to the 1980s that is understandably unacknowledged. Ironically, Robbins provided the state with the morality denied to it by the Victorians and which Robbins never imagined would be used to support the philosophy of markets and privatisation.

In the late 1950s and 1960s, there was a period of relative economic prosperity in the UK, although international comparisons showed that the performance of British economic and educational institutions was behind that of her competitors. There was a common discourse emphasizing economic expansion. Increases in the number of students occurred through the enlargement of existing institutions and the creation of new ones. Eight new greenfield universities were being built by the time the Robbins Report was published in 1963 and more were being demanded. These included what are sometimes known as the 'Shakespearean Seven': Sussex, Essex, York, Lancaster, Kent, Warwick and East Anglia. These were built on greenfield sites near smaller cities. There were Oxbridge influences, collegial forms and experimental humanities and social science programmes. In 1966, ten technological universities, including Aston, Salford and Brunel, were designated; these were based upon existing colleges of advanced technology, mostly located in larger cities.

In 1964, Harold Wilson's Labour government established 29 polytechnics based on existing technical colleges with which, over time, many colleges of education merged to form the second half of the binary system. The government's hope was that this sector of higher education would not only be cheaper to run than the universities, but also more amenable to public control and more responsive to the needs of industry, science and commerce (Robinson 1968). In terms of governance and financial control, the polytechnics remained under the aegis of local education authorities (LEAs) until the 1988 Education Reform Act, which gave them independent corporate status. Thus, although by 1981 the expansion in student numbers in higher education had come close to that projected by Robbins (i.e. 560,000 full-time students), their distribution among institutions was not what had been envisaged. Instead of 80 per cent of students attending universities, as Robbins had proposed, only about 50 per cent did so. By 1987, the traditional universities took less than half the overall student population.

From the early 1970s, the expansion in British higher education failed to keep pace with most other industrialized nations, and in the mid-1970s, faced by the energy crisis and pressure from the International Monetary Fund (IMF), the Labour government began a process of cuts in education and other social services. This was dramatically accelerated by Mrs Thatcher's first Conservative government of 1979, which enthusiastically espoused monetarist doctrine. The 1981 cuts in university funding were part of a general process of cuts in public expenditure.

Crucial in terms of the political rationale behind the cuts with all its confusion and paradoxes, was the collapse of a progressive, optimistic political economy which loosely related investment in education to the prospects of economic growth, and the creation of a more meritocratic and fairer society. This was replaced by a much tougher negative political economy, a monetarist theory and practice drawing on the writings of Milton Friedman. Here a distinction was drawn between the benefits of private wealth-creating industries and expenditure on services which fuelled inflation. High taxation to meet such expenditure in turn reduced incentives for 'wealth-creating' entrepreneurs. Within this context, education – including higher education

– would have to bear its share of cuts in public expenditure, in particular where it did not directly serve the needs of industry. In the UK, contradictions emerged. In practice, the logic of 'monetarist' cuts was mediated by an academic establishment which tended to protect the older universities and subjects through reliance on established and largely unexamined criteria of academic excellence. This had consequences which did not fit with a government rationale emphasizing wealth creation, as the cuts fell most heavily on the technological universities and hit science as well as social science.

A good account of the cutbacks in provision for universities at the national level has been provided by Maurice and David Kogan (1983) in *The Attack on Higher Education.* As the 1980s drew on, it became clear that the 1983 financial cuts were only the first stage of a process to reduce universities' dependence on government funding. Universities were encouraged to build stronger links with industry and to seek alternative sources of financial support. In 1974, block grants from central government accounted for 77 per cent of total university income and by 1987 only 55 per cent. From 1986 onwards, the basis for funding was changed. It was now to be based on student numbers for teaching and on research reputations and the amount of awards from independent research grant-awarding bodies for research.

The impact of these changes on academics in both the 'old' universities and the 'new' (ex-polytechnic) universities has been complex and profound (Miller 1991a), but certain trends are clear. There has been a worsening of salary and promotion prospects, which neither successive settlements reached by the AUT and the Committee of Vice-Chancellors and Principals (CVCP), nor negotiations between the unions and employers in the other half of the binary system up to 1992, did anything to improve. In both the old and new universities, there has been a growth in the number and proportion of staff employed on short-term, temporary contracts with no tenure provision.

The 1988 Education Reform Act was a confirmation and crystallization of the policies that had been developing over the previous decade. The polytechnics and other higher educational institutions were removed from local authority control, further education colleges were given control of their budgets and responsibility for staffing matters, the University Grants Committee (UGC) was replaced by the Universities Funding Council (UFC), and arrangements were initiated by the appointment of university commissioners to abolish the tenure of academics. These reforms, together with a changed emphasis on the criteria for funding, were central to the changes in policy and structure of higher education. The UGC had not had any statutory authority. It had been an advisory body to the Treasury and was later transferred to the Department of Education and Science (DES). The UFC was smaller than the UGC and was statutorily incorporated, with significant industrial and commercial representation. The new polytechnic and colleges funding council had a similar parallel constitution and it replaced the National Advisory Board (NAB) which had had a strong local authority representation. The UGC had 18 members, of whom 13 were academics, three were industrialists and two local authority representatives. The UFC, chaired initially by the vice-chancellor of Cranfield Institute of Technology who had strong industrial links, had only 15 members, of whom six were from business.

These measures legally formalized emerging power relations. The strong emphasis on business involvement fitted with government ideology, policy and practice as it had developed throughout the 1980s. It could be seen as a distorted echo of the sort of business involvement in the establishment of civic universities like Birmingham in the 1890s.

The proposals to change the criteria relating to academic tenure was seen by many as a potential threat to the freedom of academic research and teaching. The 1988 Act appointed commissioners to ensure that university statutes make provision for the dismissal of staff on the grounds of redundancy – that is, when the institution ceases to carry on an activity, teaching or research, for which a person was appointed. This was additional to provisions for dismissal for good cause, which already existed for tenured staff.

In the White Paper *Higher Education: A New Framework*, published on 22 May 1991, the government stressed that its chief aim was to increase participation rates in higher education from one in five 18-year-olds in 1990, to one in three by the year 2000. The main body of the White Paper then proposed a series of structural reforms which the government believed would facilitate this expansion, the most important of which was the removal of the 'binary line' separating universities from polytechnics and other colleges.

The White Paper, and subsequent 1992 Education Act, which enacted the removal of the 'binary line' entailed:

- Abolition of the universities funding council and the polytechnics and colleges funding council, and their replacement by a single funding structure for universities, polytechnics and other colleges.
- The creation of separate higher education funding councils within England, Scotland and Wales, to distribute funding for teaching and research.
- The extension of the title of university, and of degree-awarding powers, to those polytechnics and other suitable institutions which wished to use them.
- New arrangements for quality assurance and quality audit of teaching and research which would be common across the restructured higher education system.

The White Paper stressed the need for increased efficiency in higher education, if expansion was to be achieved without loss of quality. In this context, the government proposed to:

- Maintain differentiated tuition fees, which permitted a major element of funding allocated for teaching and general purposes to be linked to assessments of quality.
- Increase competition and selectivity in research funding. The student-related element of research funding, allocated to universities by reference

to student numbers, was to be phased out. Resources for research were to be allocated to higher education councils, against judgemental criteria, for use at institutions' discretion, and by research councils, on a competitive basis, for specific projects.

In the UK, until the 1992 Act abolished the binary divide, all universities had a Royal Charter and were technically independent private institutions, although in practice largely publicly funded, whereas polytechnics were clearly public bodies administered by local authorities (the London polytechnics were incorporated companies). The polytechnics were all given separate corporate status under the 1988 Education Reform Act, and designated universities after the 1992 Education Act. All have changed their names on becoming universities, but most have retained a geographical marker so that, for example, Sunderland Polytechnic simply became Sunderland University. For other polytechnics where there was an established university in the same city, the change of name has been a little more complex, so Sheffield Polytechnic became Sheffield Hallam University, distinguishing it from the established Sheffield University.

These historical and legal differences are deeper when we consider the different situation of higher education in Scotland, Wales and Northern Ireland as compared to each other and England. For example, Scotland has four very long established universities (Glasgow, Edinburgh, Aberdeen and St. Andrews), rather than two as in England (Oxford and Cambridge). Scotland had a number of central institutions like Moray House College of Education. There have been rather more amalgamations than in England, involving institutions like the technological universities of Strathclyde and Heriot Watt, or the several times renamed Glasgow Polytechnic. This has produced universities new and old which remain different in structure and ethos to those in England. The difference in length of degree (four years rather than three), structure (ordinary and honours) and age of entry (17 rather than 18) mean that higher education in Scotland retains distinctive features, which in some ways are more similar to the patterns in Australia and Canada than the English system.

Similarities and differences

We can at this stage identify a number of common features and significant differences in the development and current character of the higher education institutions in the three countries under consideration. For example, the Canadian and Australian systems are similar in that each has a legal federal structure with practically all higher education institutions (except for the National University in Canberra) being established and/or run as legal entities by the province in Canada or the state in Australia.

There are also a number of features common to all three systems. At the end of the Second World War, each country saw an expansion in the provision of higher education to cater for returning veterans. This was followed by a period of much slower growth up until the mid- to late 1950s. The pace of expansion then increased markedly throughout the 1960s and early 1970s, and the number of higher education institutions – universities, colleges and polytechnics – increased, whether by the redesignation of existing organizations or the establishment of new ones.

From the early 1970s on and certainly after the OPEC oil price rise of 1973, higher education came under increased financial constraint. The central state, whether based in London, Ottawa or Canberra, became increasingly important in the strength, scope and detail of its regulation of higher education in both financial and administrative terms. In the case of Canada, significant variation in the pace of funding and expansion occurred between the different provinces. In the UK, the cutbacks of 1981–83 had very different effects on different universities but were administered through a single centralized mechanism, the UGC. In both Australia and the UK, unified systems were established. Thus by the beginning of the 1990s, higher education was being conducted overwhelmingly in institutions called universities, although in both Canada and the UK significant numbers of students were undertaking degree work in local colleges. Each system is composed of publicly funded, state institutions. There are few private universities – only the University of Buckingham in the UK, and a handful in Canada and Australia, the only significant ones being Trinity Western University in Canada and the Catholic University and Bond in Australia.

Many of the 40 Australian universities were created by amalgamations of colleges of advanced education with each other or with existing universities subsequent to the creation of the unified system in 1989. While they are formally state institutions, funding and control is very largely in the hands of central government in Canberra. They are fairly large institutions with at least 4000 students.

In contrast, the Canadian higher education sector is much more varied, reflecting in large measure the degree of control and finance and governance still exercised by the provincial governments. In Ontario, there are nearly 20 institutions with university status with programmes that emphasize their independence from community colleges, while in Alberta and British Columbia there are a few centralized universities that have a transfer credit basis with colleges to create a higher education system (Pedersen 1991: 16). Quebec has its own distinctive system and in the maritime provinces and elsewhere there are a number of relatively small colleges and universities of religious foundation, sometimes with a continuing religious affiliation. Consequently, Canadian institutions vary in size from a few hundred students in small liberal arts or theological colleges, to more than 30,000 full-time students in multi-faculty and college mega-universities. There were 55 Canadian universities in 1993–94, excluding federated and affiliated colleges and institutes. If the constituent units of the University of Quebec are counted separately, the number increases to 60 (Cameron 1992: 51).

The higher education system in the UK, although governed by a unitary rather than a federal state because of separate arrangements made for Northern Ireland, Wales, Scotland and England, lies somewhere between the centralized control of Australia and the provincial decentralization of Canada. The establishment of a unified system after the 1992 Act replaced the UFC and PCFC with separate funding councils for universities and colleges for England, Wales and Scotland. The unified system comprised 44 old universities in England and Wales and two in Northern Ireland, and included 32 'new' universities – redesignated English and Welsh ex-polytechnics and colleges. In Scotland, in addition to the eight old universities, five central institutions (some designated polytechnics) and a number of colleges of higher education – after some amalgamation – have formed new universities. In 1993, there were 90 or so UK universities, over half of which were UK 'old' universities. Compared with Australia, there have been relatively few amalgamations, and there remains a diversity of institutional cultures and management styles.

The difference in the scale of amalgamations in Australia and the UK has been the main difference in the establishment of unified systems of higher education. In Australia, at the insistence of central government and under threat of withdrawal of funds, there have been 40–50 amalgamations, sometimes between smaller colleges of advanced education geographically widely separated; for example, Charles Sturt University has campuses more than 100 miles apart. More often, however, colleges of advanced education have been amalgamated with an existing 'old' university. By 1990, 35 publicly funded universities (four specialist colleges) had replaced the 90 or so education institutions, universities and colleges of advanced education that existed before unification. In the UK prior to the 1992 Act, amalgamation had most notably been between colleges of education and polytechnics. Some colleges were affiliated to universities (e.g. Westhill College and the University of Birmingham), but there had been only one amalgamation between a polytechnic and a 'new' university in Northern Ireland to produce the University of Ulster. By 1994, there have been a few amalgamations following the establishment of the unified system, rather more in Scotland than in England, for example the amalgamation of Glasgow Polytechnic and Queen Mary College to produce Glasgow Caledonian University.

Perhaps more significant are the 30 or so smaller colleges in the UK with a significant proportion of students undertaking degree courses, and which are funded by the higher education funding councils. Although they are allowed to compete for research funds, they do not have university status, and their degrees, previously monitored by the Council for National Academic Awards (CNAA), now come under the aegis of a university. Those which aspire to university status will need to meet certain criteria.

In the UK, student bodies range in size from 4000 to 5000 at some of the smaller old universities and ex-polytechnics to over 10,000 at the University of Birmingham, 14,000 at the Universities of Oxford and Cambridge to approximately 50,000 at the University of London. Many of the larger ex-polytechnics have between 5000 and 10,000 full-time and several thousand part-time students.

The typical management structure in the three countries, although by no means uniform in its pattern or functioning, comprises three main parts. First, there is a university council, usually called a board of governors in Australia and Canada, its 30–60 members composed usually of a majority of lay members variously appointed, the vice-chancellor and other senior and some representative academics, and often one or two students and graduates. The council has responsibility for the overall financial, constitutional and legal well-being of the institution. Second, the senate, sometimes known as the academic board, is composed of ex-officio academics and administrators, pro-vice-chancellors, deans, the registrar, the librarian, a substantial number of elected academic staff, together with a small number of students. This body, usually chaired by the vice-chancellor or president, has prime responsibility for the academic affairs, teaching and research of the university. This body is usually larger than the council or board of governors. Third, there is the executive embodied in the person of the vice-chancellor, assisted by senior academics and administrative staff.

At the level of argument and rhetoric about higher education and universities and their purpose, and the implementation of policies in the three countries, there have been a number of similar dominant themes. The first is the need to shape higher education to meet the needs of the economy. The second is the feasibility of increasing the use of market mechanisms in the provision of higher education. The third, and often related to the previous two, is the need for increased managerial efficiency and effectiveness at the level of the institution. The fourth somewhat paradoxical theme when related to the emphasis on market mechanisms or autonomous managerial efficiency is the increasing involvement of the state in the regulation and governance of universities. This theme is addressed in the next chapter.

2

The State and Universities

This chapter discusses the relationship between the state and universities. A number of everyday concerns inform the general discussion about the role of the state as they do the perception by academic managers of the pressures from the state on universities. The first of these is the expansion of student numbers. This feature is often linked to the maintenance of standards of education in systems moving from the education of an elite to a larger proportion of the population. Then there is the cost of such expansion, particularly when compared with other calls on the public purse, for example health care or provision for the elderly. This leads on to the related concerns of value for money and accountability. These concerns translate into both specific and broader questions about the contribution university education and research does or should make to the needs of the economy and society.

These matters help constitute the argument about the legitimacy, degree and type of government control and pressure on universities. They have been part of the dynamic behind the 'corporatist' formulation of policy in Australia, and the restructuring of higher education in both Australia and the UK from a binary to a 'unified' system. In the first part of the chapter, these topics are addressed by examining the nature and extent of state participation, in particular by analysing how the federal states of Canada and Australia operate, as compared with the unitary state in the UK, and the significance of 'corporatism'. The rationale behind, and implementation of, the unified systems of Australia and the UK are compared with each other and the situation in Canada. In the second half of the chapter, these same issues are discussed, but this time drawing on interview materials which express the views of university academic managers and union representatives.

These concerns – finance, student numbers, value for money, accountability – are perceived by both commentators and academic managers as having considerable implications for the role of universities in general and for the nature of their management. However, some general discussion of the nature, extent and organization of the state itself with regard to different territories, regions and their peoples is necessary if we are to appreciate how these processes affect universities.

The constitution of the state

The different forms and practice of federalism in Australia and Canada, the relationship of the states to the commonwealth in Australia and of the provinces to the federal state in Canada are of importance beyond the specific sphere of university/state relations, for they crucially affect the governance and financing of, and recruitment into, universities and therefore the pattern of their overall management.

The UK, compared with the federal constitutions of Australia and Canada, has a highly centralized state with an unwritten constitution. Power is concentrated at Westminster and through party dominance of parliament (the Conservative Party since 1979) is effectively in the hands of the Cabinet and prime minister. This power is modified to a certain extent by the UK's membership of the European Union, so that, for example, as far as higher education policy is concerned, EC students are entitled to take courses at UK universities at the same (below cost) fee levels as home students.

The UK was largely constituted by the dominance of England over Wales, Scotland and Ireland. These are distinct countries with their own history, culture and character. As such, the state has developed a range of political and administrative structures which relate to that diversity, including ministers of state for Wales, Scotland and Northern Ireland. The different histories and cultures are significant for the nature, purposes, organization and governance of higher education. The reorganization of the funding councils following the 1992 Further and Higher Education Act in part recognized some of the differences between England, Scotland and Wales by giving them their own funding councils, while the separate administrative arrangements for Northern Ireland were retained.

The nature and extent of the state's relation to universities can be examined in terms of the legal and political realities of federal and unitary structures, the policy implications of corporatism and the analytical distinctions between state, economy and civil society. However, it is also worthwhile placing these discussions within a broader historical framework of different conceptions of the state and its relationship to capitalism and democracy. In his account of the debates about democracy and the state on either side of the Atlantic, Smith (1990) provides a useful framework and categorization of different perceptions and an analysis of the state and its role. This draws on the actual operation of the state within capitalist liberal democracies. It also sketches different models of the relationship of the state to civil society, classes, economic organization and political democracy. By extrapolation, it is possible to apply the analysis to the relationship between the state and universities. It provides a way of understanding the various views of the role of the state that government policy makers (politicians and bureaucrats), university managers, administrators and academics hold. These are sometimes explicit, often implicit, but in either case they inform their behaviour, decisions and strategies.

Smith distinguishes 10 different models of the capitalist state which have explanatory and analytical force and prescriptive and policy implications. They extend in a loose chronological sense from early nineteenth-century participatory and paternalistic versions, through mediatory and manipulatory models to elitist, hegemonic and regulatory accounts of the first half of the twentieth century, to contemporary compensatory or minimalist types with a final futuristic category of conservatory.

While it is the latter models which are most useful in attempting to understand contemporary state/university relations, some of the perspectives and assumptions of the earlier models are still relevant. So that within the mediatory model, there is emphasis by John Stuart Mill and Joseph Chamberlain on the role of 'the educated university graduate within the central bureaucracy' and 'the successful industrialist or professional practitioner in municipal government', respectively. Both Mill and Chamberlain placed great importance upon the expansion of educational facilities (including universities) so as to raise the intellectual and moral standards of the citizenry (Smith 1990). Mills' views on the role of the graduate and Chamberlain's on that of the businessman have been expressed strongly in twentieth-century state and university governance and administration. Graduates have increasingly come to dominate the civil service bureaucracies of the UK, Canada and Australia, and the university link and ethos variously expressed (not always positively) is still a feature of state/university bureaucratic and administrative arrangements. In the UK, there was political and constitutional representation (over-representation) of graduates in the university seats in the House of Commons until 1945. And businessmen are well represented in government agencies, including those dealing with the funding and governance of universities; for example, the increased representation of industrial and commercial personnel on the funding councils in the UK since1988. Also, historically, they have been well represented on the governing councils of universities in all three countries – in the UK, Joseph Chamberlain was the first chancellor of the University of Birmingham and contributed substantially to its foundation. The role of business leaders has gained substantially in importance in the 1980s and 1990s; while in some ways this is related to the developments of minimalist state policy, it also relates to an old paternalistic tradition. Thus it is difficult to ascertain which is the dominant ethos when the chancellor of Aston University (a member of the quaker, Cadbury chocolate family) endows a lake. Is this part of the nineteenth-century paternalist tradition or a contemporary business response, filling the gaps left by restricted state funding?

To turn to the regulatory, compensatory and minimalist models of the state within liberal democratic societies, what are the features and powers of the respective models and what implications, if any, do they have at the level of understanding and policy for state/university relations?

The regulatory model developed in both intellectual and practical terms in the 1930s and 1940s, and its rhetoric still informs 'corporatist' debates in Australia and some aspects of state policy towards universities in all three countries, particularly with respect to research and the improvement of economic performance. Smith (1990: 192) believes the model 'assumes that the task of government is to use expert knowledge in order to minimise social tension and optimise economic growth'.

Keynesian policies in various forms in the UK, USA and even Germany were central to the development of the regulatory relationship between the economy and the state. Keynes life was the epitome of the relationship between government, state and university academic: adviser to the Treasury in London part of the week, lecturer in economics at Kings College, Cambridge the rest (Skidelsky 1992). Smith (1990: 192) notes that 'the object [of the regulatory model] is to generate feelings of economic security (preferable prosperity) and psychological contentment among the population at large, especially those sections who are most closely connected to the current political establishment and those most capable of threatening the position of that establishment'. In the UK, Australia and Canada, universities and their graduates were seen up to 1968 as more a part of the political establishment than a threat to it.

The compensatory model develops some aspects of the regulatory model, mainly in what could be termed a welfare state direction, and this certainly had implications for universities as well as education in general. Two main protagonists discussed by Smith were C.A.R. Crosland in the UK and John Kenneth Galbraith in the USA. They were both concerned to analyse the balance between public and private enterprise. They saw a role for education in promoting economic growth and social justice. Smith (1990: 192) gives the following definition of the compensatory model of capitalist democracy: 'it assumes that the state will restructure the public sphere, intervene in the private sphere and rectify any imbalance between the two. As necessary it will also reduce the relative degree of advantage enjoyed by the minority benefiting most from the unequal distribution of private property'.

While it has been in the sphere of taxation policy rather than regulation of access to higher education that the policy has sought to compensate for market failure and the unjust patterns of economic distribution generated by a market economy, nevertheless providing access to universities for underprivileged groups has been an important feature of higher education policy. Even when accorded a minor role within an overall policy emphasizing minimum state intervention and the superiority of market solutions for economic and educational health, this aspect remains significant in terms of government pronouncements. In the UK, the commitment to increase the participation rate in higher education to one-third of those eligible by the end of the decade can be seen in this light. The commitment in Canada and Australia by both government and university academics and administrators to improve access for aboriginal peoples, women, ethnic minorities and rural populations can be seen as part of a 'compensatory' educational mission. This has had significant effects in terms of the policy and management of some universities.

The 'minimalist' model of capitalist democracy is in many ways a critique and rebuttal of both the regulatory and compensatory schemes. It is significant as the dominant form of political rhetoric, if in varying degrees in the UK, Canada and Australia – as well as in the USA – throughout most of the 1980s:

> It assumes that the regulatory function of government will not involve compensatory activity (which is regarded as counter-productive for all involved) but will be restricted almost entirely to enforcing a body of law. The laws enforced by the state will maximise the chance for achieving the goals of minimum social tension and optimum growth as predicted in the regulatory model.
>
> (Smith 1990: 192)

In its crude form, it assumes that practically all state action and activity by public bodies will be less efficient, effective or just than private individuals relating through the market. Its most influential intellectual protagonists were Friedman (1962) and Hayek (1976), its foremost political champions Margaret Thatcher and Ronald Reagan.

One of the paradoxes of this approach apparent in state/university relations (as elsewhere in the public sphere) has been that, in order to promote the free market, it has been necessary for the state to take strong action to attack and dismember established monopolies and professional privilege.

The distinctive features of regulatory, compensatory and minimalist models can be seen in the policies of governments on research grants, student fees, national wage negotiations and the granting of charters to new private universities. They are also often implicit in the responses that university managers make to state pressures. Sometimes there is outright resistance in the name of an alternative ideal of what a university is and how it should relate to the body politic. More often there is accommodation, a recognition of *Real politik*, and of the financial and administrative power of the state. Attempts are sometimes made by academics and other managers to channel these pressures to their own versions of the purposes of the university. Sometimes there is enthusiastic endorsement of managerialist or market messages emanating from politicians or state agencies.

The literature on the nature and extent of the state and its relationship to the economy and society is considerable, and includes conservative, liberal and socialist political perspectives, as well as the associated Weberian and Marxist approaches (Poulantzas 1973; Galbraith 1974; Bowles and Gintis 1976; Hayek 1979; Giddens 1985; Middlemas 1986). In a discussion of the management of higher education in relation to the state and the economy, a number of perspectives do offer insights into the character of the state in advanced capitalist democracies. They allow an analysis of the structure and dynamic of the connection between state and universities, while recognizing the crucial relationships to the economy.

A useful analysis of the nature of the state and its relationship to the economy and to universities must define the state as something more than just a particular government. The administrative apparatus of the civil service, as well as the military, the police and the legal system, can all be included in an even quite restricted definition of the state. A more extensive definition was offered by Althusser (1972). He developed a distinctive theory of ideology and how it works on the individual through the processes of socialization to produce 'socially appropriate subjects [who] acquire various technical and interpersonal skills, the internalization of various attitudes and a submission to the dominant values systems' (Grosz 1990).

Althusser's argument was that the state in society constitutes this subjectivity, primarily through ideological state apparatuses (ISAs). These ISAs do not function through the overt exercise of force but through values, ideas and ideologies that are less visible. The functions of ISAs are wide-ranging, including the religious, educational, familial, political and cultural. The repressive state apparatuses (RSAs) and ISAs work together to ensure that there is a congruence between the needs of the economy and society and the subjectivity of individuals.

The problem with this account is that it is too inclusive; it blurs the contrasts between different spheres of society. It also has a tendency to be functionalist and to reduce the individual to a passive subject, thus ignoring the capacities for resistance and conflict, and restricting the recognition of human agency. Nevertheless, there is a utility in Althusser's formulations, in that they direct attention to institutions which are not formally part of the state – quasi-state institutions like funding councils, and other bodies such as committees of vice-chancellors and principals. Such institutions work in practice to connect the purposes of the state with the practices of those working in higher education. Bertramsen *et al.* (1991) discusses the work of Poulantzas (1969: 76), Jessop (1985) and Laclau and Mouffe (1985), all of whom argue for an analytical distinction between state, economy and civil society. Political processes structure all three realms, and penetrate the boundaries between state and civil society and between both of these and the economy.

Institutions such as universities, churches and trades unions, although primarily located within civil society, are a terrain on which different forces operate, on which specific hegemonies and settlements are established; these reflect the dominant power and discourses within state, society and economy. These institutions have their own structures, ideologies and cultures. Political actions are mediated through state agencies; for example, political decisions and policy emanating from ministries of education are articulated with universities in civil society through such intermediate bodies as funding and research councils. Sometimes, these articulations may be very direct and obvious, as in the promotion of defence research; at other times, they may be more indirect, as with funding formulae that operate in an attempt to affect student numbers or subject preference in a particular way. Influence is exerted on the composition and/or ethos of intermediary agencies like funding councils through choice of personnel and terms of reference. These articulations produce practices which mould the identity of the institution and its culture (Laclau and Mouffe 1985: 105).

Accounts that pay due regard to the complexity of the relationship between the state, dominant classes and elites and the interaction of these with the governance, culture and pedagogy of British universities include those by Tapper and Salter (1992) and Halsey (1992). Their analyses provide a basis for understanding the reactions and responses of British academic managers to the pressures and opportunities which they see as largely emanating from state action. While Halsey's analysis focuses on the specific character of British academics, and the importance of Oxford and Cambridge, his account helps to explain the not dissimilar ways in which colleagues in Canada and Australia react to the demands of their own provincial/state and federal/commonwealth governments.

Tapper and Salter accept the importance of the economic dimension, of 'capital needs' as Marxists call it. However, they attack functionalist reproduction theory (Bowles and Gintis 1976) when it attempts to explain through the changing needs of capital what is happening in education and schools and, by implication, universities. They wish, as does Halsey, to retain a degree of autonomy and independence for the state and bureaucracy and also to recognize the importance of politics and the ideological factor. Thus they can claim that:

> . . . the state bureaucratic apparatus has assumed the task of helping capital to define what its needs may be, of reconciling the tensions inherent in the definition of those needs, and demonstrating in more precise terms the ways in which schooling [and presumably university courses and research] must change if these needs are to be met.
>
> (Salter and Tapper 1981: 31)

In the liberal democratic states, higher education – and its provision, control and nature – can be seen as constituting part of the problem and perhaps potentially part of the solution to what O'Connor (1974) describes as 'the fiscal crisis of the state' and Habermas (1975) sees as a 'legitimation crisis'. From a more right-wing market or monetarist position, the state is seen as being 'overloaded' with social demands, which include the costs of public education and within that higher education (Brittain 1988: 255).

Thus it is argued that the government, civil service and quasi-state institutions like funding councils are faced with linked pressures. There are pressures to limit increasing public expenditure, which is itself fuelled by rising popular expectations of access to higher education, resulting in either higher student numbers or increased numbers of frustrated applicants.

Corporatism and Australia

The relations between the state and universities, and the associated debate about 'corporatism' and corporate management as it developed in Australia in the late 1980s, encapsulated many of the themes, alternative ideals and political pressures already alluded to under Smith's categorizing models and provides a more concrete base to explore the issues of state and university management.

In his discussion of the relative power and autonomy of the Australian state *vis-à-vis* civil society and the world economy, Pusey (1991) notes a number of features which make it distinctive when compared with the UK and Canada, let alone Eastern Europe or Latin America where the meaning and reality of state/civil society/economy relations are quite different. In a sense, Australia was born a modern state by the time of its federation in 1901. It had a well-established trades union and political labour movement, and a Labor government had been elected in Queensland in 1899, the first popularly elected Labor government in the world:

> Australia then had the highest living standards and most equal distribution of income of all the developed nations. Federation in Australia had very different significance to the same constitutional form in the United States or Canada where it was a means of limiting and dividing state power. In Australia it was a consolidation and aggregation of five states which had exercised a sort of 'colonial socialism' where state governments exercised a general management role in their economies and took direct action to attract both capital and labour from abroad, mainly from Britain.
>
> (Pusey 1991: 213)

Pusey points out that Australia was the last of the new nations colonized by Britain, and in contrast to the USA and Canada was a predominantly secular society. He argues that a combination of the secularism of a colonial past and the 'tyranny of distance' contributed to predispose contemporary Australians towards a positivistic understanding of politics and society.

The discussion about corporatism and its policy implications is most developed in Australia, but it is of interest not only because of its prominence in debate in Australia, but also because of the questions it raises in all three countries about the nature of the relationship between the state and economic and political interests, capital and labour and how these shape higher education. There are connections as well as confusions between 'corporatism' at the state level and 'corporate' or 'corporatist' styles of management perpetrated in the universities. The arguments about corporatism connect with the more general debate about the nature of the state and its relationship to the economy and society, and this in turn has implications for how universities and their management are seen in relation to government.

Corporatism as an analytical tool as classified and developed by Cawson (1986) complements the descriptive, polemical, prescriptive or perjorative way in which it has been used by some Australian academic commentators (Smyth 1991: 31). Cawson distinguishes three levels of corporatism: macro-, meso- (or middle) and micro-corporatism. The state remains central at all three levels. At the macro level, there is a process of negotiation and implementation of policy between representatives (in the ideal-typical case) of business and trades unions. At the meso (middle) level, interactions occur between the state and representatives of a particular sector; for universities, this might be committees of vice-chancellors. More generally, the commercial sector might be represented by an employers' association or a dominant multinational which negotiates directly with the state. At the micro level, there is negotiation and implementation of policy between the state and an individual institution, for example a university, local authority or corporation.

Cawson extends the notion of corporatism from an emphasis on national corporate tripartite deals between the state, capital and labour to one that recognizes that corporatism may operate with only two partners or be extended to several. The first condition may approximate to the coalition which some neo-marxists analyse in the relation of the state to capital and the second to pluralist analysts. Cawson's emphasis on the different levels at which corporatist processes may operate is particularly useful when examining state/university relations, as is the emphasis he places on corporatism being not only a process of negotiation of policy between state representatives and other policy formulators, but also a process of policy implementation by those who have negotiated the policy.

Representatives not only have importance in using their power to protect and project monopoly interests, but also because effective representation is signified by an ability to control and shape their constituents' activities. This is important whether it is trades union leadership representation of labour unions or of vice-chancellors representing universities. Bargains are not only negotiated and struck, usually from positions of unequal power, but are implemented. To take a crude example, pay and conditions may be negotiated by the state, university management and trades union representatives with the proviso that a proportion of payment be related to performance and that quality assessment and audit procedures are implemented. Once a deal is struck, it then becomes the task of the academic institution's representatives in their role as managers to implement the deal.

The range of meanings associated with 'corporatism', 'corporatist' and 'corporate' can be quite various, with many nuances and connotations. For instance, in England and Wales, the incorporation of polytechnics as a result of the 1988 Education Reform Act took them out of the control of LEAs, both in terms of financial control and the severe reduction in representation of LEA nominees on governing bodies. It established 'corporate' status for polytechnics and made them legally independent, autonomous institutions with greater control over their financial affairs. Directors and deputy directors, or chief executives and their management team as they increasingly called themselves, received substantial increases in salary in the first few years after incorporation. The image and style of the polytechnics in their new corporate status was one that moved towards the world of business and commerce, enterprise and market and away from local authority administration and public service. 'Corporate' here was used in a limited institutional, often legal, sense and meant separate corporate status with analogies to business organization.

The more general 'corporatism' has had distinctive power in Australia. Contemporary corporatism, whether in the UK, Canada or Australia, has roots in European history and political economy; 'corporatism' has both a right, fascist heritage and a left, social democratic one. In both cases, the crucial element was some sort of nexus between the state, business and the unions. The balance of forces was various, as was the degree of democratic control and accountability within the various corporate sectors, but there was usually some notion of a labour presence. There has been a union presence based on the varying power of trades union organization in different occupations, industries and regions in the UK and Canada as well as in Australia, but it is strongest in Australia. Some of the differences are discussed briefly here.

For the UK, Middlemas (1986, 1990) has recorded and analysed the rise and fall of various forms and experiments which might be deemed corporatist under both Labour and Conservative governments up until 1979. That date marked a crucial divide. Thatcherism was defined not only in terms of monetarism and a belief in the market, but also by its opposition to what it saw as the excessive power of the trades unions. There have been changes in the law that have altered and restricted the framework within which trades union activities can take place. Equally important was the refusal to involve trades unions or their leaders in negotiation or even consultation in the formation and implementation of economic and public policy. 'Thatcherism' and 'corporatism' were not seen as compatible by Margaret Thatcher at least during the last days of her ascendancy; when fighting a challenge to her leadership by Michael Heseltine she characterized his views as 'more akin to some Labour party policies, intervention, corporatism, everything that pulled us down'. This attitude has not changed much under the Conservative administration headed by John Major. Indeed, one of the few remaining 'corporatist' institutions, the National Economic Development Commission (NEDC), where state employers and trades union leaders did meet periodically and which commissioned useful reports on the economy, was abolished in 1992. We are not likely to see a return to the degree of consultation of negotiation with trades unions that characterized the Labour administrations of Atlee, Wilson and Callaghan or even the Conservative ones of Macmillan and Heath.

In the Australian case, under the Labor administrations of Whitlam, Hawke and Keating, the government has had a commitment to a corporatist model involving some sort of partnership between the state, business and the unions. Radical critics characterize this as a process of incorporation of the leadership of trades unions, which is designed or at least has the effect of neutralizing union power or of bending it to accommodate to the needs of the market or the state. Nevertheless, in political and ideological terms, public recognition is given to notions of partnership, consultation and joint decision making with trades unions or their representatives, which is very different from the UK scenario.

Smyth (1991: 32) points to the involvement of the trades unions and a Labor government along with representatives of private capital in crucial documents and policies concerned with economic revitalization and education. *Australia Reconstructed* (1987), a report that was the result of a joint mission by the Australian trades unions (ACTU) and the Trades Union Development Council (TDC) to Western Europe in 1986, along with the accord between the state, trades unions and employer organizations, provided the corporatist basis for the Dawkins reforms of higher education. Furthermore, in salary negotiations, industrial relations and arbitration awards, the Australian model is one which employers (universities), the trades unions and the state are all involved. Moreover, because of the power of the labour movement in Australian history and the election and re-election of Labor governments in the 1980s and 1990s, key ministers such as ex-Prime Minister Bob Hawke were officials in the trades union movement. Mr Crean, appointed education minister in January 1994, was formerly head of the Australian Council of Trades Unions.

One might reasonably ask what is the significance of this variation in the power of national corporate culture and structures between Australia and the UK at the institutional level? Are the dynamics of corporatism or the alternatives played out at the central state level, whether in Canberra or London, replicated at the institutional level? In the case of the formal federal states of Australia and Canada, what is the impact of the different state entities on university administration? Some of the answers to these questions emerge in the responses made by academic managers to questions about the nature and effect of state pressures on their own universities. Before engaging with this, it is worth describing some efforts by the Australian and UK governments to regulate student members and research provision. This provides perspectives that indicate the practical problems with which university managements are faced.

The state and the universities

The universities and the state increasingly have to not only meet the expectations and demands of those who receive higher education, but also those who pay for it. This in part explains the changes in policy of both the UK and Australian governments in 1992 and 1993 regarding the provision of undergraduate places. The way in which public demand is balanced against economic cost is influenced by the imminence or otherwise of elections. Governments in Australia and the UK have, through state agencies, directly influenced universities admissions policy (Maslen 1994). This is one of the sharpest ways in which the reality of state power is manifested to university managements. On a year-to-year basis, changes in government policy with regard to student numbers and funding affect university policy regarding the two crucial management tasks of balancing the budget and maintaining viable courses.

If we compare UK Department for Education initiatives on university finance linked to student recruitment promulgated at the end of 1992 with

Australian Department of Education policy on undergraduate recruitment in 1993, we see strong similarities in the action of the state and its impact on universities and their managements despite Australia having a Labor government and the UK a Conservative one. Between 1989 and 1992 in the UK, government promulgated strategies designed to increase higher education student recruitment. These included a combination of ministerial rhetoric, financial measures designed to reward institutions taking increased numbers of 'fees-only' students, and the administration of structural change abolishing the binary system.

There was a change of emphasis in 1992. The expansion of higher education student numbers was not to be pursued so enthusiastically and the open-ended financial commitment was reviewed. There was a switch of emphasis to further education provision. Measures on university student fees signalled the shift. Fees that were banded in levels between clinical, science and technology, and humanities and social science subjects and which are paid by local authorities on behalf of eligible (practically all) home UK students were not increased in line with inflation. There was a reduction in the humanities and social science fee levels. Admittedly, the impact was limited to new 'fees-only' students through central government balancing transfers. It is extremely unlikely that these relatively marginal changes will be effective in shifting to a significant extent the pattern of university student recruitment from the humanities to the sciences or from the social sciences to technology. However, this could be seen as a symbolic representation of the government's view of what type of expansion it deemed desirable and of an attempt to limit 'excessive' and 'expensive' increases in the number of higher education students.

In the UK in the early 1980s, there were heavy financial cuts accompanied by a reduction in recruitment in student numbers in the 'old' university sector, but not in the 'public' polytechnic sector where government saw expansion as being cheaper. By the end of the 1980s, there was a wider commitment to the expansion of student numbers with a target of one-third of the age-cohort in higher education by the year 2000. For a variety of reasons, student demand for university places exceeded government expectation; indeed, in Scotland and Northern Ireland, it was already over a third by 1992. Subsequent to the establishment of the unified system in 1992, the expansion of demand proceeded, but initially with a rather different pattern to the previous decade. For the academic year 1993–94, there was an 11 per cent increase in student numbers compared with 1992–93, which was not matched by the 7 per cent increase in funding. From 1992, the minister responsible promised a 3 year period of consolidation for universities; the expansion in demand had outstripped government forecasts and certainly government willingness to fund the expansion without further squeezing the unit of resource. The pattern of expansion had varied across different types of higher education institutions. The new universities (ex-polytechnics), which had previously recorded the fastest rates of expansion in 1993–94, experienced a 1 per cent fall in recruitment (nevertheless, overall student numbers for these institutions still rose because of previous high recruitment rates). The old universities experienced a 7 per cent increase in entrants, but the highest rise (27 per cent) was in higher education colleges (some of them aspiring to university status, partly on the grounds of size) and in further education colleges offering franchised part degree courses.

The scale and pattern of student demand presented problems for the state in terms of the provision – and in the UK case, a particular problem in the control – of funding. Student fees in the UK are paid by local authorities, entitlement to which has been based on obtaining a recognized degree place. Furthermore, there has been entitlement to means-tested maintenance grants, which are similarly administered. This meant that although central government through Treasury reimbursements to local authorities had been responsible for funding up until 1993, it had little direct control over that expenditure. There have been attempts to affect the pattern of student recruitment by the universities by altering the level of fee provision between different subject bands. Now there is direct negotiation between individual universities and the state agency, the UFC, over the numbers of students to be recruited in specific categories – full-time, part-time, sandwich, European Union, undergraduate, postgraduate as well as within-subject groupings. The control has become precise.

Thus over a period of time, the UK government has attempted to set overall policy on student recruitment. By limiting overall funding and influencing the market of student demand and supply, government did influence the overall pattern. While overall direction was largely imposed, the impact on individual universities and colleges was often arbitrary, not only because of changes to state funding policy exercised by the funding councils, but also because of changes in student demand. With the changes in 1993, government control became more exact and the degree of autonomy and discretion of the funding councils was severely limited. Whether policy will become more consistent is difficult to predict.

In this situation, individual university managements are often faced with difficult decisions in working out a strategy which will ensure financial and academic integrity because of the vagaries of government policy. In the UK case, these have lacked long-term consistency; this situation has been exacerbated by the existence of a market-like situation in terms of student demand for particular courses or institutions. While there are some long-term trends and patterns, over the short-term student demand for particular courses is subject to changes in fashion, unemployment rates and perceived job prospects. Thus university management in the specific area of student recruitment in the UK struggles to develop even short-term plans. It is constrained by government policy, particularly changes in funding policy. At the same time, universities are competing for students.

In January 1993, the commonwealth government in Australia indicated the type of university recruitment it required universities to pursue in 1993–95. It made clear that it wanted universities to increase their intake of school leavers to cope with increasing demand. Peter Baldwin, higher education minister, told vice-chancellors that they would have to restore their intake of school leavers to at least the level of 71,000 students in 1990. Although the universities had enrolled slightly more undergraduates in 1991 than in 1990, the proportion of school leavers in universities fell from 77 to 74 per cent of total places, that is, about 6000 fewer places were available to younger students. At the same time, new postgraduate places had increased by about 8000 places or by 53 per cent. Baldwin stated that the commonwealth government's intention was to make sure its policy was adhered to by the university system as a whole: 'If the number of places for young people does not improve significantly in 1993, the commonwealth will review funding for 1994 and 1995 to ensure undergraduate growth is allocated to institutions that have protected and intend to continue to protect opportunities for young people' (Maslen 1993a).

Further specific areas and institutions were being targeted by the commonwealth government. It was proposed that over half of the A$43 million of growth funds would go to 10 universities in designated areas, which included the disadvantaged suburbs of Sydney and Melbourne and the population growth area of southern Queensland. Funding allocations for 1993 differed from previous years when money was distributed to the states according to their existing student numbers (Maslen 1993a: 1). As in the UK, it appears that the Australian government is attempting to limit expansion in the university sector and switch demand and resources to further education. Maslen (1994: 6) reports that Ross Free, minister for education and training, announced a 12 month, A$3 million publicity campaign to inform school leavers, parents and careers teachers of the opportunities in technical and vocational education (TAFE). The government was committed to spend an extra A$1.1 billion between 1994 and 1997 to create an additional 173,000 places in TAFE colleges. It would appear that the Australian government, which expanded university provision between 1984 and 1994, faced with a demand from school leavers in excess of the university places being funded and increasing problems of graduate unemployment, has attempted to switch resources and demand to sub-degree technical and vocational education offered in colleges rather than universities. It is striking how similar the developments are in the UK and Australia.

Whether looked at from the perspectives of a fiscal or legitimation crisis of the state or of an overloaded state, government is faced with interlinking economic and political problems. On the economic side, there are difficulties with the shape and weight of taxation and its relation to expenditure on higher education, with a range of strategies being explored in the three countries: various types of grants, loans, graduate taxes and differential fees to name but a few. This is in the context of more deep-seated economic problems involving budget deficits, periodic inflation, balance of payments problems and mass unemployment. These all affect the way in which government formulates policy. This relates directly to funding, and to the expectations of universities for a contribution to economic welfare and competitiveness in world markets. Specifically, this means the production of a skilled, trained workforce and of research which is seen to meet the needs of the economy.

Becher and Kogan (1992) describe how research selectivity increased throughout the 1980s and how the UGC undertook to report annually to the secretary of state on universities' plans. They point out that it was assumed that research can be planned and could and should be controlled by committees appointed by the UGC. They go on:

> This is central dirigisme in which a predominantly academic committee acted as if it were appropriate to report to a minister on the managerial competence of fellow academics. It leaves no doubt of the growing reach and authoritarian stance of the central authorities over what had come to be regarded as the terrains of disciplinary groups acting through peer review.
>
> (Becher and Kogan 1992: 46)

Like the UGC, the advisory board for research councils was attempting to set objectives for research, but they themselves were increasingly being influenced by the government, in particular by the prime minister and the Cabinet Office, and the Advisory Council on Science and Technology, described by Becher and Kogan (1992: 46) as 'a body designed to promote research strategically tilted towards the needs of the economy, chaired by an industrialist'.

Besides investment in universities for economic reasons, there is another pressing reason for expenditure on higher education. The provision of degree course places meets the aspirations of potential and actual students and their parents for a university education. There is also pressure for 'value for money', 'efficiency', 'effectiveness' and 'accountability' and 'curbing extravagance', which is in part a response to that part of the population and their political representatives who see neither themselves nor their children benefiting directly from university education.

This sort of analysis of the state, of economic pressures and popular expectations and the strategies adopted by politicians and civil servants in an attempt to reconcile or at least accommodate often conflicting interests, applies at the local as well as the national level. In the case of the UK, this has focused on LEAs and the provision of schooling (Miller 1988; Carspecken 1991), but the issues are more general, as Cockburn (1977) and Castells (1978) discuss. These relate essentially to the question of how, with limited – often diminishing – economic resources, the national or local state can retain legitimacy by providing an adequate service, whether it be refuse disposal, social service provision, housing, or school or university education. In the UK, the different histories and identities of the peoples of Northern Ireland, Wales, Scotland and England and attendant political demands for increased local control, have affected and continue to influence the structure, form and process of education in general, including higher education and its administration. In Canada and Australia, despite a similar federal legal structure, there are considerable differences in the way in which the systems actually work in terms of finance and control. In Canada, the provinces possess considerably more autonomy and control with regard to higher education than do the states in Australia. This means that in Canada analysis has to be applied at the provincial government level, as well as at the level of federal government.

Academic managers and the state

The themes discussed in the first part of this chapter – the nature and extent of the state, its relation to civic society and the place of universities within society – were not usually dealt with directly by the comments of senior academics, administrators and managers. This was partly because my questions were not posed in such terms, but also because in dealing with the 'state', which they usually defined as government or 'the government' or 'Canberra', university managers were more pragmatic. They were typically concerned with how to deal with financial constraints, rising student numbers and pressures from funding organizations to engage in excellent and relevant research. There is a distinction between theoretical discussion and the largely descriptive reporting of university managements' concerns and procedures. Nevertheless, common sets of questions and assumptions can be discerned below the surface: To what extent can a university be independent of the state if it is in large part publicly funded? Must or should universities respond to what amounts to market pressures in terms of increasing student demands? Do universities have a duty to pursue non-economic or even critical or 'irrelevant' research? These issues and the varying stances taken on them by university managers do imply particular positions on the relations of the university to civic society, the state and the economy even if they are not initially conceptualized in these terms.

A number of questions were posed (see Appendix) to academic managers relating to the state and its actions in terms of its effect on the management and functioning of their universities. Some of these were concerned with pressures from the federal government and from state/provincial governments or in the case of the UK pressures relating to the institutional situation in England, Scotland or Northern Ireland. In the case of Australia and the UK, there was the question of the effect of unification of the system. In all three countries, an open-ended question on the significance of developments in the previous 5 years for the academic's own institution often elicited responses directly related to state action, particularly concerning issues of student numbers, resources and research.

In using the responses from individual academics to illustrate the relations between the state and universities, I am not claiming that these are statistically representative nor that they reveal some deep reality. They are perceptions of the situation which catch something of the attitudes of senior academics to the issues raised. Those interviewed were, for the most part, influential figures in the management structures of their own institutions. It is likely that their attitudes and perceptions informed the strategies their universities adopted in dealing with the various manifestations of state policy. These areas of policy, strategy and management included not only the direct relationship with the state, but also fund-raising activities and the type of internal regime relating to research, teaching and consultancy activities promoted within the institutions. The remarks of senior academics explicitly or implicitly show how closely these spheres of activities are interrelated.

We see in the academic managers' accounts not only that the local and national state and its agencies are perceived in different ways, but also the foregrounding of different types of interaction between the state and universities. These may be analysed in terms of the Marxist structuralist and Marxist instrumentalist approaches identified by Smyth (1991; see also Poulantzas 1969; Milliband 1969) as well as the bureaucratic (Weberian) perspective. These different perspectives provide useful insights into aspects of the development of state policy. Thus a Marxist instrumentalist might emphasize the way in which state action aims to produce certain types of educated labour that will contribute to the accumulation process and the needs of the dominant economic elite. A structuralist Marxist would emphasize how state policy legitimates and reproduces a particular class balance through the technologicalization of curricula and separation in the academic structure between researchers and teachers. And a Weberian would emphasize the way in which state policy develops administrative structures which enhance calculability, systematization and control (Smyth 1991: 66).

Their responses relate to the degree of legitimacy of state action and to the way in which structural constraints work to meet the needs of the economy through the implementation of funding policy which affects the direction of research. An issue already touched upon which is central, is the regulation of student numbers in terms of state policy on equity and/or to provide particular flows and types of trained workers. Some respondents referred to the importance of personal interactions and mutual influences of senior political and civil service personnel and academic managers. This can be analysed in the context of the literature on elites and state policy formation and implementation (Wakeford and Wakeford 1974). Frequently linked to this view is an emphasis on administrative imperatives which acknowledge the bureaucrats' and bureaucracies' preference for simplicity, consistency and quantification, whether in research funding or the abolition of a binary system.

Pressures and problems

In the UK, Professor Martin Harrison, vice-chancellor of Essex University and at the time chairman of the CVCP, in an article entitled 'Crisis deepens on Britain's campuses' (*The Observer*, 10 November 1991), wrote: 'The central problem springs from an attempt to achieve simultaneously three policy objectives: to increase access to higher education, to constrain public expenditure severely and to maintain quality'. A dean at the University of Ulster assessed the pressures from central government like this: 'The pressures will continue to be of a conflicting kind, namely a desire for expansion of student numbers and more industry-oriented research coupled with a continued unwillingness to pay for either'. An editorial in the *Times Higher Education Supplement* (15 November 1991) supported this assessment and summarized the situation in the UK in 1991 as follows:

> Overall the picture is of expansion of student numbers faster in polytechnics than universities (45 per cent as against 9 per cent between 1979 and 1989), with a declining unit of resource and the expectation by government of continued efficiency saving of 1 per cent or 2 per cent each year. So that in the Autumn 1991 government public expenditure plans polytechnics will be expected to take 9 per cent more students and get a 7.4 per cent increase in funding while universities will be expected to take 5.8 per cent more students and get an extra 3.8 per cent funding.

When asked about the range of recent developments affecting university management, it emerged that only some emanate directly from the state. Developments that are of significance to university managements are many, various and interrelated. One member of the central administration of an Australian university listed the following as current pressures: (1) unified national system; (2) adverse economic conditions; (3) lower priority to higher education; (4) demographic changes; (5) instrumentalist approach and pressures; (6) national industrial system; (7) state interference; (8) amalgamations; and (9) industrial training.

Some of these pressures and developments are specific to one country or a particular set of institutions. In Australia, the imposition of a single unified system was generally recognized as being of major import, although perceived as having differential effects on different types of institutions. There was agreement among university managements in all three countries that a reduction in resources in relation to the tasks expected was a central feature of the state/university relationship. A dean of a university in Western Australia said that there had been a:

> Continuing downward spiral of funding since 1975. We've had fifteen or more years of continuous belt tightening, we've well and truly pared away any fat that was there, we keep searching for new and more efficient ways of doing things and this has led into a range of administrative and teaching practices which are far from desirable. The major one is the gradual move away from a collegial model of decision making towards a more management-dominated mode.

He thought that there might have been some time saved on committees but was unhappy about the effect on the quality of education, and said that in the university:

> There would be a strong perception that more and more of the important decisions have been taken out of the hands of the academics and placed in the hands of the central administration. So there has been an increasing development of a 'them and us' mentality. This has been exacerbated by shift at national level to an employer–employee relationship, from an academic salaries tribunal to an arbitration commission.

Here we can see the relationships and interactions between the redirection of resources and the changes at both the local and national levels leading to a more managerial system of governance within the university.

A dean of a new university in New South Wales saw the development of the unified national system as the major recent development in his institution. It had precipitated a three-way merger, which created its own administrative and cultural problems in terms of establishing an integrated, coherent institution, but he also said: 'Flowing from the new system was pressure for more staff to be more active in research and the need to generate our own funds . . . to engage in entrepreneurial activities and develop fee paying courses'.

In a university in Western Australia, a member of the central administration saw recent major developments in the following terms. First, the provision of facilities had fallen behind the growth of student numbers, graphically illustrated by his own position in a prefab! Second, there had been a significant growth in his institution of distance learning and, third, there was an increased emphasis on working more closely with industry. In 1978, the institution had explored ways of becoming more closely involved with industry, which had resulted in the formation of a Technology Park in the early 1980s. A Product Innovation Centre was also established to enable ideas to be evaluated and to provide marketing and financial skills for entrepreneurs. A number of short courses in entrepreneurship have also been offered both within the university and to the community at large.

In what were sometimes described as the more experimental, democratic and critical universities established in the 1960s and 1970s (e.g. Murdoch in Western Australia, Simon Fraser in British Columbia, Essex in England), consequent upon problems either of attracting student numbers and/or cuts in funds in the early 1980s, there were moves away from the more experimental courses and curricula to more traditional and vocational courses. This is reflected not only in the disappearance of courses and even faculties, but also in the dropping of less traditional names; for example, at Murdoch University, the School of Human Communication became the Humanities and the School of Social Enquiry became the School of Social Sciences. At Simon Fraser, Interdisciplinary Studies was discontinued and a Faculty of Applied Sciences was created. Harvey (1988: 14) notes that: 'They were highly visible changes, with an emphasis on the "high tech" aspects of the university. One reason for their adoption was the desire to show government that the university was "paying its dues" in making cutbacks, and in providing the province with much needed expertise and skills training'.

These moves to the more traditional and vocational were often accompanied by changes in methods of assessment. So that at Murdoch, where previously some courses had had no formal examination and had been assessed continuously through assignment and tutorial, now each course in the institution was to have a formal examination unless there was some sort of special case.

The configuration of institutional development in relation to the state can be quite complex. For example, a dean at Murdoch University pointed out that the threats to the continued existence – or of the amalgamation – of the university because of its relatively small size, together with a mission which stressed serving the needs of the community, meant that it could now emphasize business as part of the community, and the institution has been relatively successful in increasing the proportion of its funds from non-federal sources. The following suggests someone with a radical perspective can be quite enthusiastic about business or local state funding in order to reduce dependency on federal government:

> Institutions that will do best in the long run will be institutions that can diversify away from federal reliance . . . which is sometimes a politically unpredictable and wilful monster. Relative to the influence of the state there is an enormous imbalance . . . ultimately if there is dependence on a single source of funds there is a threat to university autonomy. If the order of the day is that education must serve the economy – these funds are driven by government policies which are driven by economic imperatives – then you can become a victim. No-one had envisaged that government would intervene to the extent of imposing profiles on institutions. If state government had been involved with some funds this could have been resisted. Schools have done better with dual support.

Canada

In Canada, while most of the senior administrators I interviewed saw pressure for increased student numbers and the provision of a reduced unit of resource, there was significant variation between provinces and even between institutions in the same province. Some institutions, like Simon Fraser in British Columbia, are now experiencing expansion, which is in marked contrast to the cuts experienced in the early 1980s (Harvey 1988). In fact, the full-time student body increased from 9858 in the academic year 1986–87 to 13,011 in 1990–91, and the budgeted faculty complement from 482 to 571, so that the staff/student ratio increased from 20.47 to 22.79. Thus a senior dean could say, 'Problems are to do with accommodating growth, not downsizing'.

In other Canadian universities and provinces, the picture is different. For example, at the University of Alberta at Edmonton – which to an Englishman seems a very large and rich institution – considerable concern was expressed about current budgetary cuts in the unit of resource and plans to cut some specific programmes. As early as 1987 in a university document entitled 'The Next Decade and Beyond', there were plans to stabilize the size of the student body, then running at about 25,000, but switch to a greater proportion of graduate students (i.e. 20 per cent). One academic administrator was fairly pessimistic, though not all of his senior colleagues were so. However, his comments give a flavour of how difficulties are perceived in a major research university in one of the richer Canadian provinces: 'Erosion of quality . . . increased workloads for staff members . . . deterioration of equipment that can't even be repaired . . . deterioration in the library and a lack of addition of new things, basically physical plant and intellectual resources are in decline'.

He reported plans to downsize the university from 31,000 to 24,000, but recognized that there might be problems in doing so because of the 'access' problem. The university was being squeezed in terms of the federal funds available to it, not only because of the perceived need to reduce the federal budget deficit, but also because of competing demands from health care, its success in raising research funds and the fact that it was redoubling its efforts – with some success in the business faculty – to raise money from industry. Nevertheless, he warned: 'This university which is complaining about the good old days in actuality is seeing better days today than it is going to see tomorrow'.

A professor of industrial administration in Alberta's business school described the relationship with the provincial government in the following way: 'There is a direct line – its physically just across the river – there is a closeness between the university and government. Local elites go to local universities. Politicians teach on courses. The networks are very close'. And a vice-president in charge of research said of the provincial government:

> . . . they are having difficulty in deciding how much they should support a research university. In Alberta in the 70s there was continuing expansion . . . a great deal of money . . . nurturing research. There was a downturn in the early 80s, but the Heritage Medical Research Fund (funded from oil money) supported outstanding achievements in science. As the province had less and less money – they had a hard look at the infrastructure. The province wants us to be concerned with teaching and accessibility, but are concerned to maintain momentum as a research institution – there is some slippage – its a pressure point. The province provides major grants for research funding. Less and less research is done in government departments and more is contracted to universities, particularly in more applied areas.

The ex-president of the University of Alberta said he:

> . . . felt good about the relationship with the provincial government, some saw it more negatively, but I had to relate, sometimes fight, with

> the politicians and civil servants. There was a natural tendency for the bureaucracy to get more involved, my job was to see that there wasn't unacceptable intrusion. Pretty good friends with deputy ministers.

And, he continued:

> We were set up by the state. We have to be on guard, be careful the relationship doesn't change to a point where we are simply an agency of government. Those people who see the model at the other end of the continuum and that we simply are sent a cheque and that's the last we hear from the minister or his civil servants, are a bit unrealistic.

A head of department at Alberta said:

> I imagine things here in one sense are no different to anywhere else. As you take money out of the system the quality of education declines. It is unfortunate that it's rather difficult to get hard measures of that to prove to government that it is hurting and that it is the students that are getting screwed. There are beginning to be signs of student revolt, not political . . . expecting student pressure.

This prognostication compares with a degree of protest in Australia in 1991 and 1992 around the issue of student overcrowding, something which has yet to happen in the UK. Staying with the issue of the relationship of student enrolment and resources in Canada, at Queen's University in Ontario a professor saw the situation in the following way: 'Enrolments are going up – and resources down and down'. Some departments operated quota systems for entry to courses in the first year, others like his own in the latter years, and this in a Canadian context which he saw as emphasizing access and opportunity rather than institutional variation or quality.

Paralleling the departmental consciousness of many in universities was a provincial focus, so that many academics in Ontario did not, he asserted, know what goes on in Quebec. Nevertheless, he asserted that in Ontario, with the biggest provincial higher education system, there was the second lowest per capita support per student of the 10 provinces. This had been going on for 10–15 years; it was, he said, a 'sick system', and he held out little hope for change from the New Democratic Party (NDP) provincial government. There had been effective budgetary cuts for several years, which had wiped out the casual academic budget and now buildings were starting to fall down. One could find more optimistic views at Queen's, notable among those most senior in the university administration, but all acknowledged the budgetary pressures under which they were managing.

At l'Université de Quebec à Montrèal with 36,000 students in 1991, the expansion plans were manifested in an ambitious building programme. A research director and industrial liaison administrator both asserted that the province of Quebec was more generous in providing a funded research structure than the other provinces. Nevertheless, concern about the pressure of increased student numbers on staff time and research capacity was something that was common to a range of Canadian universities across the provinces.

In Australia, Canada and the UK, a recurring theme in perceptions of current problems was the formidable external pressures on universities and polytechnics, often increased student numbers, reduced resources and an increasing commitment to research. All these changes required more institutional management and planning. The chair of the CVCP in the UK commented:

> ... most of those involved in the management of UK universities would not have made frequent use of the terms 'cost-effectiveness' or 'efficiency' before the start of the 1980s. Indeed, even the word 'management' itself was generally avoided in the university context until fairly recently ... during the 1960s and 1970s ... the rhetoric was primarily that of 'quality' and 'academic freedom' rather than that of 'management' and 'efficiency'.
>
> (Harrison 1991: 2)

Unified national systems: Australia

A major organizational change in the structure and funding of higher education in Australia and the UK was the establishment of a unified national system. In Australia, this was largely in place by the academic year 1990–91, and in the UK was presaged by a 1991 White Paper and enacted by the Education Act of 1992 and implemented in the academic year 1993–94. In the reactions of senior administrators and staff representatives to these changes, there is evidence of the changing nature of management, both within the institution and between universities and the state. This is succinctly summarized by Laurens (1990: 219) when commenting on the Australian context:

> In just one year (89–90) the number of institutions in higher education has halved. Almost all colleges of advanced education have amalgamated with, or converted into, universities. The binary system has gone. Multi-campus universities are now common. The size of universities has shot up to 13,000 or more students in many institutions. New modes of management are necessarily being considered to cope with this revolution.

As one might expect, attitudes to the unified national system in Australia vary depending on the type of institution – established university or former college of advanced education (CAE) – in which academic managers are located. In general, in the two former CAEs, where I interviewed senior staff, the attitudes towards unification were positive in so far as the promise of 'a more equal playing field' in competing for resources was believed. The conferring of the title 'university' was almost universally seen by members of these institutions as positive. It was felt that it made the institution more attractive to both students and staff, particularly those from overseas, and it recognized the level of work being undertaken.

At the new Charles Sturt University in New South Wales, the amalgamation process – including two colleges more than 100 miles apart – was seen as very much a product of the unified national system. The most important management development was the administration's decision to adopt a centralized, unitary system rather than a devolved, federal system based on the pre-existing colleges. A union representative noted the difficulties of negotiating transitional claims for new conditions in the new university and the different styles of management and strength of union influence in the different pre-existing constituent colleges. He saw the unified system as being 'based on an untested assertion that bigger will be better and on a managerial notion that as long as you are a manager, whether it's a chicken factory or a university, you can still manage it'. There was 'a change to consultation, and some of that rather minimal, rather than negotiation and an increased pressure for research to ape traditional universities'. He was sceptical whether barriers of distance could be overcome and feared the jettisoning of things they were really good at, in particular teaching. Some of these concerns were shared by heads of department and deans. Besides these pressures, there was also for them the challenge of developing research activity among staff who already had heavy teaching loads.

At many other institutions not studied directly in the research, CAEs were amalgamated with nearby existing universities. Here problems of differential status, power, organization and culture could sometimes be quite considerable. Teacher (1990) gives an interesting account of the tensions attending the amalgamations at the University of New England, Armidale and Northern Rivers, where in 1993 there was the first disaggregation of a unified university with the Northern Rivers component breaking away from the University of New England to form the new university of the Southern Cross.

At all former CAE institutions, staff and administrators have had to deal with difficult transitional arrangements that were favourable to some but not others; for example, designating some staff as 'professors' and establishing comparability in terms of status, academic record and capacity with professors in the pre-1987 universities. A central administrator of a former CAE stated:

> . . . the research profile will build up . . . [designation as a university within the unified national system] has done a great deal for staff morale . . . [it has had] a galvanizing effect for the institution . . . four years ago there was still some residual resentment about amalgamation back in 1982. Some people still identify with the old teachers college rather than the CAE, let alone the newly designated university.

He thought there still ought to be a strong mission for teaching, 'so that we do not become a third-rate university rather than a first-rate teaching university'. In an interview with another central administrator, the recent changes in ethos and institutional structure wrought in part by the establishment of the unified national system produce a preference for a managerial style which is at odds with an older type of administrative or collegial governance:

> Traditional universities are not a good model for us. There are unsuccessful practices bordering on incompetence. I sense Dawkins is right, he would want a stronger administrative leadership in Australian universities. That would be the best way to go rather than the hands-off, or hand in velvet glove, approach that perhaps traditional communities of scholars would think is appropriate. That's the ivory tower, nineteenth-century way of doing business. There are a number of universities and chief executive officers who are probably adopting a more modern managerial role, they are entrepreneurial, they make things happen, they break down barriers that staff would want to put up and continue in some form of splendid isolation.

He hoped to have more vice-chancellors in this chief executive mode who 'would force the universities to play in a different game, with different rules and different teams . . . the scenario will change'. He thought that 'the primary objectives of a university education will be better provided for than through the old-style traditional Australian university'.

If we turn to the views of senior staff of the pre-1987 Australian universities, we find a considerable variation in attitude, in part deriving from the different types of 'older' universities. There are three broad groups: (1) old universities like the Universities of Western Australia, Sydney and Melbourne, all established before the Second World War; (2) newer universities like Murdoch or MacQuarie, established in the 1960s and 1970s as the second university in the state; (3) institutions like Curtin and the Royal Melbourne Institute of Technology, formerly technological institutes – in a sense, acting as forerunners to a unified system. These have recently been constituted as universities under the unified system, but are discernibly different from the former CAEs with their strong teacher education component.

A dean at the University of Western Australia said that: 'The things that affect the faculty and others is the competition for students for particular types of courses. Institutions which have become overnight universities were competing in that way for a number of years'. He felt the pressure would increase, although within his own institution there was 'some reluctance to advertise its wares'. He thought funding under the unified system would mean less money for the older established universities, but he pointed out that his university had a number two account which it could draw on and vast resources of real estate if something specific needed to be done.

A number of deans and central administrators in a range of old and new universities pointed out the new arrangements for research funding after unification: 'Canberra has sought to withdraw general research funding from universities so as to direct such funding more sharply to larger research units, and so as to better serve national needs' (Laurens 1990: 225).

A dean at Murdoch, one of the 19 older universities, saw his university as a victim of the change to a unified system, on the wrong side of the binary divide in terms of resources. The unified system, he argued, really redistributed the existing cake from the existing universities, which were essential research institutions and funded as such. It carved out the research component from the operating budget, placing it in Australian Research Council (ARC) control, a body that was funding everybody on the basis of bids. He saw 'a lot of good researchers not getting research grants from ARC and in the process they are going to be deskilled'.

In national terms, he thought research was being taken away from some of the old universities, which was where the great bulk of it was being conducted by virtue of the criteria by which people were recruited. This was the effect of a form of research funding that concentrated on specific areas, emphasised size, 'bigger is better' and teamwork. All these criteria he saw as simply being asserted by central government rather than argued. He said that this had had 'a terrible effect on morale . . . a terrible waste'. It would be fair to say, however, that those in the natural and applied sciences, engineering and business were much more optimistic about the effects of changes in research policy under a unified national system.

A central administrator at the University of Western Australia (UWA) felt that the establishment of a unified national system had affected his own institution 'adversely'. It obscured roles, opened a new gap in the provision of higher education and tended towards uniform prescriptive treatment of non-uniform roles – for example, in terms of salaries, industrial conditions, funding and management. Laurens' deputy vice-chancellor at UWA and since 1993 vice-chancellor at Edith Cowan University, expressed unease about aspects of the centralization and power of the unified national system: 'The potential use of a uniform nationalized system – or corporatist model – to achieve social and political objectives cannot be ruled out in the future' (Laurens 1990: 218). On the other hand he recognized the need for university research to be more closely involved with economic development (ibid.: 223).

Comments from senior administrators at Curtin are interesting in that Curtin's designation as a technological university predates by a number of years the establishment of the unified national system. This is rather like the situation of the University of Ulster in the UK. One person claimed: 'Curtin precipitated the unified national system – whether its good or bad for Australia history will show'. The implications for the former CAEs may parallel the experience of Curtin, which as a central administrator put it were:

> Firstly, the ability to attract staff – we can attract better staff particularly from overseas to a university rather than to an institute of technology. Secondly, it forced us into accepting university procedures and nomenclature . . . Pushed us into research. In the past research was largely undertaken with industry and it was industry supported . . . now it's diversified. The culture has changed . . . research is more visible.

He saw several advantages to the unified system, particularly the recognition that there should be equal funding for equal teaching, so that if 1000 engineers were being taught under the same conditions, he saw no reason why one institution should receive more funding than another. He asserted that the relative funding model revealed that there were differences of up to 40 per cent between the best funded of the old universities and the worst funded of the old CAEs: 'In Western Australia, the relative funding model showed that Curtin, Edith Cowan and University of Western Australia were 8, 7.4 and 3.3 per cent below the norm with Murdoch 10 per cent better than the norm. This was hard to justify'. He understood that the unified system would aim to even out funding within 3 years to plus or minus 3 per cent of the norm. This would be done by slowing the growth of underfunded institutions, while 'overfunded' institutions would have to take more students for the same amount of money.

In summary, the establishment of a unified national system in Australia has had considerable effects on the size, shape and culture of institutions, with implications generally for more directive management. Smart (1989: 11) has argued that the real reasons for the amalgamations and establishment of a unified system were 'to do with costs and a belief in the economies of scale and the fact that Canberra needs a more manageable (i.e. smaller) number of institutions which it can more easily coordinate and control under its intrusive plans for direct negotiations and profiling'. Furthermore, Smart, an 'old university' academic, argues that Dawkins – the minister responsible – 'through abolition of the binary system, has been able to skilfully exploit the sharp divergencies of interest between university academics (for whom the reforms have minuses) and college academics (for whom the reforms have pluses)' (Smart 1989: 16), and thus effectively strengthen commonwealth control over all universities within the unified system, both new and old.

Constraints on overall funding, the increase in student numbers and a more directed and concentrated research policy could be seen to underlay the specific institutional changes of establishing a unified system, but these factors interact and it is difficult to disentangle their effects. Amalgamations may allow rationalization of teaching, which facilitates the development of a focused research effort. Overall, there is a complex pattern of winners and losers; the older established research universities are holding their position, some arts, humanities and social science research may suffer in the newer of the pre-unified system universities, and the former CAEs may gain some research but a range of mission and status remains.

Unified national systems: The UK

In the UK, the establishment of a unified system was seen by polytechnic and university administrators as likely to replicate many of the processes already under way in Australia. In Northern Ireland, through the establishment of the University of Ulster – by amalgamating the polytechnic with the new University of Ulster at Coleraine – the abolition of the binary divide had already happened by 1980. Ex-polytechnic administrators in the UK saw their reclassification as universities as facilitating their recruiting efforts, in particular for foreign students and staff. They welcomed a more even playing field, particularly the opportunity to compete for research funds. The existing infrastructure in the already established research universities, together with their domination of peer-review committees of staff, means that under new unified research funding arrangements, with resources for teaching and research more clearly separated, that a group of a dozen or so universities already strong in research had by 1994 already strengthened their position. Some of the former polytechnics now designated universities have increased their research funding. This has been at the expense of the weaker 'older' universities.

The amalgamation that took place among colleges to produce the CAEs have some parallels in the incorporation of polytechnics following the 1988 Reform Act, removing them from LEA control and producing new management structures and styles. At a broader level, in both Australia and the UK, central government can be seen to be taking an increasingly interventionist stance in the organization of the structure and funding of higher education, despite, in the UK case, elements of a free-market rhetoric.

Canada and Quebec

In Canada, despite the variations between provinces – particularly Quebec and British Columbia in terms of the role of colleges in providing the first part of degree courses – Canadian higher education has been dominated by universities. Although new universities have been created (e.g. in British Columbia in the 1990s), there has not been the sort of major reorganization experienced in Australia and the UK. There are parallels in the way the system is treated as a whole; for example, the way in which research funding from the federal government either directly or through research councils has been concentrated and directed for specific purposes.

In Canada itself, while formally each province has the same degree of autonomy, the distinctive historical, linguistic, economic, religious and cultural differences between Quebec and the rest of Canada has meant that Quebec might constitute itself a separate state. This illustrates the tensions and variations that co-exist within established state forms. But Quebec, which has both Anglophone and Francophone universities with management problems not distinctively different from those in universities in other provinces in Canada, or in Australia and the UK, illustrates how state/university relations have common features in industrialized, liberal democracies. However, by focusing in more detail on state/university relations in specific regions it is sometimes possible to see more clearly the pattern of state pressures and the possibilities presented to university managements. Quebec, with its differences and contrasts with the rest of the English-speaking Canadian provinces, is difficult to understand for those only familiar with the history and society of Australia or the UK. It might be seen as including many of the differences between Wales and England, Scotland and England, Northern Ireland and England, in terms of language, history, culture and religion.

Regional differences

In the UK, the effect of differences in ethos, tradition and culture has meant that Scottish higher education is still different from that in England. There are more differences than there are between Western Australia and New South Wales, but less than those between Quebec and British Columbia. In a different mode and to a lesser degree, is the federal University of Wales, with its use of the Welsh language on many official occasions and its foundation as in some sense representing the Welsh nation. The Welsh Polytechnic, with its distinctive, some would say anomalous system of governance, was also different from apparently equivalent institutions in England. In Northern Ireland, the different governmental structure affects the administration of Queen's University Belfast and the University of Ulster. The latter was the first and up to 1993 the only university to have been created from an amalgamation of a polytechnic and university.

It is worth analysing the University of Ulster in order to show the influence of a specific local political, economic and geographical situation in the relation of the state to a university.

Northern Ireland and the University of Ulster

The position of the University of Ulster within Northern Ireland, beset by 'troubles' for the last 20 years, is complex. On the one hand, some senior management saw the troubles as affecting the recruitment of staff and students. The establishment of the 'New University of Ulster' at Coleraine roughly coincided with an escalation of violence in the late 1960s and early 1970s and this, lecturers believed, affected student recruitment from mainland Britain. A professor at the McGee College campus of the University of Ulster in Londonderry thought the continuing conflict affected recruitment of lecturers and research assistants, because spouses might be fearful of the violence, and because there were few integrated schools. On the other hand, property prices were low, the scenery is breathtaking and Belfast and Derry were lively civic centres. Moreover, the sectarian violence, high unemployment and peripheral geographical situation, which undoubtedly affected the social, cultural and educational life of staff and students, was perceived by several senior managers as being the background – even the basis – for rather more generous funding and positive action by government in supporting the institution.

There are a number of different aspects to this, some of them unique. For example, the establishment of the University of Ulster was described as an amalgamation of a failed or at least struggling university at Coleraine and a successful polytechnic based at Jordanstown. The difficulties and costs of merger were seen by management at the University of Ulster as being reasonably well dealt with by government. A number of senior academic staff contrasted the relatively healthy funding of the University of Ulster in the mid-1980s with the cuts in funding at Aston, Salford, Hull and Keele in England in the early 1980s.

Some professors asserted that the Northern Ireland government's positive role in funding and encouraging economic development would not have occurred if it had not been for the troubles. But had there been no troubles, Northern Ireland would still have been the most disadvantaged region in the UK, requiring more development aid than elsewhere. Arguably, the Scottish Office has been more assiduous and successful in pursuing developmental policies than government in Northern Ireland and the same might be said of some of the larger city councils in the English Midlands and north. Even more significantly, the government of the Republic of Ireland pursued an effective policy of industrialization during the 1970s that swung the industrial balance from north to south in one decade. That stark contrast led to the establishment in 1983 of the Industrial Development Board.

Regional government agencies in Wales, Scotland and Northern Ireland were more developmental than central government throughout the Thatcher years. Several members of senior management agreed that government in Northern Ireland was more pro-active in terms of economic development than elsewhere in the UK. The relatively small scale of the province meant that decision makers – politicians, senior civil servants, academic managers and business leaders – formed a more closely knit social network than in mainland Britain. It would have been interesting if difficult to explore how far this local informal closeness reinforced protestant ascendancy, or whether this has been mitigated by government policy and/or the emergence of catholics in senior positions in the university and government bureaucracies.

The proposal in 1993 to establish a fifth campus for the University of Ulster at a disused engineering factory in the predominantly catholic west of Belfast illustrates the complexity of political, financial and institutional management interactions. Apparently, although negotiations between the university management and the Northern Ireland Office had reached quite an advanced stage, members at a university council meeting on 22 September 1993 were unaware of them (*Times Higher Education Supplement*, 24 September 1993). It was reported that funds for the £104 million project would not come directly from the education budget but from a mixed source, including the Department of Economic Development, the European Community and the International Fund for Ireland.

It is instructive to contrast comments from politicians from the two communities in Belfast. Cecil Walker, MP for North Belfast, said that 'to take a campus and put it into west Belfast is unforgivable and would give rise to allegations of discrimination in education towards catholics at the expense of protestants'. But Alban Maginness, chairman of the Social Democratic and Labour Party, the main nationalist party, said that 'the plan was an innovative step which deserved serious consideration' (*Times Higher Education Supplement*, 24 September 1993). It was planned that the new campus would have up to 4000 places and concentrate on running engineering, science and business courses. Improved access roads would also encourage students from outside the area to enter west Belfast, reducing any possibility of ghettoization of the campus.

On several occasions, the impact of EEC legislation and funding were mentioned as significant generally, but also specifically in relation to the University of Ulster. Priority funding for Northern Ireland as a peripheral region was important, as was legislation allowing students from one EC country to study in another at the prevailing level of local fees, and they were usually also eligible for mandatory awards. This was seen as important in attracting students from the Irish Republic, now comprising 9 per cent of the university's student body, as well as other EC countries, particularly as the cost of living in Northern Ireland was lower than in the Republic. Senior management seemed pleased at staff success in bidding for EC funds for a variety of research and exchange programmes, including the ERASMUS programme.

Although there is optimism about the funding of the University of Ulster, the sectarian violence continues, unemployment remains high (especially among catholic youth) and there is a flight of capital from the province. A fact of direct relevance to universities is that one in three qualified 18-year-olds head for the mainland, only 60–70 per cent of whom return to the province. In comparison, Scotland retains 93 per cent of its entrants to higher education, importing substantially from England and Northern Ireland at the same time (Gavin 1992).

As has already been noted, some of the differences between England, Scotland, Wales and Northern Ireland have been recognized and formalized in a sort of quasi-administrative federalism by the back door, as part of the 1992 Act on higher and further education. And at the level of the European Union, arguments about federalism will continue.

Within the UK, Northern Ireland represents the most distinctive interaction between state, civil society and university provision. Northern Ireland shows the extent to which specific, regional and national factors can shape the character of university governance, funding and relations with the state. The extent to which the UK government's national and regional bureaucracies dominate and displace local control contrast with the degree of provincial control exercised in Canada, as opposed to federal government control. In Canada, the powers of the state do seem to have been significantly decentralized and there is a degree of democratic control at the regional level. In the UK, neither Wales nor Scotland appear to have the degree of autonomy exercised by the Canadian provinces.

Extending state control

It seems appropriate to conclude this chapter on the relationship of the state to universities by reference to two proposals rather incongruously linked in a bill which started its journey through the British Paliament in 1993, and which will be enacted in much modified form in 1995. It provides an example of how the state under a conservative government has attempted to extend its control into the areas of professional training of teachers and the regulation of the activities of students unions. One proposal, the establishment of a Teacher Training Agency (TTA), has emanated from the Department for Education. This suggests centralizing the funding of all types of teacher training in England, whether run by schools or higher education institutions. This proposal has followed increasing intervention by the ministry in matters to do with teacher training. The increased use and formal title of 'teacher training' as opposed to 'teacher education' is itself symbolic of a more instrumental and vocational view of the preparation of teachers. This contrasts with a previous move, where the designation of 'education' or 'teacher education' replaced teacher training in the 1960s. Teacher training colleges had been renamed colleges of education. There are parallels in Australia.

The 1993 government proposals included an increased emphasis on school-based training; the transfer of resources from universities and colleges to schools involved in training; and the extension of the teaching year for the primary postgraduate certificate of education by 2 weeks. The proposal to introduce a one-year training to provide a 'mums army' of primary school teachers met united opposition from teachers' organizations and all those concerned with teacher training and education, and was modified to provide training for teachers' assistants, a very different proposal which does not dilute the graduate base of the teaching profession. Together with the successful opposition to some aspects of testing and the national curriculum in schools, this illustrates the capacity of professional academics and educators to criticize, resist and sometimes successfully oppose government 'reform'.

In the UK and Australia there has been increased government intervention in teacher education and training. This has been subject to critique from university academics on the grounds of the inappropriateness of particular proposals and the trend towards increased centralized state control. Nevertheless, the state has intervened where in the 1950s and 1960s professionals in schools and universities had considerable autonomy to develop training, pedagogy and curriculum in a broad and sometimes experimental way, which focused on the needs of the individual child or student and a range of societal needs. This contrasts greatly with the proposals of the 1980s and 1990s.

Another example of the British government's attempt to extend its control was the proposal that students unions be centrally regulated. The implications and assumptions of this are made very clear by a conservative ex-minister of higher education in his submission to the Department for Education consultation exercise. He argued that the proposed legislation on students unions raised basic questions about the government's commitment to freedom of association. More generally, that it was inconsistent with conservative principles and human rights and would, if passed, lead to an appeal to the Strasbourg court as being inconsistent with the European Convention on Human Rights. The legislation proposed involved distinguishing between 'core' and 'non-core' student activities, those permitted to be publicly funded and those not. The Conservative Party document preceding the Bill stated that candidates for election to posts as campus union officials should not stand on political platforms. This conservative critic argued that: 'A fundamental concern of Tories is to maintain and strengthen civil society. We believe the state should impose upon itself a self-denying ordinance "interfering" in the operation of civil associations only where there is some clear and powerful public interest'. He asserted that:

> Historically, Tory governments have always been very concerned to preserve universities' independence, autonomy, self-government and morale. But since the mid-1980s, we have got into the habit of increasingly involving ourselves by legislation and executive action in university matters which should cause us concern.
>
> One aspect of university as a civil association is that it imposes rights and obligations upon individual students. Many of these are not strictly academic – obligations of residence, obligations to eat meals together, or even (at Oxford and Cambridge) in aspect of dress. Among the rights and obligations on individual students as members of the civil association of the university is the right to participate in electing students representatives.
>
> . . . the present position is that universities and their student representative bodies are free to determine the institutional forms through which the 'citizenship' of the institution is expressed. This proposal is fundamentally inconsistent with the idea of university independence and with our general Tory [*sic*] commitment to the freedom of civil association.
>
> (Jackson 1993: 13)

This illustrates the fundamental theme of this chapter, that whatever the free market rhetoric, there has been an increasing tendency in the 1980s and 1990s for the state to intervene in regulating the activities of universities.

If we conceive thc university as one of the major institutions of civil society, what we see is the encroachment of the state within the realm of civil society. The rationale and justification for this has been in large measure drawn from the economic sphere. This has been expressed in a variety of often linked ways. First, there has been a requirement that universities meet increased student demand. Then attempts have been made to regulate the provision either through state manipulation of the nature and amount of fees, or more directly through the monitoring and direction of the universities. Paradoxically, this state intervention has often been undertaken in the name of introducing market pressures. There are two further broader economic elements: one is the increasing concern to regulate and restrain public expenditure in what has become an increasingly expensive sector; the second is the increasing preoccupation by politicians, policy makers and bureaucrats of a need to shape the research activities of the university to the needs of the economy in a competitive world market.

3

The Economy and Universities

This chapter discusses the relationship between the economy and universities. First, there is a discussion of how the economy and state policy can be conceptualized. This provides the basis for an examination of how universities in Australia, Canada and the UK relate to the economic context as well as to state and society. This economic context for universities comprises a range of markets, themselves partly the product of the current shape of state financing and control of universities. Specific mechanisms like research organizations and science parks designed to supplement or structure market relations in the interest of promoting national competitiveness are described and discussed. The problems associated with the relationship between universities and the economy are seen through the eyes of academic managers in the three nations. They were asked to respond to the following four interlinked questions: What are the pressures from industry and commerce? Has the institution developed strategies relating to corporations and the market? Do these strategies affect the pattern of teaching and research? And, finally, what strategies have been undertaken to gain or maintain funding?

Economies, states and universities

A fundamental question in any discussion of the relationship of states and universities to the economy is what is the nature and extent of the economy under consideration? Many writers from different standpoints (Wallerstein 1974, 1979; Giddens 1985, 1990; Kennedy 1989, 1993; Held 1991) have noted the increasing globalization and interdependence of the world economy. As Held (1991: 151–2) puts it:

> The internationalization of production, finance and other economic resources is unquestionably eroding the capacity of an individual state to control its own economic future and multinational corporations may have a clear national base, but their interest is above all in global profitability, country of origin is of little consequence for corporate strategy.

Some advocates of *laissez-faire* policies in the UK in the mid-1980s did not see this as a problem. They advocated the maximum possible reduction in the individual nation state's regulation of the economy, including deregulation of monetary markets, so facilitating the free movement of capital as well as trade. They argued that trade always balances and that the decline in Britain's manufacturing base mattered little and that the people could exist on service industries, finance and tourism. In contrast to its minimalist *laissez-faire* economic policies, the Thatcher government pursued strong national policies in relation to foreign policy, the Falklands War, the European Community and the development of social policy informed by traditional moral codes. However, the government did not allow individual universities to founder in bankruptcy as the result of the cuts in state support in 1981–83, as might have been expected from an undiluted free market approach.

A more common position held by commentators like Giddens (1985) and Kennedy (1989, 1993) and by politicians, policy makers and the majority of the populations of Australia, Canada and the UK, is that while in principle free trade and the free movement of capital and labour is desirable, this ought to be modified by government action in what is seen as the interests of the nation state's population. This action may be protectionist, and in the past often was. More recently, it has involved deregulation in significant areas, including the Australian Labor government's policies of the late 1980s in deregulating banking and trade, which sought to encourage investment and research. Even if the policies have been ineffective or counter-productive, they have had effects on universities. State policies were designed to increase the competitiveness of home-based companies or to attract multinationals to establish plants in their particular national territory. As we saw in Chapter 2, this often involved the state taking a proactive role to encourage universities to provide relevant, economically desirable research and an appropriately trained workforce.

Kennedy (1993: 127) argues that with the ending of the cold war, 'military rivalries and arms races are being replaced by economic rivalries, technology races and various forms of commercial warfare'. The language of economic rivalry has become increasingly military – industries 'under siege' and markets 'captured' or 'surrendered'. Kennedy continues: 'The nation-state is still at the centre of things engaged in a ceaseless jostling for advantages . . . A neomercantilist world order remains' (p. 127). Giddens (1985) emphasized the continuing importance of the nation-state in the contemporary world. He identified four institutional dimensions of modernity: industrialism, capitalism, military power and surveillance. In all of these dimensions, he argued the state continued to occupy a central position.

Industrialism is seen as the transformation of nature and the development of a 'created environment'; *capitalism* as the process of capital accumulation and production for profit in the context of competitive labour and product markets; *military power* as the control of the means of violence in the context of the industrialization of war and *surveillance*, the control of information and social supervision. These dimensions intersect. Capitalism, for example, has clearly become the dominant form of industrialism with the collapse of the planned, state-owned economies of the USSR and Eastern Europe. It is also implicated in the industrialization of war through the armaments industry and the development of the means and practice of surveillance.

The nation-state has been central in the development of the different dimensions of globalization, so that we can speak of a nation-state system, a world capitalist economy, a world military order and an international division of labour. This is the product of the actions of the governments of nation-states, some more powerful than others, as well as of the directorates of multinational corporations. The balance of power and influence between individual states and corporations is influenced and mediated by a range of material, organizational and knowledge resources, as well as alliances, regional groupings, cartels and the operation of the market.

It is within these configurations (state and corporate) of local, national and international interaction that universities, their staff, students and managers operate. Universities are at one and the same time international, national and local. The flows of knowledge and research, staff and students are in part international, partly because of changes in technology which make communication easier and faster, partly because of the international mission of most universities and partly because of the universal nature of much knowledge. However, practically all universities in Australia, Canada and the UK are public state institutions. Most funding comes either directly or indirectly from national state taxes and the source of funds means that the state is able to exercise predominant control over the broad parameters of student recruitment, academic salaries and, in a more mediated way, research policy.

While universities do have a national and international identity, they also have a significant local identity specific to the economy of the city, county, state or province in which they are located. Sometimes, this is reflected symbolically in the name, representing civic pride – the University of Birmingham, Melbourne or Quebec à Montreal. Often students are recruited locally, particularly undergraduates. Faculty and support staff live locally and together with the students and associated service industries they constitute a substantial part of the local economy. A large university may be very significant for the local economy; a recent study by Strathclyde University in Glasgow showed that it contributed £230 million to the local Scottish economy and created almost 5500 equivalent full-time jobs. Most universities' revenue comes from central government, national charities and large companies, but this national or international revenue is mainly spent on local goods and services; staff salaries are spent locally and students coming from outside the region could even be viewed as tourists (*Times Higher Educational Supplement*, 21 May 1993). Even the curricula and professional schools of the university may reflect the character of the local economy, so that at the end of the nineteenth century in England there were degrees in brewing at Birmingham and in textiles at Leeds, while it is not surprising that Curtin University of Technology in Perth undertakes research and teaching in agriculture and minerals and mining, and UBC in Vancouver in forestry and marine biology.

One of Giddens' dimensions of modernity, *surveillance*, is represented in universities in a variety of ways. Research on surveillance is part of the very considerable budget devoted to military matters, which are undertaken by some staff at most universities. Surveillance also has a more general but less obvious dimension in that universities and their research staff are involved in the collection and interpretation of a wide range of social statistics concerning, for example, demography, family structure, housing, education, criminal activity, consumption expenditure, production and economic performance in general, all of which are used by state agencies to regulate economy and society.

The institution itself is being subjected to increased surveillance. This is expressed in terms of different types of accountability. This can be around research performance, teaching quality, value for money and fitness for purpose. In turn, this is translated by academic managers into increasingly elaborate systems of data collection and accounting. The university and its management in the end engages in surveillance of its own staff and students. Increasingly, students give their view of the fitness and performance of staff. When these processes became glaringly apparent with the demise of Eastern European communist regimes, there were some in western universities who were surprised at the degree of complicity of academic staff in the universities there. But questions can be asked about the effect and consequences of the subtler, softer forms of surveillance legitimated by notions of public accountability or market performance characteristic of universities in western liberal democracies.

The main dimension of modernity that this chapter addresses is the economic one. This is expressed in Giddens' terms mainly as industrialism and capitalism rather than surveillance or military research. Within this economic sphere, the governments of the nation-states attempt to implement economic, monetary and fiscal policies which, in an uncynical view, are in the best interests of the population as a whole or at least those that elected them. Another more critical view would be that government's economic policies serve the interests of the dominant class or elite within which capital and corporate interests are usually predominant. However, whatever the rationale or provenance of economic policies, they are constrained by a number of forces.

First, there is the power of the financial markets. The national currency of a state is often taken as a symbol of the state's legitimacy and worth, and political and economic considerations are inextricably interwoven in the formation of monetary policy. This can be seen clearly in the history of sterling and the UK state and more particularly in the leaving of the exchange rate mechanism (ERM) in September 1992. In 1947, the Bretton Woods Agreement – influenced by Keynes – provided for semi-fixed exchange rates. The International Monetary Fund (IMF) coordinated adjustments to the value of currencies, pegged to the US dollar, when justified by a fundamental disequilibrium in the balance of payments of a member country. Bretton Woods broke down in 1971, leaving exchange rates to fluctuate.

In 1979 with the election of the first Conservative government headed by Mrs Thatcher, the UK abandoned the last vestiges of currency regulation, freeing capital movements and allowing a free hand to speculators. There had already been a turn to monetarist policies. From 1976, under pressure from the IMF, the control of money became the main means of regulating the economy under Labour Chancellor Healey. Thompson (1984) makes the point that with respect to the influence of the state in economic policy in Britain in the 1980s, there was a constellation of differing perspectives. This ranged from more or less full-blown monetarism and supply-side economics to the liberalism of Hayek's position. There were considerable differences in philosophical assumptions and policy implications. However, all of these positions share a belief in the importance and superiority of markets over state planning. The historian E.P. Thompson provides a striking account of the market. He suspects that:

> The market economy is often a metaphor (or mask) for capitalist process. It may even be employed as myth. The most ideologically, compelling form of the myth lies in the notion of the market as some supposedly neutral but (by accident) beneficent entity; or, if not an entity (since it can be formed in no space but the head) then an energising spirit – of differentiation, social mobility, individualism, innovation, growth, freedom.
>
> (Thompson 1993: 305)

He continues:

> This 'market' may be projected as a benign consensual force which involuntarily maximises the best interests of the nation. It may even seem that it is the 'market system' which has 'produced' the nation's wealth . . .
>
> Market is indeed a superb and mystifying metaphor for the energies released and the new needs (and choices) opened up by capitalist forms of exchange, with all conflict and contradictions withdrawn from view. Market is (when viewed from this aspect) a mask worn by particular interests, which are not coincident with those of 'the nation' or 'the community', but which are interested, above all in being mistaken to be so.
>
> (Thompson 1993: 305)

Thompson was concerned that historians should show how such markets actually existed, and in his account of 'moral economy' and the effectiveness of riot in controlling food price fixing in the eighteenth century, showed that they were then much modified. In the 1980s and 1990s, one may recognize the power of the market rhetoric of the World Bank, national politicians and policy makers, corporate apologists or academic managers, but question how markets really work for lecturers, students or researchers. How are these markets managed and are their effects wholly beneficent? Indeed, assessing benefits and losses is precisely what admission tutors or research administrators actually do when faced with the reality of managed markets, whether students seeking places or funding bodies seeking research results. Gray (1992: 174) argues that:

> The market itself is politically and culturally constructed and may, even with capitalism, be constructed in different ways distributing advantages differently. On the other hand markets do have a real existence, resist attempts to mould them in certain directions and even have a disconcerting habit of re-emerging in spheres where they are supposed to have been abolished. The task for a critical social theory is to grasp these realities – for example, the way that economies *appear* to behave autonomously, and to confront states and governments, even 'capitalist' governments, as awkward and intractable givens – while avoiding their reification.

In practice, in the late 1970s it was the:

> . . . actual circumstances and constraints in the economy combined with the onset of recession which was of crucial importance rather than the changes in ideological outlook on the part of policy makers. It was this matrix of events that provided the conditions for a different ideological explanation to be given for the economy's decline and for a different set of remedies to be thrown up that would solve these problems.
>
> During this period the whole area of 'public expenditure' came under increasing scrutiny and was considered as the major problem of the economy.
>
> (Thompson 1984: 287–8)

Free market monetarism took a full-blown form in the early period of Thatcherism from 1979 to the mid-1980s. The value of the pound fluctuated quite widely, being at one time nearly equivalent to one US dollar. Deregulation and the availability of credit, particularly in relation to the housing market, led to the boom of 1986–89, but British manufacturing industry was severely reduced in the 1980s and imports of manufactured goods grew faster than exports. The Conservative government seemed at times to think that the British economy could be sustained primarily on the sale of services and overseas investments. Increasing Japanese investment in the UK, while strengthening such manufacturing industries as car production and electronics, meant that profits were exported and there was little concomitant growth in research and development.

The Chancellor of the Exchequer Nigel Lawson decided to shadow the Deutschmark in the mid-1980s boom, and his successor John Major took the UK into the ERM at two marks to the pound. While Britain's trade deficit was at the time £12 billion a year, about £15 billion was spent to prop up the pound, about 40 per cent of reserves.

The basic problem for the control of any national economy or currency is that the volume of currencies circulating on the world markets is many more times the volume of trade or indeed the reserves of any single central bank. Nine hundred billion US dollars in foreign currency were traded daily in world markets in 1992, a quarter in London. That exceeded the gross national product of all but the biggest states. As one Canadian journalist put it:

> Surely some degree of national economic sovereignty is the price for having a political system at all. What appeared to be at stake in the crisis of September 1992 was not the fate of a particular government or the individuals who composed it, rather the real issue was whether the British state still had the capacity to revive its own economy or not. Pressures for economic nationalism may be back with a vengeance.
>
> (Ignatieff 1992: 21)

Economics and national policy do seem to have to deal with rampant 'internationalization'. Increasingly, the solution to economic problems is seen as lying outside the capacity of nation-states and their governments. But while international organizations like the G7, OECD, GATT, IMF, World Bank and European Union (EU) may appear powerful and to be controlling the institutions of individual governments, they seem less effective in solving or controlling major world economic problems of famine and debt repayments or the problems of inflation, unemployment or regional development in any particular country. This applies not only to weak undeveloped countries but also to the relatively powerful, advanced industrial economies like the UK, Canada and Australia. International currency movements or the strategies of multinational companies may in the end be more important in determining what happens on the ground than either national government policy or regional pacts.

Nevertheless, next to the financial markets and the policies of multinationals, international agencies and agreements are important. Some are on a world scale, like the International Monetary Fund (IMF), World Bank, General Agreement on Tariffs and Trade (GATT) and the United Nations. Often just as significant are regional groupings with economic powers, like the group of seven major industrial powers (G7) – the USA, Japan, Germany, France, the UK, Canada and Italy – the countries of the European Union (the European Economic Community prior to 1993) or the North American Free Trade zone (Mexico, the USA and Canada). These regional organizations do affect economic policy in specific countries and have particular effects on universities. Thus for the UK, membership of the European Union has presented considerable opportunities for both research and the recruitment of students.

Between 1987 and 1991, British academics and industrialists secured just under 20 per cent of all the contracts by value awarded under the European Community Research and Development Framework Programmes. The fourth framework indicated several areas for the EU commission's spending proposals, which is scheduled to run from 1994 to 1998. The commission wants to spend ECU 13.1 billion (£10 billion) on the programme. The research ministers have managed to agree how the eventual framework budget should be split among the commission's proposed programme 'actions'.

The 'Action I' programme, dealing largely with work to bolster long-term industrial competitiveness, will receive 87 per cent of the budget; 4 per cent will be devoted to boosting international collaboration; 6 per cent will be directed at improving researcher mobility and training. Measures to disseminate research results and improve their take-up by industry will attract only 2.5 per cent. Within the action on industrial competitiveness, 28 per cent will be earmarked for information technology and communications; 16 per cent for industrial technologies; 9 per cent for the environment; 13 per cent for life science technologies; 18 per cent for energy; 2 per cent for transport; and just under 1 per cent for socio-economic research (Patel 1993). These percentages give an indication of the relative priority and importance given to different research areas. This distribution of resources inevitably has its effects on the research bids and profiles of universities, departments and research groups.

In the UK, European Union regulations mean that students from any EU country have the right of entry to courses in UK universities on the same criteria and at the same fee level as home students. The 1992 devaluation of the pound effectively reduced the real cost of fees for many overseas students from outside the EC, and should have made recruitment of these students to UK universities easier, thus benefiting the finances of some universities, assuming they were charging at least the real marginal cost of tuition. The UK government's decision to reduce fees in 1993 in order to control the recruitment and finance of home students, may well have the paradoxical effect of increasing the attractiveness of UK degree courses to students from the EU. The UK government, through the funding councils, may attempt to regulate EU students by setting quotas, in complete disregard of the market.

The North American Free Trade zone may affect student recruitment in Canada and have implications for the long-standing restrictions on the recruitment of faculty to Canadian universities. In Australia, there has already been major controversy about how the recruitment of overseas students paying market or full cost fees should be regulated. The investment of Japanese capital in Bond University has raised questions about the national and public control of higher education. The dispute between Australian Prime Minister Keating and the Malaysian government about the non-attendance of a Malaysian representative at a meeting on the Pacific economy in Seattle in 1993, led the Malaysian government to restrict the number of their students attending Australian universities. All these instances show the complex interaction between state policy and the market for students.

In some parts of the world, pressure from below from smaller national, regional, religious or ethnic groups has challenged the authority, influence and even the existence of larger often federal states like the Union of Soviet Socialist Republics and the former Yugoslavia. This has been of decisive economic and political significance, in some cases with bloody and catastrophic consequences. Such change has had profound effects for lecturers, researchers and students, which puts the problems and pressures on western universities in perspective.

In the case of the three countries under consideration here, the situation has not been cataclysmic, although local, regional and national identity has been of some significance in terms of both economic and political policy and the governance and character of universities. This is most marked in the case of Quebec, but in the UK the specific history, culture and economic conditions of Northern Ireland, Wales and Scotland have been important in both economic and university policy (the case of Northern Ireland and the University of Ulster was discussed in Chapter 2). In the European context, local, regional and national pressure groups often seek support from the supra-national bodies of the EC. In practice, ERASMUS and university exchange programmes are between universities, their staffs and students. Cities and universities are twinned and links established between local, economic, political and educational institutions.

Nevertheless, the central state – certainly in Australia and the UK – through administrative and financial controls, has extended its control at the expense of local, city or state control. This has been done primarily through the establishment of unified national systems which gave university status, autonomy and self-governance to former CAEs and polytechnics. The administrative control by the Australian state or the English or Welsh local education authority has been reduced. The legislation necessitated universities negotiating directly with a central funding council or national ministry of education. Student numbers have been regulated nationally and institutional profiles monitored. In practice, this has limited the capacity of universities to compete in an open market as autonomous, firm-like corporations.

From the late 1980s onwards, the tension between central government control and a commitment, often by the same politicians exercising control, to making university institutions more susceptible and responsive to market pressures, lies at the heart of the often contradictory and paradoxical relationship of universities to their economic environment. These paradoxes and ambiguities are partly a reflection of the competing perspectives espoused by academics, politicians and policy makers. At this point, it is worth reviewing in outline some of the major viewpoints.

Economy and society

Economy and Society is the title of a book by Holton (1992), which sets out to compare 'economic liberalism', 'political economy' and 'economic sociology'. He indicates the major contributors to each tradition and their assumptions, strengths and weaknesses. Within economic liberalism, the tradition stretches from Adam Smith (1976) to Hayek (1949) and Friedman (1962), and assumes a world of individuals seeking satisfaction which is best met through the unhampered operation of the market. The major contributor to political economy is Marx (1976), and subsequently a range of Marxists, including advocates of the Frankfurt School (Marcuse 1968; Gramsci 1971; Braverman 1974) and world system theorists like Wallerstein (1974). This tradition emphasizes that social conflict and competing power relations are inherent in capitalist economy. The economic sociology tradition draws on a wide range of theorists, including Polanyi (1977), a social anthropologist, and the classic sociologists Durkheim (1933) and Weber (1948), who like Parsons and Smelser (1956) wrote books with the same title as Holton's own, *Economy and Society*. Contemporary social theorists like Giddens (1985) might also be viewed as advocates of this perspective.

This approach acknowledges the importance of economic power but does not see it as determining in the last instance. It pays due attention to other forms of power – military, political, religious and social – and takes into account the importance of cultural processes and institutions in shaping not only individual consciousness, but also the interactions within economic institutions. Patterns of power relations are seen as deriving in large measure from the specific history and culture of different societies.

The different traditions offer different strengths for the understanding of contemporary economy and society, and while Holton's analysis is conducted primarily at a theoretical level, it does offer insights for an analysis of universities and their management. While universities are primarily cultural institutions, they are embedded in economic, political and social formations. The questions of how the state and economy are important to the university and how the management of the institution operates inevitably involve an examination of the form and relative power of political, economic and cultural elites and their influence on universities. Within the university, even if we take its prime function to be cultural (i.e. research, teaching and the dissemination of knowledge), there are problems of governance, economic support and the maintenance of a degree of legitimate consensus.

Economic liberalism

Holton points out that economic liberalism as a form of analysis and political policy remains powerful not least because of the robustness and resilience of market forms of economic organization. In the post-war period, the market, although regulated by the state, seemed successful when compared with the inter-war period. By the 1980s, the post-war boom had clearly ended. The problems of capitalism were, from an economic liberal perspective, caused by over-regulation and too much state interference and expenditure. By the late 1980s and early 1990s, with the collapse of the state-regulated economic and political regimes of Eastern Europe, the availability of a state socialist or centrally planned model as an alternative to market capitalism was largely removed from the political, ideological and economic agenda.

Economic liberalism remains a major form of analysis. It is significant as a way of analysing and understanding economics and society and the way in which universities work. But more importantly it has provided a major, in many cases, predominant ideology for key political decision makers concerned with the formation and implementation of public policy for universities as well as for education in general, health care, social services and housing.

Economic liberalism is the tradition most influential in guiding the policies of government in the UK and Canada and, despite a Labor government, to a lesser extent in Australia. In Australia, Pusey (1991) argues that 'economic rationalism' has become dominant among policy advisers and administrators in key departments in Canberra. He argues that new economic and market criteria have become dominant over traditional liberal and welfare ones, and that in practical policy terms accommodations can be made with conservatives and even some orthodox Marxists who recognize the economic trade-off. Further, as the following quotations illustrate, the 'economic rationalism' variant of economic liberalism has implications for the managerial control of universities.

Pusey (1991: 193) writes that 'the essence of the conflict of new politics and new administration with old politics and old administration, centres clearly on the changing status and institutional expression of liberalism and of liberal pluralism'. He illustrates this general shift from a social democratic or even liberal orientation to a hard market economic emphasis, by reference to the Dawkins Bastille Day (14 July 1987) reforms as an example of applied economic rationalism. Mr Dawkins, the minister of the then new mega-department of Employment, Education and Training, wanted more efficiency, responsiveness and flexibility in Australian universities and colleges of advanced education:

> The reforms are really only 'political' for as long as it takes to remove the institutional shields against the market – by the selective abolition of tenure, by giving 'merit pay' to accountants and 'marketeers', and by systematically distorting the criteria for promotion and the assignment of research monies in their favour. This has been supplemented by a clarifying letter from our vice-chancellors. Almost overnight, they became the 'chief executives' of their large new corporate enterprises and they felt obliged, with unseemly haste, to write to all their new minions informing them that 800 years of history had come to an end and that the self-governing community of scholars might no longer enjoy even a residual legitimacy. Further, all were informed that they were directly responsible to the new 'corporate structure', first to the head of department and through that person to the dean of the faculty, and thereby to the chief executive, who presides over the structure

> with the help of a radically reduced but 'leaner' and so more 'efficient' council or senate (one that invariably has fewer staff and student representatives and many more ministerial appointees).

He concludes this section with 'the marketeers get the carrots and the liberals get the stick' (Pusey 1991: 194).

Political economy

The political economy approach, as we have already noted in relation to a general analysis of economy and society, probes behind the façade of the apparent equality of contractual relations in the market economy to reveal the power of unequal class relations. In terms of its application to the processes of higher education and the governance of universities, its focus is on various manifestations of class forces. So that questions about the class background of students, the differentials of access to elite, mass or marginal institutions and the relative advantage that different types of higher education confer upon recipients emerge from a political economy perspective. These particular questions arise from a political arithmetic, social democratic tradition rather than an analytical Marxist version of political economy – the focus is mainly on individuals' progress through the system. Reform proposals include making the system fairer and more efficient rather than fundamentally overturning society or reshaping universities or recreating the institutions of economy and state.

One question concerns changes in participation rates from different social classes as the system expands. In the UK, although the proportion of 18-year-olds receiving a higher education has increased from one in seven in 1987 to over one in four in 1992, and the proportion of women and mature students has increased significantly, the ratio between students with different class backgrounds has changed little. In Australia, with the (re)introduction of fees and a graduate tax it was feared by progressives that this would have an adverse effect on the relative chances of students from working-class backgrounds. As in the UK, although the system had expanded considerably, the proportions of those being recruited from different classes remained roughly the same.

A narrowly restricted class-oriented political economy approach might tend to ignore or play down the significance of differences and changes in participation rates in terms of gender and ethnicity, let alone the different meaning and significance for men and women and different ethnic groups of the experience of higher education in general or of studying different subjects.

A more radical political economy approach focuses on the way in which universities legitimate the existing power relations of state, capital and the ruling class over the population. In the economic arena, university education has been seen in terms of the provision of a skilled workforce that is technically and ideologically proficient in supporting the private corporations and public services which maintain and reproduce a capitalist market system. Here there is a dual aspect – not only must higher education be efficient in producing trained and relevantly skilled personnel, but it must also reproduce an appropriate ideology which does not subvert the institutions of state, the corporate economy, the market or even civil institutions like the family, in so far as they are seen to support the overall system. From this perspective, the symbolic dynamic of legitimation is exemplified in the award of honorary degrees, appointments to the councils of universities and the endowment of chairs by private business interests.

A book entitled *Warwick University Limited* (Thompson 1970) explored the power and influence of business interests on the governance of Warwick University. In it E.P. Thompson presents a political economy marxist account of the working of the economy in the UK and suggests that the influence of capitalist economic power extends to the modern university:

> Capitalism is an economic system with an inbuilt drive for growth, for accumulation. In an economy based on private property, growth means the accumulation of privately owned assets. This process requires profits just as it always has done. And the drive for profits in a world dominated by a small number of firms is above all a desire for control. It is only natural that this drive for control would extend to the university. There is no area in life which is not penetrated by the needs of the giant firm. The university offers skilled manpower and research facilities. It also offers them largely at the expense of the general public: Warwick has had six times as much government money as private. The extension of corporate power over the university need not yield an immediate return for the investment of time and money; the modern giant firm takes a long term view of its activities.
>
> (Thompson 1970: 40)

Buckbinder and Newson (1988) present a similar analysis of universities, corporations and academic work based on the Canadian context.

Economic sociology

Economic sociology draws on the work of Weber (1948) and Durkheim (1933) and emphasizes the interactions of economy and culture with state power. Pusey's analysis of the Australian state bureaucracy, although not proclaiming the designation of economic sociology, exemplifies how it is possible to analyse state action in terms of the influence of ideas in the context of Australia's place in the world economy. This is apposite for comparative analysis of the management of education, because it can show not only how state and economy influence universities and their managements, but also how cultural traditions in Australian society and within its universities form the bureaucratic elite and furnishes their intellectual universe. Thus, Weber (1948: 280) wrote: 'Not ideas, but material and ideal interests direct government conduct – very frequently the "world images" that have been created by "ideas" have, like switchmen determined the tracks along which action has been pushed by the dynamic of interest'.

Pusey (1991: 232) argues that in the formation of the modern Australian state, its founders drew on their experience of Great Britain that the 'state would be the most likely protector against private interests' and that the 'major constraints on individual liberty were not public but private' (Rosecrance 1964: 30). Further that there is a complex history and relationship between nineteenth-century Benthamite utilitarianism and its modern market variant in Australia:

> . . . 'charter myths' are inspired more by Hobbes and Bentham than by Locke and Mill, 'metaphysical' universals are forsaken for a much tougher, and colder, reliance on the judicial and administrative arms of utilitarian state. The irony is that buried in the attitude there is cynical distrust, in Bentham's words, of the 'perplexity of ambiguous discourse that, while it distracts and eludes the apprehension, stimulates and inflames the passions' and thus of all 'ideas' and 'intellectualising'; a distrust, and in many ways an ascetic realism, that has inclined the nation to place its faith instead in the more modern universalism of judicial and administrative deliberation, decision and above all 'fair' allocation. The cruel irony is that it is the anti-intellectualism, and indeed the distance of this apparatus from the people, that now so easily allows its own very positivistic formal rationality to be stolen with the forged key of a market 'utilitarianism' that is specially in the modern international order, everything but utilitarian.
>
> (Pusey 1991: 232)

In his analysis of the emergence of economic rationalisms within the state bureaucracy in Canberra, Pusey shows how the interaction and mutual support of free market doctrines, and a private school educated, elite university, young bureaucracy and the political agenda of dominant ministers like Dawkins within the Labor government produce a set of policies, discourse and management styles that privileges economic efficiency over social welfare and citizens' rights. Thus 'for the new reformers in the Hawke period the "system" is equated with a market *economy* that defines its own *environment* quite differently, in terms that relegate "society" (if such a thing exists at all) to just another dimension of the biosphere' (Pusey 1991: 200). Shades of Margaret Thatcher's assertion 'That there is no such thing as society'.

Market, state and academy, and the control of universities

Burton Clark, writing in 1983 on higher education systems, analysed methods of integration which coordinate the purposes and character of institutions, and distinguished three ideal types of control: state authority (which includes political and administrative control), academic oligarchies and markets. Using a triangle he placed the poles of state, market and academy at the points of the triangle, representing the different principles and systems of control. In 1982, the USA and Japan were nearest the market pole, the USSR nearest the state authority pole and Italy nearest the academic oligarchy pole. Canada would have been placed nearest the centre of the triangle with the UK somewhat nearer academic oligarchy and Australia (not included in Clark's diagram) nearer state authority (see Fig. 1). However, since 1982, Canada, Australia and the UK have, to varying extents, moved towards both market and state authority control. In the perception of most academics, there has been a reduction in their own general control. However, to ordinary academics in many institutions, it appears not only that state and market controls have been increased, but also managerial control by those at the top of the academic hierarchy. Perhaps what is needed is a three-dimensional model which not only charts the relative pull and power of academy, state and market, but also the intensity of control.

Noting that Becher *et al.* (1977: 16) had asserted that 'central government has the determinant role in the overall shaping of the system', Clark (1983: 144) wrote:

> This is left neither to the market nor to academic judgement yet given the traditional respect for institutional autonomy and individual academic freedom, the government is 'coy' about stating national objectives, and the intermediate bodies, although increasingly to be seen as parts of the machinery of government, retain academic judgements and are heavily involved in resource decisions.

It has been argued that between 1983 and 1992, the UK state has become less 'coy' and more explicit, overt and determining, if erratic and vacillating, in its control of the university system.

Clark (1983: 144) wrote of Canada that it 'is located close to Britain in this three dimensional conceptual space, with a somewhat weaker tradition of oligarchical influence' and comparing the 'national to the provincial level of government – Canada's strongest level of state supervision – then we find state officials exercising considerable bureaucratic influence upon subsystems, particularly in Quebec and Alberta'. That is probably just as true in 1993 as it was in 1983, but Canada's universities remain more market-influenced than those in the UK or Australia, not least because of the proximity and competition with universities in an even more market-driven system in the USA.

Figure 1 presents some paradoxes. Surely advocates of market control are in the business of reducing state control as well as that of academic oligarchies or producer monopolies. In one sense, that is true and there are real conflicts of perspective, policy and interest between those committed to the importance of state planning and those convinced of the efficacy of market solutions for the economy in general as well as for the provision of

Figure 1 Systems of university control and direction of change, 1983–93. From Clark (1983: 143).

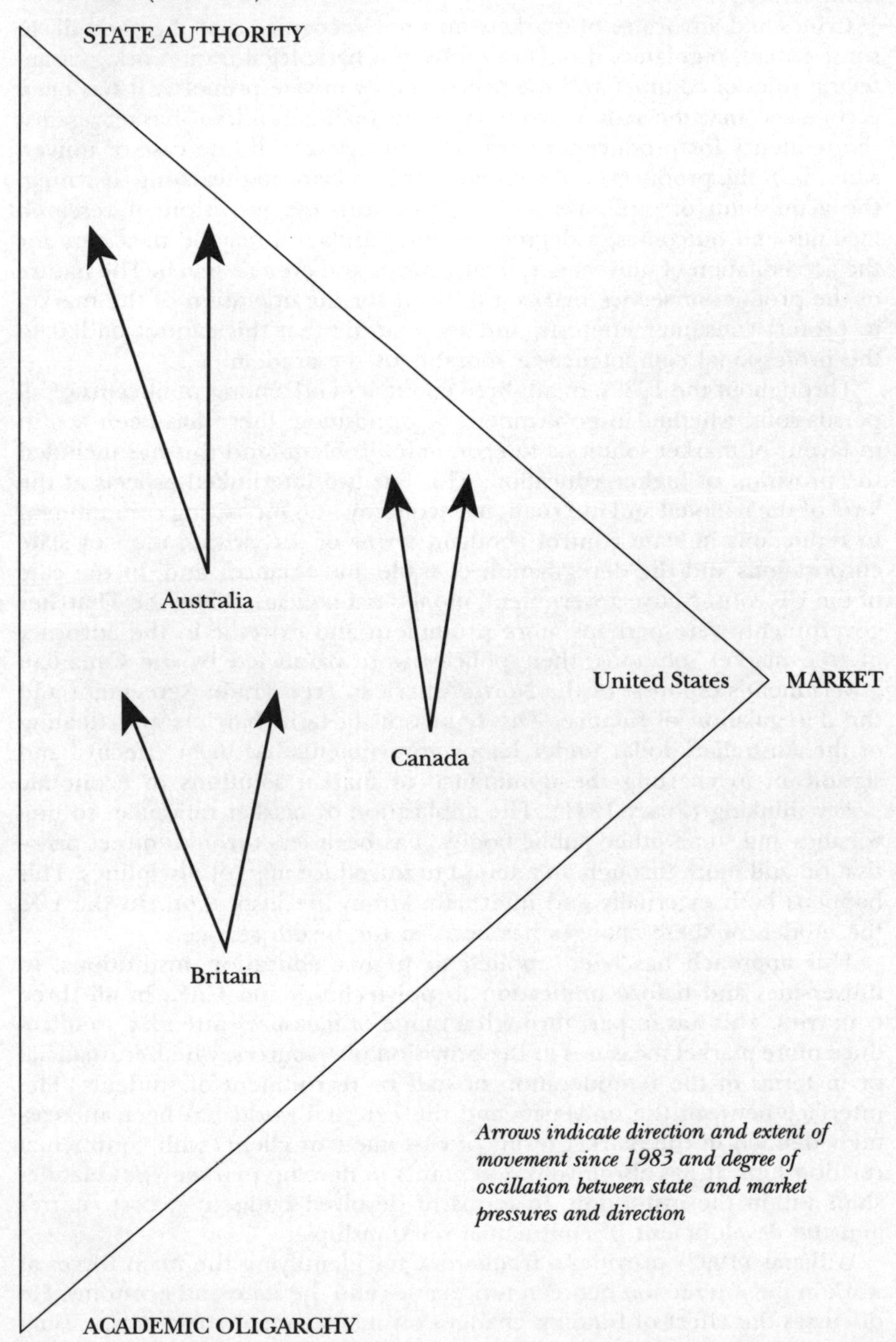

higher education. However, at another level, there is both symbiosis and compromise.

Critics and advocates of markets may not recognize that they are all, to some extent, regulated, if only in terms of a basic legal framework guaranteeing rules of contract and the protection of private property. It has been recognized that the state may intervene to maintain a free market against the tendency for producers to organize into cartels. In the case of universities, with the production of complex services involving teaching, learning, the acquisition of diplomas and degrees, and the provision of research facilities and outcomes, a degree of state regulation may be necessary for the accreditation of universities, their courses and even research. The nature of the product or service makes it difficult for the operation of the market to protect consumer interests, and some argue that this cannot be left to the professional competence or morality of the academics.

Throughout the 1980s, in all three countries and among politicians of all persuasions, whether in government or opposition, there has been a shift in favour of market solutions to economic problems and this has included the provision of higher education. This has two interlinked aspects at the level of the national and international economy – an increasing commitment to reductions in state control (both in terms of the privatization of state corporations and the deregulation of trade and finance) and, in the case of the UK conservative government, monetarist policies. While the Thatcher governments were perhaps more prominent and extreme in the advocacy of free market solutions, their policies were paralleled by the Canadian government's espousal of the North American Free Trade Agreement and the deregulation of finance. The reduction of tariff barriers and floating of the Australian dollar under Labor governments has been effective and significant in charting the dominance of market solutions in economic policy thinking (Pusey 1991). The application of market rationales to universities and some other public bodies, has been less through direct privatisation and more through an attempt to introduce market disciplines. This happens both externally and internally within the institution. In the UK, the model for these changes has been in the health service.

This approach has been applied to higher education institutions, to universities and before unification to polytechnics and CAEs in all three countries. This was in part through a range of measures intended to introduce more market measures in the provision of resources, whether financial or in terms of the remuneration of staff or recruitment of students. The interface between the university and the external world has been increasingly defined in the market terms of customers or clients with contractual relationships. It has also involved attempts to develop market-type relationships within the institution, in terms of devolved budgeting, cost centres and the development of contractual relationships.

Williams (1992) provides a framework for identifying the main forces at work in the interaction between universities and the state and economy. He discusses the effect of funding changes on management structures, raising external funds, the overseas student market, as well as the mechanism and process of allocating financial resources within the university. The aspects discussed here include raising funds from industry and the impact of these links on the autonomy of universities and academics. Science policy, science parks and MBAs illustrate how policies, institutional forms and courses relate to the needs of industry and commerce.

Raising funds from industry

In the UK, university income from industry grew substantially throughout the 1980s, from £27 million in 1982–83 to £114 million in 1990–91. The number of university-based science parks increased from two in 1980 to 40 in 1992.

One of the features of the relationship of university managements to the economy is the pressure to raise more funds from the private sector. This is partly to meet the widening gap between the reduction in state financial provision and the pressure of increasing numbers of students. It also reflects a desire by university managers to diversify their sources of finance in the hope of preserving autonomy and independence. The pressures seem similar in Canada, the UK and Australia, with Canada having the most developed free market and endowment culture and Australia the least.

In the UK, the Universities Statistical Record (1993), using figures compiled from returns submitted by the 'old' universities to the Higher Education Funding Council, showed that in the 1990–91 academic year there was a 20 per cent rise in endowment income and donations over the previous year. Income from research grants and contracts awarded by UK and EC charities also rose by 25 per cent (*Times Higher Education Supplement*, 3 July 1993). However, some of the prestigious institutions are much more successful than others in collecting donations and endowments. Nine universities attracted more than £5 million. London University raised £33 million in 1990–91 and £38.8 million in 1992–93, while Oxford and Cambridge were the next largest recipients with £28 million each in 1990–91. Surprisingly, at the other end of the scale are business schools and technological universities, which one would expect to have good links with industry and commerce. London Business School raised £26,000 and Loughborough and Aston University £17,000 and £26,000, respectively. It seems that size, status, prestige and links with established social elites are more important in the endowment business than mission statements emphasizing service to business and industry.

A pervasive part of the culture of most of the universities in all three countries has been an increasing and acknowledged orientation to 'the market'. This is sometimes explicit in terms of tailoring courses and research to the expressed needs of industry, commerce or professional groups; in other instances, it is apparent in the language, discourse and attitudes within the institution. Examples from the UK, one from an established university and another from a former English polytechnic, illustrate a phenomenon common to the universities of all three countries:

> The university is strongly market-oriented both in relation to the development of courses and research thrusts. This is built into the organizations of the institution issuing in various market strategies. They are pervasive and subscribed to at all levels in the institution from deans to heads of department, directors of research centres, senior course tutors. Relatively few academics take another view and express it privately rather than publicly.
>
> (Central administrator)

In an article in the first edition of *Alumni News* (1991) on 'Planning in higher education', a central administrator at the University of Ulster refers to other aspects of the dominant language of academic management since the publication of the Jarratt Report in 1985:

> . . . since then, planning has been in the forefront of thinking about management – no longer administration – in higher education. Concepts such as integrated corporate planning, modelled on the best practices of commercial enterprises, have become commonplace. Strategic and operational plans with well defined objectives, procedures for monitoring outcomes relative to targets, full economic costing of teaching research and other activities, the need to ensure value for money, a commitment to quality assurance and staff appraisal schemes, are but some attributes of planning which are increasingly prevalent in higher education . . .
>
> There seems to have been a growing feeling, which probably began to appear in the early 1970s, that the relatively poor performance of the UK economy since the second world war, was due, at least in part to the remoteness of higher education from the requirements of the industrial and commercial life of the country. Some would go further and assert that higher education, primarily the universities, was antipathetic to industry and commerce and had become, to some extent, a producers co-operative committed to the interests of the academic staff rather than the students, or the wider society
>
> (*Alumni News* 1991: 12–13)

What is being identified here is the need for a particular type of planning with the use of a corporate, commercial model and a need to change attitudes towards industry, students and society. Another quotation from an academic engaged in innovative research and teaching illustrates a critical perception of the prevalence of market discourse:

> It's the ethos of the market, the language being used, the management style – completely market led – almost a profit-driven type of enterprise and we thought we were academics. The talk is of clients or consumers

rather than students. But the management style is discredited; it uses techniques which are pretty naff in terms of modern business practice – the breaking up of academic community into a rigid hierarchical structure. We used to elect deans.

(Union representative)

In the last quote, the connection is made between a market-led ethos and a particular management style that is judged archaic. That is obviously not an inevitable connection, although the widespread development of more bureaucratic levels in polytechnics in the UK after incorporation in 1988 and similar processes as CAEs became amalgamated with universities in Australia was commented on by several interviewees.

What are the perceptions of academics towards the direction of research efforts and funding towards meeting economic needs? There are variations in terms of central state and federal responsibility when compared with local, provincial and state activities, and research councils, funding councils and government departments also vary in their importance and organization. However, a common theme is the necessity for the state and its agencies to develop, direct and coordinate research to promote wealth creation and improve competitiveness. Nevertheless, as an ex-president of the University of Alberta put it: 'Desirable as it is to establish a fruitful relationship with local industry, we don't want to become a slave to any other element out there, labor, business, professions or government'.

In Canada, provincial governments play a much larger part than the states of the commonwealth in Australia or the countries of the UK in channelling and controlling funding. Nevertheless, crucial imperatives as far as research and development are concerned emanate from the Canadian federal government. A central administrator at a Canadian university describes how new sources of funding for science and technology involved setting up new 'centres of excellence', which tried to network the best researchers and which involved technology transfer when possible: 'If you look at the ultimate winners (15 or so areas), they tend to have some basic science but with a lot of promise of technological developments of use to the country'. He pointed out that the national funded government agencies (e.g. research councils) were not keeping pace with inflation, and that other private corporate funds were contributing to the networks of centres of excellence.

The message being sent to research groups is, 'Look you are going to need some sort of industrial or technological pay-off' – corporate sponsorship was a key element in partnerships in these centres. That is a message that represents a pressure. I'm not going to call it good or bad particularly. It's one that some of our scientists for whom curiosity-driven research is most useful of all might worry that things could get skewed in the thrust of how quickly you can transfer out – how useful is the information.

In Quebec, it was pointed out to me by a group of university–industry liaison administrators drawn from the University of Montreal, UQAM and McGill that:

> . . . ten years ago a single enterprise might develop a research contract with a single university; five years ago the contracts were getting larger and were receiving grants from the federal government; now we see industry getting together to finance long-term larger projects awarded to more than one university . . . it leads to alliances . . . consortia, other mechanisms, new organizations.

They noted that in Quebec both the provincial and federal government were offering large incentives to encourage collaborative research between the private sector and universities. Nevertheless, they and several others across Canada quoted the low research and development component of 1.35 per cent of GNP against an average 2.60 per cent for OECD countries in 1991.

In Australia also, the problem of inadequate research and development by industry to meet the needs of a modern competitive economy was cited not only by the government but by central administrators, deans and heads of department. The incentives from the commonwealth government of allowances of up to 125 per cent of the cost of research were mentioned, and the efforts of the government to encourage industry and universities to collaborate were recognized; however, it was noted that there was a range of factors inhibiting in-house research and development and sponsorship of research in universities. The structure of major corporations active in Australia, many of them part of multinationals, who conduct their research in the USA or the UK, was seen as important, as was the historical involvement of the commonwealth government in research which had relieved Australian industry of the need to do its own research.

A senior administrator in charge of research and development in the Technological University in Western Australia said that apart from mining and agriculture, there was little pressure from industry to involve the university in research:

> Mining tends to put funds in project by project, bit by bit, specific. There is a state provision for mineral industries research fund with matching funding. Intellectual rights are divided up three ways. Results are private and confidential with three monthly reports. The report goes to the sponsors first before you can publish the results, but only after it is checked out by companies.

In the UK, there was a similar refrain. The low level of research and development and indeed training by UK companies was often mentioned, as were the efforts of central government at least at the level of rhetoric to encourage universities to develop research which would meet the needs of industry. As the deputy director of a London polytechnic put it:

> Research, consultancy, applied research – all market-led . . . We are traditionally strong in engineering – but business for overseas students and full-cost fees for lawyers are also important . . . people are good at responding to the needs of industry. For example, our Hospitality and Hotel Management degree. Hotel employers pay for about three-quarters of full-time students and there are a lot of part-time students paid for by employers on Diploma and taught Msc degrees.

This relationship can, of course, extend to various forms of endowment for academic work. 'We have employers who top up professorships and teaching fellowships, four or five thousand pounds for four or five years – we are in discussion with Unilever about an endowed chair' (central administrator of a Scottish polytechnic).

The complexity and difficulties of industry–university relations mediated as they often are by professional associations and mutual misunderstanding are illustrated by the following quotations. 'Professional institutes have acted as a break on what goes on between industry and the institution' (deputy director, London Polytechnic); 'Nearly all courses are tied into professional qualifications NOT quite the same as employers – the institution has to make links – that probably reflects the backwardness of British industry . . . Industry doesn't know what it wants' (union representative, London Polytechnic).

A realistic view suggests that courses are developed in many institutions more for their earning capacity than for their fit with the 'needs' of industry. 'You can have all sorts of good ideas about courses but the criteria as to whether or not they are useful to the institution is how much money they are going to bring in – full-cost students, overseas students . . . loads of money out of them . . . that is why the MBA is so popular – you can charge exorbitant fees' (union representative, London Polytechnic).

Extending this viewpoint, this radical unionist who was not uncritical of capitalist corporations, asserted that the 'Death of liberal education is coming from the state and the institution – what industry wants is just trained minds as they always have done – a degree as such signified a reasonably intelligent human being'.

At this point, it is useful to sketch the changes in funding arrangements and governmental control in the UK, and the range of measures taken to enhance or supplement a market orientation, often to meet the broader objective of enabling universities to meet the need to strengthen industry's and commerce's capacity to be more competitive in world economic markets. While the focus is on the UK, many of the processes, strategies and mechanisms are relevant to Australia and Canada.

Science policy

The White Paper presented to Parliament in June 1993 is a good example of the UK government's attitude to the preferred relationship of the state to the economy and research. It was concerned with government department research, which is significant in the Department of Defence, Department of Trade and Industry and Department of Health, and research commissioned and supported by major charities, in particular major medical charities like the Wellcome Trust. However, its main focus was on research carried out in universities, specifically that funded by the research councils.

Through selective quotations, it is possible to highlight the main concerns of the government. The White Paper, entitled *Realising Our Potential: A Strategy for Science, Engineering and Technology*, has been translated, amplified and interpreted by vice-chancellors and senior administrators in charge of maximizing the research performance and income in each university. However, the main message of the report is clear, and while the importance of 'freedom for researchers' is recognized, the overriding importance of bending research to the needs of wealth creation is emphasized again and again:

> The decision for government, when it funds science, as it must, is to judge where to place the balance between the freedom for researchers to follow their own instincts, and curiosity, and the guidance of large sums of public money towards achieving wider benefits, above all the generation of national prosperity and the improvement of the quality of life.
>
> (Department for Education 1993b: 2)

The role of knowledge in enhancing performance in a competitive world economy is a central assumption of the report:

> The UK's competitive position rests increasingly on our capacity to trade in goods and services incorporating or produced by the latest science and technology. This applies as much, for example, to trade in financial services as it does to manufactured goods and to both small and large enterprises. There are no captive or protected markets on which we can rely; and every year [there is] increasingly fierce competition . . . by new entrants from the Pacific . . . and elsewhere . . . [and] . . . steps should be taken which, on the basis of other countries' experience, will help to harness that strength in science and engineering to the creation of wealth in the UK by bringing it into closer and more systematic contact with those responsible for industrial and commercial decisions (Ibid: 4).

This report was produced in a context where the negotiations between the four major trading blocks – the USA, the EC, Japan and Canada – representing agricultural producers including Australia at the G7 meeting in Tokyo in June 1993, indicated the subsequent ratification of moves to reduce substantially or abolish tariffs on a wide range of manufactured goods. The completion of negotiations on services and agricultural products as part of the GATT Uruguay round in April 1995 confirmed that the

UK government's assessment of the importance of science and technology research and development was founded on a view of wealth production through competition in a free trading world economy rather than in regulated protected economies. Significantly, the means to economic competitiveness was seen to be cultural. The report asserted that 'The aim is to achieve a key cultural change: better communication, interaction and mutual understanding between the scientific community, industry and government departments' (Ibid: 5).

The report proposed a number of structural and organizational changes to the research councils, so that the Science and Engineering Research Council will be converted into an Engineering and Physical Sciences Research Council and a Particle Physics and Astronomy Research Council, and the Agricultural and Food Research Council will be modified into a Biotechnology and Biological Sciences Research Council. But crucially, 'All the Research Councils' missions will be reformulated to make explicit their commitments to wealth creation and the quality of life' (Ibid: 6).

The report goes on to elaborate its purposes:

> The purpose is to give a clearer sense of the vital national contribution made by the ideas, inspiration and dedication of our science and engineering communities, and to devise organizational structures in which the individual can flourish and national priorities and objectives can be more clearly and openly set and pursued . . . [and] . . . Over time, it will also help government where necessary to reorientate the country's research. It will enable the Government to reach a more systematic judgement of the technologies which give the best fit between researchability, technical feasibility and commercial potential (Ibid: 7–8).

While affirming that industry has a responsibility for innovation, the White Paper reaffirms its fundamental theme, that a 'closer partnership and better diffusion of ideas between the science and engineering communities, industry, the financial sector and government are needed as part of the crucial effort to improve our national competitiveness and quality of life' (p. 8). A crucial passage emphasizes control 'selectivity and accountability' and 'meeting the country's needs': 'The Education Departments are committed to selectivity and accountability in the use of public funds allocated by the Funding Councils for research, and to helping secure an adequate supply of people qualified in science, mathematics, engineering and technology subjects to meet the country's needs' (Ibid. 10).

However, there is an almost Keynesian recognition that a capitalist free market needs state intervention if there is to be an 'effective economic return to the nation' – 'circumstances can arise where market forces do not work in a satisfactory manner and investments in commercial research and development which offer a good economic return to the nation, though not necessarily to the individual firm, will not go ahead without some sort of public support'(Ibid: 15), and the implications are spelt out as follows: 'The

Government intends to work closely with the private sector and the academic community to help to increase the effective use of highly-qualified people and hence the productive potential of the economy as a whole' (Ibid: 24).

The report asserts that decisions on priorities for support should be much more clearly related to meeting the country's needs and enhancing the wealth-creating capacity of the country. Certainly, the reformulation of the mission statements for the research councils proposed by the 1993 White Paper leaves little doubt, to quote just two examples. For the Economic and Social Research Council Mission, the crucial sentence is 'Enhancing the UK's industrial competitiveness and quality of life', and for the Medical Research Council Mission, 'Enhancing health, the quality of life and the UK's industrial competitiveness' (Ibid: 29).

The UK government's stance on research and funding had already been set out in the May 1991 White Paper entitled *Education and Training for the 21st Century*, which affirmed the production of a trained workforce as the central mission of higher education. It set out the criteria – plurality, competition, selectivity and accountability – to be applied to the future funding of university research. It is likely that recipients of public funds for research have a clear understanding of the government's strategy.

Besides the research councils, research undertaken directly for government departments is a significant part of academics' research in universities. In 1993–94, the Ministry of Defence expected to spend some £2.6 billion on research and development to meet the needs of the armed services, a quarter of it being spent on research. The argument of the report was part of the conventional wisdom that knowledge had increasingly become the main component in adding value to goods and services, and that the wealth of nations has come to depend more and more on the knowledge and skills of their people.

The mandatory tone of what young people must perceive and value in the service of business exploitation is interesting: 'More young people must perceive science and engineering in industry as an attractive and worthwhile career. They must also see the value of developing the entrepreneurial skills which will help businesses exploit more effectively the results of research, science and technological development' (Department for Education 1993b).

Entrants to full-time postgraduate courses in UK universities increased by over 80 per cent between 1980 and 1990. There was also a significant expansion in the equivalent numbers undertaking a qualification by research – up by 40 per cent over the same period. Postgraduate research, its orientation and control has become recognized as an increasingly integral part of the research and development programmes of private corporations. The Economic and Social Research Council decided to target studentships in areas such as management and business studies and to favour proposals that involve links with research projects with business or policy objectives. The Science and Engineering Research Council has introduced a number of schemes to bring the postgraduate training it supports more closely into line with the needs of industry. These measure confirm the managerial view that government would also like to see steps taken to ensure that the research training itself is more closely related to the needs of potential employers.

Mark Richmond, who was chair of the Science and Engineering Research Council until 1993, states that the implications of the science White Paper are that:

> . . . wealth creation implies a mission focused ultimately in the market-place. Is the proposed research likely to enhance the UK's economic competitiveness and well-being? That could be the main test applied to grant applications in the future. At its inception in 1965 the Science Research Council [had] research in universities as its primary role and only in later years was this mission diluted by more industry-related schemes.
>
> By the end of the 1980s, SERC [Science and Engineering Research Council] had two roles: to support research in universities and polytechnics and to underpin technology based industry – for the future. The underpinning of wealth creation in the engineering, physics and chemistry based industries is to be paramount for that council and research in universities is to be a means to that end. If the missions of the research council's are to be focused on the needs of the market-place, there must be significant shifts in that direction.
>
> Those applying for grants to the councils may have to shift their focus. The whole thrust of the White Paper suggests that the government feels they should.
>
> (Richmond 1993: 9)

He concludes that the White Paper 'could signal a massively significant change: it could indeed shift the shaping of scientific research in the UK out of the hands of its practitioners to those who exploit it'.

In a critical article, Murphy (1993) points out some of the confusions and unargued assumptions lying behind the economic argument for the expansion and direction of higher education. He points out that in the UK (and the same would apply in Australia and Canada), when the economy was at a low ebb as in 1982 or 1992, the proportion of graduates without a job or in short-term employment was at its highest. Conversely, when there is considerable growth, employment prospects for new graduates improve measurably. Thus in 1982 and 1987 for the UK economy, respectively low and high economic growth periods, we find that the percentages of university, polytechnic and college graduates facing unemployment or short-term employment were as follows:

	1982	*1987*
University	23%	13%
Polytechnic	29%	19%
College	44%	25%

Murphy argues out that the employment prospects of all graduates follows the economic cycle, that the significance of graduates over non-graduates in bringing about economic growth has been exaggerated, and 'that instead of Britain needing more graduates to prosper, Britain needs to prosper before it is likely to want, still less need, those graduates it currently produces' (Murphy 1993: 19).

A view shared by Murphy (1993) and Marginson (1991) for the UK and Australia, respectively, is that the assumption that a key cause of the uncompetitiveness of the economics is to do with the quality of the workforce is too simple and probably misleading. Government policies, failure of capital investment and managerial inefficiencies may be more important as causes of economic difficulties. Murphy (1993: 25) cites a survey by Touche Ross (1992: 32), management consultants who reported that British companies were 'less positive and less enthusiastic as to the qualities of UK labour than Japanese companies based in the UK'. The Japanese believed 'that the UK continued to offer an advantage in terms of labour and transport' and they had a high regard 'for the quality and availability of labour' (Touche Ross 1992: 32).

One of the problems is the difficulty of specifying what the effect of higher education is in promoting those traits which will enhance productivity. Despite this difficulty, it has become part of the conventional wisdom in political and business governing circles that universities should do this, and if they are not they should reform their ways so they do. It seems that there is a range of 'personal and transferable skills' which go beyond the traditional qualities fostered by universities like 'brain power' and 'idea creation'. There are 'psycho-social characteristics which have to do with adaptability, flexibility and capability, with communication and inspiration, with being a team player as well as a team leader, with time management and task management' (Council for Industry and Higher Education 1992, cited by Murphy 1993: 23).

The 1987 White Paper went further than the traditional expectation that higher education would maintain and promote 'standards of attainment in specialist knowledge and competence associated with the particular subject of study'. It asserted that higher education must ensure 'the further development of skills in communication and numeracy and the fostering of *positive attitudes to enterprise and work generally*' (DES 1987: 100; emphasis added). The pressure for information and accountability is explicitly linked to the economic requirements of the country, so that 'Essential data on performance in each institution should be published so that its record can be evaluated by funding agencies, governing bodies, students and employers' (DES 1987: 2, cited by Murphy 1993: 102).

The vice-chancellors of Birmingham, Aston and elsewhere in their reception of the White Paper *Realising our Potential: A Strategy for Science, Engineering and Technology* (DES 1993b), seem to accept its 'Unmistakable theme: the need to harness scientific research for the creation of the nation's wealth. It rings with phrases such as "technology foresight", systematic interchange between industry, scientists . . . and . . . policy makers' (Birmingham University Bulletin, 21 June 1993).

One strand in the attitude of university managers to the economy is very positive – the enthusiastic endorsement of business and university collaboration. Central administrators at polytechnics and universities in the UK, Australia and Canada cited a range of initiatives, including science and technology parks, seeking sponsored chairs, teaching companies and the direct involvement of faculty with professional associations (e.g. engineers and accountants in the accreditation of courses). The links with industry and commerce for many are already close and getting closer. One polytechnic was reported (*The Observer*, 10 November 1992) as requiring all research by its staff to have a corporate sponsorship element.

Perhaps as important as direct university research and development links to corporate business are the efforts universities make to elicit extra funding from business to plug the gap left by inadequate government funding. In general, administrative leaders did not report an untoward influence on research programmes or taught courses by corporations. Rather, they complain about the lack of involvement of business in the university. More significant was a recognition that the state was interested in universities both for the research and the production of an appropriately skilled workforce able to meet the needs of the economy and the corporate sector.

Science parks

Science parks (otherwise named technology, business or innovation enterprises, or even research parks) are one of the institutional forms developed in the 1980s and 1990s that have attempted to connect universities and their research with business enterprise. The *Economist* (1993) reported positively on Warwick University's 'Warwick Manufacturing Group'. Established in the early 1980s, 240 staff at the Warwick University Science Park began to conduct joint research with industry. It compares its funding from industry with German Freehaufer institutes, from which firms can buy subsidized research which are half-way bodies funded 45 per cent from the state. It noted that John Major, the prime minister, rated the Warwick group as a 'role' model and continues:

> The customer not intellectual curiosity drives Warwick. All academics are on short-term contracts. Their performance is monitored. Degrees for managers are highly technical. The content is dictated by the firms, which share the teaching. All research is guided by companies too. Warwick insists that firms get involved. Rover spend £3m a year with the group; three profitable new technologies have resulted in the past 18 months. Inventing in-house would have been dearer, reckons Alan Curtis, Rover's Director of Product Supply (*Economist* 1993: 35).

At the core of the science park concept lies the idea that scientific knowledge leads in some natural or rational progression to technological innovation. Universities are seen as repositories of scientific expertise and research, and the view is that the UK is good at science but bad at commercializing its fruits. Science parks are a way of orienting academia more closely to the needs of industry (Massey *et al.* 1992: 34).

One index of a direct link between universities and the business of science parks is academic start-ups, that is, academic staff taking research out of the academic laboratory on to the science parks, starting up their own firms and moving on to the market (Massey *et al.* 1992: 34). In a 1986 survey of 183 establishments on science parks, one in six (i.e. 17 per cent) were university start-ups. In response to being asked about the most important factor influencing the firm's choice of location on the park, 16 per cent mentioned that a key founder had worked at the local academic institution.

The incidence of academic start-up firms varies considerably between parks (Massey *et al.* 1992: 36). Cambridge Science Park, despite having 'Laser Scan', one of the earliest and most well known of academic start-up firms, has a comparatively low percentage of such firms. By contrast, Aston Science Park has a high percentage of new start companies, and many of these are academic start-ups. A major factor encouraging new start firms at Aston was the availability of venture capital from the park's managing company, Birmingham Technology Ltd, something that is relatively unusual in the UK context. Another factor at Aston has, ironically, been the cuts made to the university occupational health and safety department following the large (31 per cent) 1981 UGC funding reductions. Some of the staff who left that department set up their own company on the science park.

Massey *et al.* (1992), in their trenchant critique of the economic, political and social assumptions and implications of science parks entitled *High Tech Fantasies*, argue that science parks embody sets of practices which are characteristic of certain features of late twentieth-century capitalism. These include a service and commercial orientation, reasonably advanced technology, a white-collar, fragmented, increasingly graduate workforce and anti-union managements. However, some of the claims for science parks – the close and substantial linking of academia with industry and the crucial improvement in the performance of the economy – are in their view overblown. Rather, science parks in general redistribute and replicate economic activity in patterns which do not fundamentally challenge or regenerate the traditional, business, social or even spatial structure of economic activity, and ironically the linking of business with universities through science parks may actually reinforce archaic social, professional and business cultures in the UK.

Science parks in Australia or Canada have not developed to the same extent as in the UK, still less the USA. Nevertheless, the new, developing incipient or planned science park was often a topic of discussion of senior academic managers in those countries where it may have more symbolic than real economic significance in linking the worlds of the university with those of the business enterprise.

The establishment of science parks is set against a background where historically Britain and its academics and businessmen had a reputation for inventiveness if not application in effective production and marketing. Trinity College, Cambridge has more Nobel-winning scientists than France. Papers by British scientists are the second most published and cited in the world. However, since 1986, Britain has been paying out more in royalties on patents from abroad than it has been earning. Of the G7 group of seven richest countries, which includes Canada but not Australia, Britain was the only one where the share of research and development expressed as a share of national income actually fell in the 1980s. Private research and development spending fell by 13 per cent between 1989 and 1991 (*Economist* 1993: 34).

Various reasons are given for the reluctance of many sectors of British industry to invest in research and development, among them the importance financiers attach to short-term profits and high dividend payments rather than long-term investment. The dearth of renewal and development is certainly of spasmodic concern to ministers as indicated by a range of projects to encourage contact between publicly funded university research and business. For example, William Waldegrave, minister with responsibility for science, has talked of wanting research to target emerging technologies (*Economist* 1993: 35). But as the same article points out, 'Business still neglect contacts with academia'. Colin Webb, a physics Don at Oxford, told a Lords Select Committee that his research group can expect two visits a year by delegations of up to twenty Japanese industrial scientists: 'The number of similar visits I get from research scientists in British industry is negligible'.

Master of Business Administration (MBA)

One of the most obvious areas where universities relate to the needs of the corporate economy is in the development of Master of Business Administration (MBA) degrees. They are ostensibly postgraduate degrees, although many entrants, particularly practising managers with a number of years of experience, take them without first degrees. Premium fees which cover the cost of provision and which generate a useful profit for the institution can be charged. In Australia, the Graduate School of Management at the University of Melbourne is now controlled jointly by the university and a number of major corporations (Marginson 1990). As in Britain there has been a proliferation of MBA courses and their direct relationship to the immediate needs of companies is increasingly being emphasized. Churchill (1993) reports the need for business school MBA courses to 'break away from traditional ideas about narrow functional specialisms' and to focus on implementation and practical experience putting students 'into the field to solve real business problems in partnership with host companies'. The head of Cranfield School of Management, which runs its own executive MBA programmes, said that 'companies are seeking MBA graduates not just with theoretical knowledge, but also with the influencing and leadership skills to put their ideas into practice; this is seen as more important than ever before'.

The majority of students on part-time 'executive' MBA programmes (usually of 2–3 years duration) are paid for by their companies as part of management development programmes. On full-time MBA programmes most students are self-funded. As fees in Britain in 1991–92 were often £6000–£7000 a year with living costs and foregone earnings on top, this represented a considerable investment.

Despite the considerable expenditure, even in the 1989–93 recession in the UK there seemed to be no shortage of candidates. This was partly a reflection of the enhanced earnings that MBA graduates have been able to command. Manchester Business School reported that the *average* salary of its 1992 graduates (two-thirds having gained offers of employment 3 months before graduation and 90 per cent immediately after graduation) was £30,000 with the top of the range being £50,000. That was higher than the top Lecturer grade (main career grade) of £24,000 and more than a full professor who, even with consultancy earnings, would not on average have been earning much more than £40,000 in 1993.

It may be that in the UK the supply of MBAs will swamp the marketplace by the mid-1990s. There has been a very rapid increase in the number of MBA courses being offered for the middle ranks of management in industry and commerce. There were about twenty in the mid-1980s producing about 2000 graduates a year. By 1992, over 100 business schools were offering MBAs producing about 8000 graduates a year (this is still about one-tenth of the 80,000 a year produced in the USA). Much of the expansion took place in the erstwhile polytechnics (now new universities), but even in those bastions of traditionalism, Oxford and Cambridge, MBA programmes were established.

MBAs are the most obvious type of course which universities have been developing and expanding which relate directly to the market and business needs. There has also been a substantial increase in the number of undergraduate and postgraduate courses, and overall student numbers engaged in business or cognate areas are up. Marginson (1990) reports that in Australia there was a large absolute and relative increase compared with other courses in the period 1979–88. Business/administration/economics student numbers increased from 7302 to 13,487, an increase of 84.7 per cent, nearly twice that of science – an increase of 42.8 per cent, from 7999 to 11,424. There was a 52.4 per cent increase in engineering/surveying students from 3268 to 4980, and a 45.7 per cent increase in arts/humanities/social science students from 13,336 to 19,426. In education, there was a small reduction of 0.4 per cent. Overall, there was a 34.3 per cent increase from 66,050 to 88,689 students.

This trend continued and in 1989 business studies students comprised 20.8 per cent of all Australian higher education students, about the same proportion as science and engineering combined. Of the new students enrolling in 1989, 22,199 (26.6 per cent) were business studies students, compared with 15,462 science students and 13,245 arts/humanities/social science students. This increase in the absolute and relative numbers of both undergraduate and postgraduate students studying subjects directly related to vocational careers in business, is likely to change the overall culture of universities and the relative influence of different groups of faculty in the governance and definition of purpose of the academic enterprise.

Accountability, value for money and academic freedom

Two consultative reports on the academic year (Flowers 1993a, b) and research accountability (Coopers and Lybrand 1993) produced for the Higher Education Funding Council for England illustrate the pressure for accountability and value for money. They exhibit a concern about the dangers of imposing economic or administrative solutions from the centre which might infringe on institutional autonomy or reduce the capacity of the individual academic to produce good research and teaching. The reports use careful language, consider a range of solutions and emphasize their advisory nature. However, the arguments are couched predominantly in the terminology of the state, manager and accountant. Their drift gives rise to the sort of fears expressed in a very different polemical style by Conrad Russell (1993: 107):

> ... the pressure on unit costs, the reduction in the amount of money per student, has been used as a battering ram to take academic judgement out of academic hands. This constitutes an assault on academic freedom. If academics cannot research, cannot decide how to teach, cannot defend the interests of their students, cannot decide the size of their institutions and cannot decide the standards of their degrees, what academic freedom is left for them.

The committee of enquiry chaired by Lord Flowers reviewed the organization of the academic year. The body of the committee's report is concerned with a fairly detailed evaluation of the costs and benefits – both academic and financial – of changing from the UK's traditional three 10 week terms (Oxford and Cambridge have 8 week terms), usually starting in October, to a two or three semester system of 15 weeks and various similar permutations and combinations. A semester system is used in most Australian, Canadian and US universities. The details of the comparisons are less important than the context, assumptions and likely outcomes in terms of intensification and control of academic work. The report notes as part of the background that it was occurring at a time when 'considerable attention was being given to the future direction and nature of higher education in the then wider context of the future role and purpose of post compulsory education' (Flowers 1993b: 10), and that this was already happening while the PCFC and UFC sectors were merging, that student participation in higher education was both increasing and widening, and the nature of the delivery of higher education was coming under examination in terms of content, method and timing.

The committee identified three features which had led to the establishment of the review. First, institutions were already considering change to the traditional three term structure with a view to improving the quality of learning, enabling staff to make more effective use of their time and 'improving the financial position – in terms of both revenue and capital' (Flowers 1993a: 3). Second, a 30 per cent (300,000) increase in student numbers was planned for the UK between 1991–92 and the year 2000, many of whom would be from non-traditional groups with new needs, and if this expansion was to be accommodated without sacrificing quality 'within the finance likely to be made available by the Exchequer structural change to the academic year may be required' (p. 3). Third, the possibility that reorganization of the academic year could accommodate more students, potentially increasing throughput without increasing institutions' accommodation. The Flowers Report (1993b: 5) considered the possibility that a three semester or four term year would allow a significant increase in the number of students within the existing available space. However, the main point of Flowers was perhaps its emphasis on the 'efficient' use of academic staff: 'Staff resources amount to about 75 per cent of total recurrent costs. The potential for increased efficiency in the area is of equal, if not greater importance than the increased utilisation of accommodation' (Ibid.).

The committee asserted that its proposals were advisory and not prescriptive, that it would be for institutions to make their own decisions on their preferred approach, that it recognized the diversity of purpose and missions of universities and it considered research-related concerns throughout its report. It noted that institutions were already considering implementing increases in the working day, working week and academic year to accommodate increased student numbers. The report concentrated on considering changes in the organization and extent of the academic year. It noted that many institutions in the traditional university sector and even more in the ex-polytechnic sector were instituting modular and semester systems, but that 'In response to the need to increase both the flexibility of provision and institutional capacity to meet the projected growth, a further question has now emerged. It concerns the extension of the academic year by using the summer period as a fourth term or third semester' (p. 7). This would extend the academic teaching year to 45 weeks, which could give the flexibility for multiple entry points for students or for more intensive courses, so that the very few institutions which currently offer a degree in 2 years might be extended.

One of the main concerns that the committee noted, expressed both by academic staff and students, was that an extension of the academic teaching year would adversely affect the research capability of staff. The report optimistically assumes 'that increasing student numbers will lead to additional resources with which universities and colleges can recruit additional staff'

(p. 52). Elsewhere, they note that 'increases in resources will in most cases lead to an increase in the number of staff, perhaps not pro-rata to the increase in student numbers, but thereabouts', and that there is a 'strong possibility that additional staff will need to be taken on with effectively teaching-only duties'.

By the time the Flowers Committee produced its final report in November 1993, some of its earlier assumptions about the continued growth of student numbers and hence pressure to use accommodation more efficiently had been undermined by the budget announcement which instituted measures to stabilize overall student numbers in universities for a 2–3 year period. The final report notes that:

> The higher education sector has experienced a period of rapid growth (student full-time equivalents have grown by 63 per cent between 1989–90 and 1993–94 in H.E.F.C.E. institutions – to a provisional total of 852,000). After a period of consolidation over the next two years, numbers are projected to continue to grow to approximately one million full-time equivalents. Providing for increasing numbers of students is already putting strain on the physical plant and on the other facilities of many institutions, and this will increase.
>
> (Flowers 1993b: 11)

Coopers and Lybrand (1993) reported on a range of possible ways of introducing greater accountability for the use of reseach funds. These ranged from very detailed monitoring of inputs and outputs to a very loose assessment of general output with the minimum of bureaucratic interference. As with the Flowers Report, the language is careful and the emphasis is on the advisory nature of the report. However, with both reports, the dominant discourse is essentially economic, with resource management and accountability the dominant themes. This language is beginning to replace that of scholarship, learning, teaching or the intrinsic benefits and delights of research within the higher education system as a whole, as well as within the cultures of individual universities.

This chapter has reviewed a variety of ways of conceptualizing the economy and its relationship to society within which universities are institutions with significant economic aspects. How these are described and understood depends in large measure on the broader analytical frameworks, so that the economic liberal, political economy and economic sociology perspectives deliver different foci of attention and emphasize different causal factors which are significant in producing the set of economic and social relations which constitute the university.

The second half of the chapter described and discussed some of these relations. This part of the account is based on government documents, some responses to them drawn from the educational press, and the views of academics – mainly 'managers', but also the managed. All these trace the impact of economic forces, in particular business interests, on the activities of universities. This, together with material drawn from Chapter 2, gives a theoretical and descriptive background for the next chapter, which focuses on analytical schemes for understanding the management of universities as institutions within the broad context of state, economy and society. These broader contexts and conceptions provide an underpinning and a framework within which particular strategies, tactics and styles of management are worked out, promulgated and applied.

4

Management in Universities

The focus of this chapter is on the management of universities at the institutional level. In previous chapters, we have seen universities as part of national systems. An account has been given of how the state and its agencies exercise influence on the purpose and practices of universities and how university managements respond to a range of pressures from government. In the last chapter, some indication of the interactions that occur between universities and their managements and the local, national and international economies was given. State and economy interact with each other and both have decisive influence and effects on how universities are managed. However, universities, their staff, students and managements are not simply passive recipients of state orders or market forces; they have their own resources, models, cultures and agendas.

Management at the institutional level has degrees of constraint and freedom. Management strategies and cultures are developed and perceived in varying ways by academic staff in different universities. In Chapter 5, a case study is presented and the final chapter extends the analysis to the implications of the changes in management, state and economy in the three countries for academic staff and university education in general.

In this chapter, in order to understand the management of universities, analysis and description from a number of different sources is presented to throw light on what are often ambiguous, paradoxical and even obscure university management practices. First, there is an account and discussion of some of the major models that have been used to analyse universities and their management. These provide different ways of conceptualizing how universities and their managements work. In practice, these models, in mixed and modified form, are used by university managers to inform their understanding and to guide and legitimate their activities. Different models and understandings of what the university is about are held by different groups, for which the institution may have markedly different realities and significance.

Some of these perceptions are embodied in the responses given by members of university managements in universities in Australia, Canada and the UK. The questions posed relate to their roles and activities as university managers responding to pressure from the state, industry and economy and to specific problems like staff recruitment, retention and removal and the promotion of research.

Finally, I draw together these different strands to comment more generally on what seem to be the main features and developments in the management of universities as they are understood by managers and academic staff at the level of the individual university.

Models of universities

Structures

When considering management of and in universities, and the different models that can be used to understand aspects of structure, process and change, one of the problems is to decide at what level to pitch the analysis. There are some clear physical and legal distinctions as well as different organizational structures. It is possible to distinguish in ascending order between the individual academic, the department in which he or she works (the faculty or school may or may not be a significant layer of organization or influence) and the university.

The university, however, has different organizational and legal forms – it may be unitary or collegiate. For universities like London, Oxford and Cambridge in the UK, for example, the college is as or more important than the university as a focus for academic organization, identity and management. This is less true of the Universities of Durham or York, which do have colleges but are less collegiate in terms of academic organization and management. In Canada, the collegiate constituents of the University of Ontario and the different campuses of the University of Quebec do have considerable, if varying, degrees of independence. In Australia, a few universities like Melbourne have collegiate elements, often derived from the merger arrangements following the establishment of the unified higher education system after 1989.

Beyond the university, the higher education system is more or less differentiated, which is in turn subject to degrees of control and influence by the state and market. Here the differences in practice between unitary and federal states have to do as much with financial and funding controls as formal legal status. On this reading, it is possible to distinguish as many as six different managerial levels: department, school or faculty, college or university, university higher education system, local state or province, national state. In reality – as far as the individual academic or manager is concerned – in most cases three or four levels are significant.

To illustrate how this works in terms of the interaction of an individual with different managerial levels, we can take a critical point in the career of an ordinary academic, say a decision at age 54 to take early retirement or to press on hoping for promotion to senior lecturer. At one level this is a personal decision influenced by the lecturer's past experience of success and frustration in terms of teaching and research in the current institutional context. Family situation, other employment possibilities and interests might have become important, so that the lecturer may have come to think of himself or herself as, say, an antique dealer, fisherman or gardener. Beyond the immediate individual experience and expectation and forming it, is the departmental context; the peer group of co-teachers and researchers, the attitude of the head of department and the power and resources available at departmental level. This in turn is determined by a range of factors: the subject taught in the department, its status and market position will affect the career prospects of the individual lecturer, so that, for example, in a business school the situation of someone in an accounting or marketing department might be very different to a lecturer in a social science area.

The faculty level in some instances may be significant in terms of status, power and resources; the obvious instance would be medicine where, in the UK, higher salaries are paid to clinical staff. In some universities, professional schools of law or engineering may have influence which is relevant to an individual's career. This works not only in terms of formal opportunities, but also decides who are the significant actors, so that a dean of a faculty may be more influential in deciding career patterns than the professor who is the head of department. Then there is the university level: in British universities with limited resources, in some cases having suffered massive cuts, there have been policies to encourage, even pressure academics to take early retirement or take 'enhanced mobility allowances' with offers amounting to two or three times annual salary in some cases. Universities will usually have institution-wide procedures for processing promotions, but there may be a degree of variation as between faculties and departments in terms of both procedure and criteria; for example, the number of references required will depend on institutional dynamics (i.e. how centralized, formalized and uniform its management practices are). Beyond the university, the resources and policies applied in the university system as a whole, in terms for example of partially self-managed areas like rating rewards for research performance, will be influential in affecting the position of an individual academic. In the UK, the research rating of a department from 1 (low) to 5 (high) will affect the prospects of an individual academic within it. In turn, higher education as a whole is shaped and limited by the policies and resources made available by the central authority. In the Canadian federal system, the provincial government provides yet another level of complexity and control.

To return to an analysis at the level of the university, there are many administrative and institutional features of universities common to Australia, Canada and the UK. Nearly all are governed by a bicameral system. This consists usually of a formally superior governing body, termed variously 'council' or 'board of governors' (or even sometimes confusingly, 'senate'), with responsibility for financial, legal and administrative integrity and with a predominance of externally appointed lay members, and a separate body charged with the governance of academic affairs composed of a mixture of ex-officio and elected academics, usually called a 'senate' or 'academic board'.

In the same way as states may be unitary or federal, so can universities; in the latter case, the constituent bodies usually bring together colleges or institutes with their own systems of governance. As with unitary and federal states, universities' formal constitutions operate in different ways, often depending more on the distribution of bureaucratic and personal power and financial control than legalistic distinctions.

One type of university administration which is similar but significantly different to the collegiate universities of Oxford and Cambridge, where historically 'prior to the twentieth century, wealth, power and prestige at both Oxford and Cambridge . . . resided in the colleges rather than universities' (Tapper and Salter 1992: 91), is what might be termed the federal university. The Universities of London and Wales are examples. The constitutions of the University of Ontario and some other Canadian universities, particularly in Quebec, are in some respects similar. Processes of amalgamation, proceeding at different rates over time but more marked around the time of the establishment of a unified system in first Australia and then the UK between 1988 and 1992, have produced institutions which, while they may not have formally federal constitutions, incorporate former colleges of education, art or music that retain a degree of identity and self-government. The crucial factor is the degree of integration or devolution in the control of finances. Where there are separate endowments or funds from central government sources which flow directly to the constituent colleges or units, their capacity for independent action is enhanced.

Tapper and Salter (1992) describe in their chapter aptly entitled 'Colleges and the blessings of endowment income' how the pressure exercised by central government through the terms of grants and through advice has enhanced the role of the Universities of Oxford and Cambridge. However, the endowment resources of the richer 20 or so colleges at both universities, together with the way in which the state has continued to fund fees to colleges through local authority grants, has allowed the colleges to retain quite a high degree of financial autonomy and power. The power of the central administrations at Oxford and Cambridge has undoubtedly increased in the last two decades. There has also been a process through the equalization of the use of endowment resources and common admissions procedures of establishing what Tapper and Salter (1992: 109) call an 'inter-collegiate' administration. However, the power of the colleges and their dons remains considerable.

The situation in the federal Universities of London and Wales is rather different. Historically, an important aspect of these universities has been their status as examining bodies, not only for constituent colleges, but, in the case of London, moderating external degrees in many polytechnics, technical colleges and colleges of commerce before the development of the CNAA and the binary system in the 1960s. Before the Second World War,

London established university colleges at Leicester and Exeter that later became fully independent universities. The process by which once dependent subordinate colleges become autonomous, grow, attain independent financial resources and exercise increasing academic self-government is complex. There may be various outcomes from complete independence to a loosening of federal ties and control. In the case of the Universities of London and Wales, discussions have been underway for some years. In 1993, it looked as though both institutions would disintegrate, with the establishment of totally independent university status for the larger constituent colleges – Cardiff, Swansea, Bangor and Aberystwyth in the case of Wales, and Imperial College, University College, Kings College and the London School of Economics in the case of London. However, the chances of this happening appear to have receded, though the colleges have attained much independence. Direct funding status and revisions of arrangements concerning governance and financial arrangements mean that the formal federal Universities of Wales and London will continue to exist with some powers. In effect, the constituent university colleges function as independent universities, but retain a degree of coordination and commonality. With collegiate federal universities of this type, there is always the possibility that under certain conditions there will be a break-away or break-up. Even where formally unitary institutions have been established as in Australia prior to and during the process of the establishment of the unified system, particularly where the amalgamations have seemed to be forced by governmental pressure or where one institution seems to dominate or 'take over' another, there have been and are likely to be further instances of institutional break-up and reformation as new institutions. This is more likely where there are geographically quite separate campuses and where the constituent parts have quite distinctive identities and cultures. An example of this process has been the case of the Northern Rivers campus of the University of New England breaking away to form a separate university.

Something of the complexity and variety of universities has been indicated, as has the range of levels from the individual, through the department, faculty and system to the state, within which universities are inserted and managed. This might seem to indicate that the university as such might not be the best or even a prime focus for an attempt to understand managerial activity. Alternatives discussed in previous chapters include the relations between the higher education system and the state and economy, or the relations of both these to individual academics or to departments, subjects or professional groups. However, when discussing state, economy and higher education generally, in all three countries one has to consider the implications for, and reactions of, particular universities and their managements' styles and strategies. As far as individual academics or colleague groups in teaching departments or research institutes are concerned, important as immediate superiors or general government and system policy may be, the crucial relations remain with the university as both employer and manager.

Fielden and Lockwood (1973) put the case for considering universities as the prime focus of management. Since the 1970s, the activities of government, system-controlling bodies and various changes in funding mechanisms have at the same time increased outside constraints and emphasized competition between universities as separate entities. They argued that:

> Universities are organisations which have corporate responsibilities, and which possess power to manage the activities of their members in order to carry out these responsibilities. Members of the academic staff collectively constitute the major element in the government of the university, but individually they are employees by contract. Members of academic staff may be influenced by, and give their prime loyalty to, the national and sometimes, international professional groups which cut across all universities. However, in terms of organisation and management, the existence of the university creates a firm boundary. Faculties, colleges, departments and other units are not autonomous units within a guild structure, they are interdependent parts of a unitary organisation.
>
> (Fielden and Lockwood 1973: 22)

This still provides a good case for considering universities as organizations. Various models, both analytical and managerial, can be applied to them. They exist as distinct and distinctive institutions for academics, both managed and managing, as well as for government, employers, students and the general public.

Models

The range of organizational analytical and prescriptive models is wide and any categorization will inevitably oversimplify and provide contentious cases. The scheme developed by Walford (1987) provides the basis for a differentiation that reflects the wide range of approaches and provides a vehicle for understanding how universities may be understood as managed institutions. How administrators and academics conceptualize their own institution and their role emerges in the latter part of this chapter in responses to questions about how managers see themselves and how they deal with specific problems.

Models with varying degrees of analytical and managerial power can be roughly categorized into four groups. First, there is a range of models that emphasize rationality in either analytical or pragmatic terms and that focus on various institutional forms and processes – administrative, bureaucratic, managerial and even to a degree collegial. Second, there are models that emphasize ambiguity, expressed in a variety of ways, such as 'organized anarchy' (Cohen and March 1974), 'garbage can' (Enderud 1977) or even as 'loose coupled'! Third, there are models that emphasize the political and interactionist aspects of the relationships between individuals and groups that constitute universities and that place less emphasis on the university as a given institutional entity. Fourth, there are a number of models that are composites, which attempt to include aspects of the other models in either a sequential (Enderud 1977) or system (Becher and Kogan 1992) perspective.

The rational models have roots in Weber's (1947) analysis of bureaucracy and rational legal authority. A bureaucratic organization has a formal organizational structure, specified roles with a hierarchy, and a clear chain of command with formalized written regulations and procedures. The authority of the official – in the case of universities, an administrator or academic – will rest on the holding of an office rather than personal charisma or traditional reverence.

In the pure form, the bureaucratic organization is dedicated to a pursuit of goals which can be rationally explained and justified and where the activities of the bureaucracy are logically related to and conducive to the attainment of these goals. Weber recognized that bureaucratic organizations usually have leaders and/or governing bodies who exercise power on different grounds. Vice-chancellors sometimes have charismatic qualities and governing bodies are composed of traditional notables from state, church or commerce, with elected representatives from local authorities and from the academic staff themselves, as well as university bureaucrats.

Halsey (1992: 36) points out that the Victorian idea of the university in England, while taking into account the rationalizing and bureaucratizing effects of industrial society, espoused a view that incorporated ancient and medieval traditions. Halsey shows the connection between the form or organization of the university and the characteristics of its graduates:

> Max Weber in Germany summarized these traditions as a cultivation of young men in the humanistic outlook and styles of the dominant strata. Charisma apart, he distinguished between two types of social personality as the products of higher education – the *cultivated* man and the *expert*, and the British Victorians had certainly made much of the correlative curricula distinction between *education* and *training*. Behind these distinctions Weber had identified two corresponding forms of power – the *traditional* and *rational* – and the twentieth-century history of universities may be understood as a struggle between drives to express their underlying forms of authority in the curriculum and organisation of the university and its claims to enter its alumni into positions of occupational and social authority.
>
> (Halsey 1992: 36)

Weber saw education as adapting to industrialism. In the contest for dominance between the cultivated man [*sic*] and associated traditional forms of authority and the expert and rational authority, the expert was likely to win because of the 'irresistible expanding bureaucratisation of all public and private relations of authority and by the ever-increasing importance of expert and specialised knowledge' (Weber, in Gerth and Mills 1947: 243, cited by Halsey 1992: 38). If that was true at the beginning of the twentieth century, it is much more so at its end.

Following Weber, there have been a range of behavioural scientists, organizational analysts and management theorists who have taken a basically rational view of organizations and their administration. Often analysis has been developed primarily with private corporations or public administration in mind (Fayol 1949; Drucker 1959; March and Simon 1985), and there have been attempts to apply the model and associated prescriptions to universities (Samut 1986; Walford 1987). The main features of a rational model of universities is that it assumes, implicitly at least, that the university is composed of rational individuals, who will have access to relevant information for decision making and through a process of reasoned discussion come to agreement about goals and strategies for achieving them. In practice, some senior managers assume that it is sufficient for them to search for solutions and that, once presented, the rest of the academic staff will see the reasonableness, indeed inevitability, of the action proposed and will concur with them.

In its more simplistic form, the 'rational' model makes the fundamental assumption of consensus. This is related to a rather naive view that a limited number of goals can be clearly identified and agreed. It is assumed that individual participants in the organization will identify with it, and that there will be a demonstrable congruence between individuals and the institutional goals. On this model, disagreement or dissidence can be put down to a failure in communication, so if the management goals and strategies are explained more clearly, the misinformed academic will see the light. Alternatively, there is an assumption that the individual is deviant and should be treated accordingly. Room for sustained, principled disagreement, which itself is rationally based, is rather limited. There are a number of problems – both analytical and practical – in coming to terms with the incoherence, confusion and conflict that actually occur in universities. Such problems with the simpler rationalistic theories and prescriptions are realized among the more acute of the universities' management echelons, some of whom have adopted a systems theory approach in an attempt to deal with the complexities of managing universities. However, systems theory (Becher and Kogan 1992) shares many of the assumptions, strengths and weaknesses of managerialist decision-making rational models.

Walford (1987: 129) has noted that there has been a development of more sophisticated rational models that attempt to deal with disagreements; hence Cuthbert (1984) discusses pragmatic–rational models which, in terms of practical policy makers, are more realistic than analytic–rational models. The pragmatic model recognizes that it is unlikely that complete agreement will be reached on organizational objectives but that decision makers will still proceed to informed choices that can be justified rationally. Brunsson (1982) makes a distinction between decision rationality and action rationality; thus, while rational decision making might consider a range of possibilities, for example in the case of UK universities in the early 1980s closure or merger with another institution, there may be strong ideological forces which prevent serious consideration of these possibilities and limit the range of action. In this way, management may still be conceived of as rational but within a limited ideologically bounded scope.

There is a strong predisposition for senior administrators and academic managers to adopt at least some elements of a rational model to inform and justify their actions; it fits with the ethos of universities and with their own training. The bureaucratic structuring and processes of university administration reflect and reinforce this approach. Furthermore, pressures from government and specifically higher education funding agencies, although they may be perceived as capricious and make irrational demands on the institution and its managers, at least in the short term promote planning and accountability procedures (HEFCE 1993) which assume a rational model. In terms of institutional life, it is likely that rational, particularly bureaucratic models, will be most influential when there is a relatively stable situation, say one of slow growth with a commensurate increase in resources. Under conditions of severe cutbacks or rapid growth, merger or changes in legal status and managerial forms, then the stresses of adaptation are likely to reveal sometimes quite fundamental disagreement about the purposes and goals of the university. Differences of interest as between different groups of academic staff emerge which cannot be resolved by rational discussion.

So far in this discussion of rational models, there has been reference to the principles of the models and to one of the major forms – bureaucracy, expressed in a range of institutions including universities. However, collegiality is another major institutional form, particularly associated with universities. It can be seen as competing with bureaucracy at least in terms of legitimacy. Collegiality embodies aspects of rationality. Although the emphasis on equality and democratic discussion is different to the hierarchy and subordination characteristic of bureaucratic forms, there is a common assumption that through the exercise of reason consensus will be reached. The institutional forms that collegiality takes can be various. Historically, collegiality based on the existence of separate colleges as at Oxford and Cambridge has been one of its most influential forms. Here relatively small groups of fellows of formally equal status deliberate and form policy and in many cases practise administration through the rotation of offices. They resolve disagreement through debate and vote for the head of college. In large non-collegiate universities or universities where the colleges do not exercise the power they still do at Oxford and Cambridge, there are institutional forms – senates, academic and faculty boards and even elements of councils or governing bodies – which are essentially collegial. The elements of collegiality usually operate through representatives of the academic body rather than through the direct active participation of all.

Harvey (1988) argues that the traditional view of the university as a college, which can be described as a community of individuals and groups, all of whom have different roles and specialities, but who share common goals and objectives for the organisation, has been superseded by a political model. There is much to be said for this standpoint and the political model will be described shortly. However, it is important to distinguish between all-encompassing models, whether analytical or prescriptive, and institutional forms and ideals. Rational, bureaucratic and collegial models cannot describe in full the culture or governance of universities, but nevertheless they have power as partial accounts and models of how universities as organizations can be managed. Before moving on to examine political models, it is necessary to describe a set of models which are in direct contrast to the rational model and which claim to represent more nearly the reality of life in universities. These see the management of universities as an ambiguous, paradoxical and disorganized arena.

Such models have been designated 'garbage can' (Cohen *et al.* 1972) and 'organized anarchy' (Cohen and March 1974), and Walford (1987) stresses they emphasize ambiguity. In the 'garbage can' model, in contrast with the rational model, there is no careful consideration of choices or strategy. There are sets of solutions and problems that are not necessarily articulated. There are a variety of actors in the university who possess problems or propose solutions. There are occasions when the organization has to make decisions in response to particular crises or pressures. At this juncture, contingent, *ad hoc* meetings of solutions and problems occur within, as the metaphor puts it, 'the garbage can' and there is an outcome. Walford summarizes the 'garbage can' model (if it can be called a model, for maybe 'model' is too rational a formulation) in contrast to the rational model as follows:

> The traditional, rational, way of thinking about choice opportunities is to suppose that a problem leads to the generation of alternative solutions, which are then examined in terms of their consequences and in terms of institutional objectives, and finally a decision is made. In the 'garbage can' model the sequence of actions is not predetermined and there is a discontinuous flow of problems, solutions, participants and choice opportunities without there necessarily being any 'logical' or one to one relationship between these four elements.
>
> (Walford 1987: 133)

A less provocative formulation of a model that in a sense encompasses the 'garbage can' situation is the 'organized anarchy' model. Here the emphasis is on the university as a very loosely structured institution, in contrast to private corporations or government departments. A wide range of individuals, some of them organized in more or less coherent colleague groups, inhabit the terrain of the university. They may have little in common, having different cultures and aims, and neither hierarchy nor collegiality effectively coordinates them in pursuit of common goals. An extreme cynical but popular expression of this view is that of a university composed of individuals and departments united only by complaints about car parking. In the 'organized anarchy' model, while individuals or groups may have relatively clear coherent goals, the institution as a whole is characterized by a lack of clear goals, let alone a subordinate one. Further crucial elements of the technology of the institution – in universities, the processes of teaching, learning and doing research – are unclear, difficult to understand, control or improve.

Those participating in the university and its decision-making procedures vary considerably from time to time. For example, in the summer vacation, with most students absent, lecturers busily writing books or articles at home, and between meetings of senates, faculty boards and departmental meetings, what or who constitutes the university? The building may be described as the 'university'. The vice-chancellor and those administrative and clerical staff who are almost continually present, in practice constitute 'the university' for many outsiders. Or does the university have a formal, abstract ideal existence which encompasses all its members and some essential ethos? Part of the attraction of the 'organized anarchy' model is that it is anti-idealist; it presents a practical material analysis claiming to represent the messy reality of life in universities, recognizable in novel form in, for example, David Lodge's books *Changing Places* (1975), *Small World* (1984) and *Nice Work* (1988).

One of the problems with the 'organized anarchy' model is that it is somewhat dated. It may have been a reasonable description of interactions in universities in the 1960s and 1970s. Even then it probably underestimated the importance of power and contractual obligations. By the 1980s, with increased government control and reduced resources, the political aspects of university governance, and in particular increased managerial control, were apparent and the 'organized anarchy' model seemed increasingly anachronistic either as analysis or ideal.

Harvey (1988), in her analysis of two Canadian universities in British Columbia adapting to reductions in resources, makes a strong case for the utility of a political model. However, she does that in opposition to a consensus collegial model and has a rather specific notion of the political focusing on overtly self-interested political behaviour. A more general case can be argued for a political model being appropriate for understanding power relations in universities and, of course, other organizations. This may apply even when there is an absence of overt conflict and the organization seems to be in a stable state. Both the limited and the broad view of the political model are worth taking seriously. The emergence and relevance of a political model of university management was accepted by key actors – academics, administrators and managers, as well as analysts – in universities in the course of the 1980s. The narrow political model assumes that individuals are motivated by self-interest; the broader model assumes that, whatever the motivation, analysis must take due account of power relations and differences in interests.

One of the most influential writers to advocate a political model is Baldridge. His case study of change and crisis in New York University (Baldridge 1971) used essentially a 'political systems' model, which assumes that complex organizations like universities can be studied as if they were miniature political systems. Baldridge *et al.* (1978: 35) distinguishes six assumptions about the political process which would apply to the interactions in and of a university. First, there is a lot of uncertainty and for much of the time most people are not involved in the policy process. Thus while a range of individuals and groups may be involved in the political/policy process over particular issues, it is those individuals – and this is the second assumption – who spend continuous time and effort, who are effective in influencing and controlling policy. In general, they are predominantly senior administrative and academic staff, usually the vice-chancellor (president) and registrar. The third assumption is that universities are composed of different interest groups with differing goals and values. Unless there are plentiful resources, these interest groups are likely to come into conflict. Thus the fourth assumption is that conflict is normal, not an aberration or necessarily dysfunctional. The fifth assumption is that the power and authority of the formal bureaucratic system within the university will be modified and changed by the political action of effective interest groups. Sixth, interest groups are located both inside and outside the university and often external interest groups – for example, political parties or trades unions – may have a powerful influence on what happens inside the university.

Baldridge's model is useful in analysing the political processes and management of universities during stress or crisis, as when there are severe reductions in resources or major reorganization; for example, at Aston in the early 1980s (Walford 1987), or Baldridge's (1971) own analysis of the reform process at New York University in the 1960s, or Harvey's (1988) analysis of retrenchment in Canadian universities in the mid-1980s. However, because this approach concentrates on showing the overt political processes and rightly identifies the importance of conflict, negotiation and control of resources between competing interest groups, it underplays the importance of the existence of more concealed implicit power relations that operate when institutions are in a stable environment. Indeed, by keeping some issues off the agenda and effectively denying the legitimacy of other interest groups, a dominant cabal can effectively maintain the *status quo* or pursue a particular course of action.

Lukes' (1974, 1979) analysis of power distinguishes analytically between three levels or dimensions. The first level concentrates on an analysis of direct observable behaviour by individuals or groups in introducing particular policies or securing specific decisions in their favour (Dahl 1961). The second level, developed by Bachrach and Baratz (1962), recognizes that power is exercised not only during direct confrontation but also when individuals or groups are able to create, ascertain, modify or reinforce political values and institutional practices in such a way that they limit or set a framework within which discussion and decisions take place.

Lukes' third level goes beyond this 'mobilization of bias'. He argues that power is exercised not only in situations of conflict – overt or emerging – but also when creating the conditions to ensure that conflict does not arise. This is not simply because subordinate groups do not engage in conflict because they judge they have little chance of success (a common enough situation in universities), but also as Lukes (1979: 23) puts it, peoples' 'perceptions, cognition and preferences have been shaped in such a way that they accept their role because they cannot imagine any other or see it as natural and unchangeable'. Because of their intellectual training, it is unlikely that many university academics will be totally uncritical or accepting of their role; moreover, it is difficult to apply the general ideological analysis that Lukes' third dimension demands at the level of the university as an organization to be managed. Nevertheless, this dimension is apposite for consideration of the general relations of academics and universities to polity and economy described in Chapters 2 and 3, and will be used again in the final chapter.

In this chapter, the first and second dimensions are clearly relevant to a consideration of how universities are managed as perceived by their managers but, in some ways, it is the way in which the third type of power works that is the most interesting.

Walford (1987) groups together political and interactionist models, and in the sense that both give credence to the individual's perception of his or her own interests, this is clearly justified. Drawing on the work of Mead (1934), Becker (1961), Blumer (1969) and, as far as sociology of education in Britain is concerned, Woods (1983), a symbolic interactionist perspective places a strong emphasis on the individual's construction of reality. Political model perspectives emphasize the importance of the group and the realities rather than the perceptions of power. A symbolic interactionist or phenomenologist perspective will stress the meanings people give to their own actions and those of others. This is important because the meanings people hold, even if mistaken, will inform their actions and influence their behaviour. Thus if, for example, disgruntled academics wish to believe through a combination of their own frustrations and a reading of the vice-chancellor's intentions that he is shortly going to resign or accept another job, this may reduce their efforts to gain control over the university's policy-making apparatus – no need to make an effort, happy days will be here again. However, of course, the reading of the vice-chancellor's intentions may be mistaken; he may intend to stay and their perceptions paradoxically will have strengthened his position. One of the difficulties with a symbolic interactionist perspective is that it tends to take each individual's perceptions and interests as of equal value. While this may have moral value, in practice as Walford (1987: 138) succinctly puts it: 'While everyone may experience the organisation in a different way and define his or her own reality, some people have more power than others to make their interpretation persuasive'.

Some of the more sophisticated analyses of university organization (Enderud 1977; Clark 1983; Lockwood and Davies 1985; Becher and Kogan 1992) recognize that different models will reveal different aspects of the university, and furthermore that they may be more or less apposite at different times. One way of accommodating the different models is to relate them as a sequence, so that 'organized anarchy' models which emphasize ambiguity might be followed by political models emphasizing power and negotiation, in turn followed by a collegial phase where legitimacy for policies is obtained, and concluding with a rational bureaucratic phase where more or less agreed policies are implemented. This sort of sequencing can be presented as an actual account of changes (e.g. Enderud's description of changes in Scandinavian universities in the 1970s) or as a prescriptive account (e.g. as a guide to managers, as in Lockwood and Davies 1985). The difficulty with this approach is that it can easily fall into a Whig interpretation of history, where the sequencing is progressive and the end state is deemed to be superior to that which preceded it. An inverted form often adopted by radical critics of university management might be termed the 'golden age' model: 'In the beginning was democratic collegiality, which has been diminished by the encroachments of bureaucracy, state power and subservience to a market ethos'. There are some elements of this in Halsey's (1992) *Decline of Donnish Dominion*, as the title suggests.

While it is true that if we look at particular universities, certain decisions may proceed through a sequence of ambiguity, political activity, collegiality and bureaucracy, as described by Enderud (1977) and advocated by Lockwood and Davies (1985), in other cases it does not work like this. In practice, the pattern of interaction and the dominance of one form and style of management over another and hence the applicability of a particular model will depend on the balance of power and influence of the particular actors, individuals and groups. In the end, one is driven back to a political model, while recognizing that dominant political groups may mobilize particular apparently non-political models to facilitate and legitimate their own activity.

There is a tendency of advocates of complex sequential models in the end to see the situation from a management perspective. This is also true in large measure of systems theorists. Becher and Kogan (1992) are clear that they are presenting a model to aid an understanding of the relationship between different levels of reality – individual, basic unit, university and state – and that the model sheds light on some areas and not others. Their account presents in more manageable form an analysis similar to the complex structural functionalist analysis of Parsons (1951) and Parsons and Smelser (1956). This analysis attempted, through the identification of four basic functions – adaptation, goal attainment, pattern maintenance and integration – to present the analytical features of social systems, large and small, including universities (Holton 1992: 21).

'Goal attainment' involves the political articulation and achievement of goals. Adaption concerns the deployment of resources – land, labour and capital – to meet the goals. 'Pattern maintenance' involves the institutionalization of values into stable cultural patterns. 'Integration' concerns the creation of a balance between the other three functions so as to manage conflict and tension. Parsons and Smelser used their analysis at the level of societies to include the political, economic, religious and educational subsystems. It has also been used at the level of particular institutions, including the school (Parsons 1951); in principle, it can be applied to the university.

The power and influence of this approach can be noted in the work of Holton (1992) and his conceptualization of economic sociology, but it also finds echoes in Becher and Kogan's (1992) analysis. They make a convincing case for treating the university as a significant institution worthy of its own level of analysis alongside the individual, basic unit (department) and the central level of 'various authorities who are charged with overall planning, resource allocation and the monitoring of standards' (Becher and Kogan 1992: 9). These elements are meant to represent functions rather than entities, so that people may operate sometimes as individual academics, but they also sometimes represent basic units or even institutions as a head of department or chair of a university committee.

Becher and Kogan (1992) distinguish between two modes relating to the academic or the university as an organization, which they argue can be analytically separated but which in practice are not sharply distinguished in the everyday life of the academic or the university. The first mode, the *normative* mode, relates to the monitoring and maintenance of mode values – what people in the system count as important. The second, the *operational* mode, refers to the business of carrying out practical tasks at different levels within the system – what people actually do or are institutionally required to do (Becher and Kogan 1992: 10).

These two modes can be analysed as having internal and external aspects. Becher and Kogan (1992: 12) state that if we take the normative mode, the external aspect for the institution would be concerned to take cognisance of current social, economic and cultural values. Internally, the university would meet the requirements of the external authorities and set and monitor rules of procedure and due process. The institution would seek to ensure that the basic units (departments) carried out proper procedures as far as academic appointments, student recruitment and the use of funds were concerned. Increasing pressure from central authorities means that the university exercises increasing control in these areas and develops policies and norms around 'enterprise culture', 'managerial efficiency' and 'criteria for excellence'. While adumbrated at a national system level, these norms are articulated and take specific form at the level of the university.

The second, operational mode involves internal university operations concerning the maintenance and development of its constituent elements and its range of established activities, through the differential allocation of money and personnel:

> It has a key role in planning and implementing policy decisions coming from the central level in return for resources. Extensive pressures on the university at the operational level might involve specific proposals for research on industrial projects, the solution of social problems or expectations that the university promote cultural development.
>
> (Becher and Kogan 1992: 14)

This sort of system analysis provides a framework for relating the individual academic to the department, the university and the pressures coming from central government in terms of a range of goals, aspirations and activities. This in turn facilitates the conceptualization of the university's problems as an institution adapting to external and internal pressures. However, when applied at the university level, there is a tendency for a process of reification (e.g. Rex 1961): the university becomes an entity rather than a collection of individuals. Then anthropomorphism occurs, in that the university somehow acquires a spirit, mind and purpose independent of its members. Conveniently, this model can be used persuasively by senior academic administrators to equate their own interests as managers with that of the university as a social system. This legitimates their own actions and can reduce the force of alternative views. Thus the statement that '. . . the university needs 12 redundancies to meet its operational budget and fulfil its purpose as an ongoing academic institution' may be credible from a systems perspective. It delegitimizes the perspective of individual academics or even academic departments which argue that they need the security of tenure arrangement to pursue the true purpose of the academic enterprise and their commitment to professional values in terms of teaching and research.

In considering these models, the political ones are most useful in explaining what goes on in university management and not only during cutbacks or restructuring. Walford (1987) argues that managers and those managed display their own understanding and use various models to analyse the situation and intervene in policy making. But also, and maybe more important, by promulgating a particular model – a rational or system type – they can legitimate or at least neutralize the activity and criticism of actual or potential opponents. Walford (1987: 145) puts it like this:

> Individuals and groups have their own interests which may well develop into clear, observable conflicts. They also develop their own definition of the situation, their own ideologies or models of university organisation which structure the way in which they view real or potential change. The various actors have different resources which they can draw upon to make their definition of the situation stick. They can reinforce their own particular way of looking at the world such that barriers are erected to limit the scope of the political process such that some issues are simply not discussed [e.g. the remuneration of the vice-chancellor]. Further, those with power in the organisation are able to selectively draw upon and use to their advantage the models of organisation held by others.

Thus those in power may be able to appeal to the ideal models held by others (e.g. a collegial model) to invoke cooperation or allegiance. At other times, they adopt a system or rational managerial model to push through decisions in the face of opposition. They may thus retain a degree of legitimacy and rule out effective opposition. The skilful use of a particular range of models of the organization can itself be a powerful management tool and one not easily challenged.

So far, we have considered models for understanding universities and for managing them that pay little attention to the actual or ideal purposes of the university. There are, however, prescriptive models that promote particular ideals with attendant and organizational forms. The controversy and confusion about these models, both outside and inside the university, is viewed by Scott as one of the causes of the crises of confidence he sees as endemic in universities in the 1980s. Scott (1990) distinguishes five models which have operated over the last century and a half in the UK, in the USA and Canada, and in Continental Europe and Australia.

The first of these models might be termed the 'liberal university', as advocated by Newman (1910) in his *The Idea of a University*, where knowledge is pursued for its own sake, not for its utility:

> If then the intellect is so excellent a portion of us, and its cultivation so excellent, it is not only beautiful, perfect, admirable, and noble in itself, but in a true and high sense it must be useful to the possessor and to all around him; not as useful in any low, mechanical, more mercantile sense, but as a diffusing good, or as a blessing, or a gift, or power, or a treasure, first to the owner, then through him to the world.
> (Newman 1910: 164)

This model has usually been seen as elitist but, as Scott (1990: 131) points out, 'in nineteenth-century Scotland a different but equally liberal tradition of university education developed, which is generally summed up in the phrase "the democratic intellect"'. This was a more open tradition but equally suspicious of utilitarianism.

The same could not be said of a second major model, that of the 'research university'. Here research might be in search of truth and beauty or quite utilitarian ends, but the emphasis and overriding purpose of the university is research for knowledge rather than teaching or the formation of students' characters. This model found its institutional form in nineteenth-century German universities, in some universities in the USA, and in London University and the large civic universities in the UK. The prototypical academic figure is the powerful and eminent research professor with assistants and postgraduate students, who conveys an image of formidable intellectual power.

The third and fourth models, which Scott identifies as the 'composite' and 'multiversity', reached their most developed forms in the USA, but exercise an influence in the UK, Australia and Canada. The university combines or attempts to combine a variety of aims and functions – strong research, postgraduate and professional education, courses for undergraduates, extramural activities and service to the community. Scott notes that a major proponent of this view, Clark Kerr, chose *The Uses of the University* (1966) as the title of his book; this contrasts with Newman's (1910) *The Idea of a University* in that 'uses' is plural and 'idea' is singular. Scott (1990: 132) asserts that Kerr's formulation 'seemed to gather up all the aspirations of mid-century society for scientific excellence, economic growth and efficiency, social reform, and individual advancement and fulfilment'.

A fifth tradition, which can be termed the 'people's university', developed in the UK from the open traditions of further and technical education. It found expression in higher education in the London polytechnics like Borough and Regent Street. Because of the elitist and restricted nature of much of the older established universities in the UK, this model found clearest expression on the 'public' side of the binary divide between the mid-1960s and the end of the 1990s. In Canada as in the USA, this tradition or model is largely subsumed under the multi-university. In Australia, it was largely carried within colleges of advanced education and technological universities until they attained university status or combined with established universities on the unification of the system after 1988. In all three countries, it is a powerful model; professed by egalitarian politicians, espoused by some managers and administrators, as well as many academics and students. 'Diversity and flexibility are the main characteristics of this model. [It affects] A much wider variety of courses, at different levels and taught in different modes, designed for a more heterogeneous student population' (Scott 1990: 132). Here the idea of the university serving the needs of disadvantaged groups within the population – women, ethnic minorities, mature students, the working class and, in Australia and Canada, rural students – is strongly represented.

Such models are drawn on by academic managers when describing how they manage and with what objectives in mind. This is true even when they see themselves as largely responding to outside pressures. The model of the university they espouse explicitly or implicitly shapes the sort of responses and strategies they see open to them. Even more important than the range of models used in an analysis of how universities, their staff, managers and basic units interact, is how these models are taken up and acted on by managers and others.

At one level, a particular strategy and individual ploys will be seen as the product of the personal stance and the practical exigencies of unique situations. But there are patterns of action and reaction and lying behind these are implicit and sometimes explicit assumptions about how the university is, how it works or should work, what are legitimate ways of conceptualizing the institution and its purposes(s), and thus what action is justified. It is here that we can see the relation between the somewhat abstract models – rational, collegial, bureaucratic, which are often translated into personal policies – and the more or less complex 'garbage can' or 'organized anarchy' model, popularly expressed as a 'complete mess up'.

It is important to remember that the managers of universities are not usually familiar with current social scientific literature, particularly the more analytical or critical sort. There has certainly been an increasing use of and familiarity with managerial literature and practice, but some of it is drawn from popular and arguably inappropriate sources, whose prime focus is on the management of private corporations. Inevitably, senior managers will draw on past schemes, half-remembered sources and, of course, on practical experience. There is no reason to expect that an eminent scientist, physician, engineer or lawyer who has attained a position of power and influence in managing a university should be particularly familiar with current debates on organizational analysis or contemporary evaluations of managerial style and strategy.

Styles and structures in 'new' and 'old' universities

This section draws on a paper by Landman and Ozga (1992) who were, respectively, chair of the faculty board and dean of the faculty of education at the University of the West of England, Bristol, formerly Bristol Polytechnic. They drew on their experience at the University of the West of England to consider three interrelated issues. First, what is the relationship between increased participation in higher education and enhanced opportunities? Second, how does the difference between 'public' and 'private' sector higher education affect provision for equality of opportunity, particularly concerning widening participation? Third, and a prime focus of discussion in this chapter, what is the potential of formal structures and processes of policy making and academic governance as mechanisms for the enhancement of democratic participation? The concern about the relationship between a public sector mission which included commitment to equal opportunities and extended access, and particular management styles and structures, and how both may be changing as 'old' polytechnics become 'new' universities, is paralleled by the experience in Australia of those in former CAEs becoming new universities or amalgamating with existing ones. In Canada, although there is not the structured shift from a binary to a unified system, the different styles of management and the varying degree of commitment to open access provision for students co-exist between, and to some extent within, institutions.

In the UK, and in particular in England, the contrasts between some of the traditional old and new university forms of governance, the styles of management and the recruitment and experience of students are probably sharper than in either Australia or Canada, although the differences in management and the student body of, say, Charles Sturt University and the University of Melbourne should not be underestimated. In the context of the expansion of higher education and the potential for increased opportunity, Landman and Ozga recognize that there is 'concern that more may have access to a diluted experience', but they go on to add (and this was a view expressed by many of the academic administrators interviewed in the former polytechnics) that:

> . . . there are considerable problems for under-represented groups in the conventional (i.e. old university/polytechnic/college) construction

> of higher education, particularly in its definitions of knowledge, in its hierarchy, in its arcane and often gender and class specific rituals. The richness of the traditional higher education experience can be exaggerated and its competitiveness, snobbery and dullness overlooked. For mature students, for many working class women and for black students, the conventional university is far from ideal.
>
> (Landman and Ozga 1992: 3)

The definition of the purposes of the university, and its reformulation beyond the statements in original charters, provides an instance of how senior management attempt to shape and control the university culture. Often this is done in response to perceived pressures from the state or 'customer'.

Mission and strategy statements became increasingly fashionable in the late 1980s and have been produced by the managements of both old and new universities to define the purposes of the institution for fund providers, for staff, present and future students, and for general public consumption. In the UK, mission and strategy statements were required by the Polytechnics and Colleges Funding Council (PCFC) after incorporation from 1988. A comparison is made between the content, rhetoric and process of production between Bristol Polytechnic, now the University of the West of England (UWE), and Aston University, one of the new technological universities within the 'old' university sector.

Landman and Ozga point out that there was a good deal of scepticism about institutional mission and strategy statements. This scepticism seems to be shared by many ordinary academic staff in both old and new universities in all three countries, partly because such statements often seem to be overblown rhetorical statements of purpose for public and governmental consumption, which bear little relation to what many academic staff perceive themselves actually or even ideally doing. Second, the production of the mission statements, although ostensibly involving many academic staff in democratic discussion, in practice usually involve relatively few senior academic managers. They are then promulgated and unenthusiastically accepted by the body of staff more concerned with increased workloads, and who in any case do not feel they are in control of the process or outcome.

One may compare the role of the mission statement of UWE with Aston's culture, recent changes and the proposals for mission and vision statements contained in the vice-chancellor's memo to academic and administrative managers. Landman and Ozga (1992: 5) write:

> In our own institution we feel that the Mission and Strategy statement is important as a public statement, to other providers and to the region generally, of the intended positioning of the former polytechnic. It is also, in the process of articulation and then as a formal record, an attempted framework that, theoretically at least, could hold together the expanded institution and act as a counterbalance for the potential atomisation caused by devolution of academic planning, and associated policy activity to Faculties.

The Aston vice-chancellor's memo on 'vision and mission statements' asserts:

> Aston is developing towards an entrepreneurial culture, particularly through adoption of the Trading Company Model (TCM) and implementation of the principles of Total Quality Management (TQM). The one encourages local understanding of how funds are generated and spent in furtherance of the university's academic objectives. The other emphasises continuous improvement of the crossfunctional processes by which those objectives are approached. Service Level Agreements (SLA) can be used to define customer–supplier relations across interfaces, but must be formulated carefully if we are to break down barriers rather than harden them.
>
> The greater the degree of devolution aimed for in decision making and accountability, the greater the necessity for fostering university-wide understanding of its shared values and purposes.
>
> Aston needs then to articulate a powerful set of superordinate objectives (our Mission) that can easily be remembered by every one of its staff, and can readily be communicated to its customers and stakeholders. We also need to express to our staff, customers and stakeholders those shared values (our Vision) that will determine how we are going to treat each other.
>
> (Crawford 1992: 1)

Again it is worth comparing the perception of the revised 1992 Bristol Polytechnic mission and strategy statement with the Aston vice-chancellor's account of the only public mission statement that his university possessed in 1992. Landman and Ozga (1992: 5) note that the Bristol statement has:

> Strong emphases on the continued role of the new university as a comprehensive provider. The statement is a strong reiteration of the former polytechnic's mission, with a pronounced equal opportunities theme; much emphasis is placed on changing modes of delivery to meet a changing student population, and on a marked regional dimension.

They comment that this indicates the persistence of the old public sector/public service ethos revised and re-articulated in line with the 1980s drive for formulations of dynamic purpose, effective and efficient provision, embedded in the market ethos and attendant metaphors of the 1990s. There is more of the latter ethos and language in the Aston vice-chancellor's statement of 'Where are we now?':

> Throughout the 1980s, Aston has taken as its compass the idea that it wished to be a *university*, interpreting that description as being in the business of creating and marshalling knowledge (research and scholarship), transmitting it (teaching), and applying it (services), e.g. through consulting or clinics. Within the vast domain of human knowledge, it has chosen a portfolio of subjects to offer which can be broadly characterised as readily applicable in the world of work, or *technological*, in

> which it can achieve critical mass and aim for selective excellence. Aston has aspired to being a provider of high-quality, innovative programmes, with a demand-led, quality-driven ethos that will give it a *leading* position in its market sector. In short, Aston has expressed the Vision and Mission that it aspires to in just three words – 'Leading Technological University'.

There is little mention here of the features of the Bristol statements, with their public commitment to what Landman and Ozga (1992: 7) see as 'unfashionable principles of equality of educational opportunity and public service' which are 'specific to the institution and yet provide some insight into the transition the higher education system finds itself in'. The absence at Aston until 1994 of a public statement on equal opportunity was the more unusual position; certainly if one scans advertisements for posts or students, most universities in Australia, Canada and the UK include some statement about equal opportunities. An example is an advertisement for a post in the humanities faculty at UWE, which stated: 'We particularly welcome applications from members of minority ethnic groups and people with disabilities as these groups are under represented within the Faculty'. This is typical of UWE's presentation and fits its equal opportunities stance.

The process of formulating mission statements and their discussion within UWE and Aston indicates the relationship of management and academics with the mode of implementation of particular policies. At Bristol, it seemed that there were considerable obstacles to the generation of debate in the academic board, the formal forum roughly equivalent to a senate in an 'old' university. The management (the executive) made efforts to overcome reluctance to participate due to 'diffidence-cum-deference'. While there seemed to be little dissent or disagreement with the principles of the draft mission statement, there was concern about ensuring appropriate frameworks for its application in the devolved faculties. There was debate about admissions policy and about the resources available for 'non-standard' entry students. However, at UWE, Landman and Ozga's impression was that a major problem in generating debate was a lack of confidence in the majority of the committee in the process and structures available to them, and a lack of capacity for, and experience in, making use of their opportunities for general debate.

On the other hand, at Aston, despite the massive restructuring of the 1980s, there are established committees – senate, academic planning committee, faculty boards – with academics with plenty of experience of deliberation. Here the problem of scepticism and refusal to become enthusiastically involved in discussion arose out of a perception by many academics that effective power was in the hands of the vice-chancellor and relatively few senior administrators and academics – the registrar, finance director, the pro-vice-chancellors – and that they would get their way whatever the discussion. This perception is worth setting alongside the vice-chancellor's statement about the formulation of vision/mission statements:

> A university-wide Vision/Mission statement is likely to be short. Cascading down from it must be a set of compatible, faculty, departmental and personal Vision/Mission statements. Again, they should preferably be short and easily remembered if they are to act as a constant guide to coordinated planning and action. The task of producing such statements requires considerable effort and local discussion, some of which has already been contributed. Over the next few months, we must finish the job; there are no short cuts if a high level of commitment is to be achieved.
>
> (Crawford 1992: 4)

Let us now spend a little time outlining the public sector (polytechnic or CAE) structure of administration by citing as an example the system of governance of one institution in the UK, the University of the West of England.

Bristol Polytechnic was a former LEA institution. Then, after the 1988 Education Reform Act, it became a higher education corporation and there are many features of its structure and governance that are generalizable to other such institutions. The board of governors was the supreme governing body; it took advice from the academic board on matters directly related to the formulation and implementation of academic policy. The Articles of Government stipulated the composition of the academic board. Half its members were executive heads of department (recruited by the governors) and others nominated from related groupings, i.e. deans of faculty, other heads of department and members of the directorate. The remaining members were elected officers, returned via three routes: as elected chairs of faculty boards, as representatives elected by each faculty and a small number of others elected by the body of lecturers.

Besides the formal representational governance structure, there is also for any institution a formal executive and management structure. In the case of the polytechnics, this was dominated by an executive head (the director) and the heads of department, who were usually appointed rather than elected, who had a separate salary grade and the power and responsibility at least equivalent to a professorial chair within a large 'old' university department, who might only occupy an administrative position for a limited period and might have peers of professorial rank. As the polytechnics acquired corporate status in the late 1980s, many developed several tiers of administration, typically deputy and assistant directors and deans, again appointed rather than elected and establishing a 'managerial' rather than a 'collegial' culture. There was a similar structure and culture within many of the Australian CAEs.

In the UK, it is from the public sector 'polytechnic' administrative and managerial culture that some of the most challenging forms of new managerialism and market orientation have developed, which nevertheless still retain aspects of commitment to public responsibility and student access.

The vice-chancellor of what is now Liverpool John Moores University, in a paper entitled 'Appropriate structures for higher education institutions', presented in 1991 when he was Rector (Director) of Liverpool Polytechnic, sets out some of the features of educational administration and management and the changes emerging from the perspective of the 'new management' from the point of view of a polytechnic executive. He asserts that dramatic changes have been occurring in higher education in the UK:

> A whole new approach to what we do has come about and with it we have all been looking for new organisational structures in which to bring about many changes. Most rectors and vice-chancellors tend these days to go around saying, 'We must reorganise, let's restructure'.
>
> (Toyne 1991: 54)

In describing the institutional organization and culture, he argues that:

> Each institution has tended to structure itself, has been essentially producer led, based upon the assumption somehow or other that those who run the place will actually make the structures work for them.
>
> (Toyne 1991: 59)

He continues in what might seem to be something of a caricature for comparative effect:

> . . . those structures, particularly in the 1960s and 1970s, have increasingly involved in their processes hugely democratic, participative, consultative and collective decision-making systems. No decision, or at least very few, would be taken by a single person without it having been through endless committees, endless debates, endless hierarchical decision-makers each of whom could prevaricate and did, so that ultimately very little decision-making would take place rapidly. Vice chancellors and rectors were, and sometimes still are, largely impotent. Because while the Academic Board, the Senate or some other group has the power and the authority to take some decisions they often, because of those democratic processes, rarely do or, at best, they take a long time to make decisions.
>
> (Toyne 1991: 60)

Here speaks the voice of the frustrated executive manager. The features described:

> . . . assume that accountability and managerial responsibility are somewhat secondary and are subsumed in the collective decision-making. They do not need to be overtly accountable, overtly making managerial decisions because the collective will make them. Thus colleague administrators are subservient and often not directly themselves involved in decision-making, that comes back to the academic community of scholars.
>
> (Toyne 1991: 60)

He concedes that this picture might be an over-generalization, but argues it is a fair representation of the organizational structure in higher education institutions.

This view is shared by many university chief executives in Australia and Canada. Toyne asserts that higher education in the UK needs to move from being 'producer-based to being customer-based or if you like led by market forces', and that 'as well as being customer-orientated, we should all work and operate as an accountable business'. This is a very different view of the university as a community of scholars with democratic processes:

> Accountable business involves essentially managerial responsibility and accountability, of the person labelled, legally – chief executive. This leads to a rise in the central importance of administrative support and administrators in turn become more significant not subservient. Customer-based, accountable businesses is what we are asked to be.
>
> (Toyne 1991: 61)

Then, referring to the conditions necessary to bring about this managerially desirable change, he refers to the importance of the already discussed 'mission statements':

> There are two stages in undergoing this conversion. Stage one is to identify mission. To establish corporate aims and clearly spell out what it is to be customer-led; this will inevitably include reference to customer-orientation and to effective management. The identification of missions and corporate aims is something which has proceeded apace. Practically every university and polytechnic has something they will proclaim on noticeboards. It is important in this corporate culture that everyone must own that mission statement.
>
> (Toyne 1991: 61)

Indeed, but it is not at all clear how the process produces 'ownership' among academic staff. He cites hiring the Philharmonic Hall and 'pontificating' [*sic*] 12 commandments, which range from 'think positively' through 'develop a sense of vision and commitment' and 'secure new sources of funding' to 'put our aim of being customer orientated into effect'. He continues:

> Stage two, to reorganise the structures internal to the organisation of the polytechnic or the university to facilitate the delivery, the mission statement and all the rest. It will certainly devolve. Because it is no longer an academic community of scholars, it is business orientated and customer and student led, it will eventually involve the devolution of managerial responsibility. Second, you should have what business people refer to as flatter structures, reduce the chain of eternal decision-making. Third, structures involving devolved responsibility or flatness must also be simpler. They must be minimalist, not complex. Fewer units, fewer committees, fewer complications to make for simpler straightforward responsiveness, involves in turn empowering managers. A concept often referred to is total quality management, which, again,

> has been embraced by many of the polytechnics and universities in recent years. To deliver you have to have increased power, certainly [for] the chief executive and the new managers who often now rejoice not in the titles of deans, or of heads of departments but of the new corporate management team . . . [they] . . . will be directors not deans because that implies that they are collective. New corporate management teams, CMTs, or SMTs, abounds [*sic*] now and have replaced much of the power of other consultative bodies.
>
> (Toyne 1991: 63)

These quotations catch in vivid form both the language and preferred practice of the 'new management' as do Toyne's comments on 'collegial' forms:

> The democratic, participative, consultative, collective decision-making is being significantly reduced. Senate or academic board is no longer essentially the powerful decision-making unit it once was. It is advisory and in the Reform Act of 1988 affecting the polytechnics, it was legislated for. Academic boards were reduced in power from being decision-making and all important to being advisory to the chief executive.

This view may be an exaggerated one based perhaps too closely on English ex-polytechnic experience to be true of the range of universities in the UK, let alone Australia and Canada. Nevertheless, it does represent the changing reality in many institutions and illustrates changes in structures reflecting a new managerial style. Toyne (1991: 64) refers to his own institution:

> The Academic Board, which had all the power, consisted of 78 members. It was the 'Academic Board', therefore the academics were in charge. It was huge. The new structure we brought in came in 1987 following the Educational Reform Act or in anticipation of the Reform Act. It moved from a two-fold structure of 7 faculties, 29 departments to ten simple schools and their heads were not called deans, they were called directors. The rest of the hierarchy was reduced to two assistant rectors, a deputy and myself. The Academic Board was cut at a stroke in the legislation from 78 to 22 of whom only 4 were ex officio, me, the two assistants and one deputy, all the rest elected by the staff. The CMP, however, now became important. The corporate management team became the driving force.

He proposes that 'the best structures last about a year and you revise them every other year', and recounts: 'Our revised structure has now moved further to 6 schools and 4 service teams, an Academic Board reduced yet further from 22 to 16. It still is only advisory'. He concludes:

> We have moved away significantly from original structures based on the academic community into ones that are customer-based accountable businesses in which the chains of command are shorter, devolved responsibility for management goes on and the like.

This contrasts with another view of the development of governance in the ex-polytechnics represented in part by Landman and Ozga's account, which while recognizing the continued and indeed maybe increased importance of bureaucratic controls, also recognizes that attaining university status may strengthen the claims for academic, collegial control.

Toyne claims not to have moved away from academic community to something 'more managerial' because the schools are still essentially 'collections of academic community', but this seems a rather tenuous claim in view of the detailed account that he has presented of the development of a managerial, customer-oriented, higher education institution reshaped by a powerful directorate.

At this point, further extended quotations give another perspective to the changes affecting 'public sector institutions', but this time from the point of view of some ordinary academics who have been working in Australian CAEs. Although the place and perspective are different, some of the features of the increased managerial control are similar. The first case reflects the views of an academic engaged in teacher education previously undertaken within a teachers college, but now undertaken within a faculty of an amalgamated university:

> Academics see much in their immediate environment that seems detrimental, even if they are not sure or cannot discover whether the government or their own institutional policy is the cause. Staff are urged to seek research grants; they do so in increasing numbers with the result that the failure rate is dispiriting at around 80 per cent. Class sizes increase so there is more marking and pastoral care. Support staff, especially tutors and demonstrators are the first victims of budget cuts. Staff in former CAEs now classified as universities are urged to add research activity to their job description if they want further promotion. Teaching and research that doesn't coincide with a national economic or utilitarian agenda appears to be devalued or discouraged. The managerial prerogative challenges the collegial tradition. Salaries decline against national and international indicators. Students are growing more argumentative and litigious as they are forced to pay a share of the cost of their higher education. There is endless talk about quality monitoring and measuring indicating an extramural and maybe internal lack of faith in what is being accomplished; the accountability rhetoric is omnipresent. Whatever the truth of any or all of these matters, they are the stuff of daily campus discussion, and influence the climate in which academic attitudes develop.
>
> (DEET 1993: 136)

Another comment:

> Ten years ago teacher education was mostly conducted in small colleges. There was more cohesion. Less rush. Ten years ago in a hypothetical eight hour day [we] would spend an hour on administration

> and seven hours teaching or planning what to teach, marking and giving students feedback on their work. Times have changed, promotion criteria have altered. Now in an eight hour day, 40 per cent is spent on research, writing articles, planning conference papers, 10 per cent is spent on administration and 50 per cent on teaching. Suddenly, in the last year or so research, consultancy and publications count as much as teaching and the job becomes a juggling act.
>
> (DEET 1993: 133)

And finally in this section:

> The shift to a university culture combined with large numbers of students and less money per student has meant teaching models have had to change. There are more big lectures and less time for small intensive workshops and tutorials. There is less time to get to know students when you have to do a PhD, finish a collaborative proposal or a book chapter is behind schedule. Many of my colleagues trying to change and do it all, feel at a loss because of the tension between thoughtful, caring teaching and the pressure to publish. Many feel the teaching core is in danger of being eaten away.
>
> (DEET 1993: 133)

In the next section, we move to a more general account of managerial roles and practices in both 'old' and 'new' universities, in Canada as well as in Australia and the UK.

Managerial roles and practices

The questions addressed to senior academics about their assessment of their role and how it had changed over the last five years mentioned a range of possibilities including executive, academic leader and scholar. Often their perception of managerial roles was related to specific management problems. A dean of education at a former CAE in Australia characterized his role as manager and academic leader. He felt there had been a devolution of responsibilities since designation as a university and this enabled him to act as a 'facilitator in an outward looking way'. The head of research in the same institution characterized part of his role as 'organizational gadfly'.

In the nearby old established university, a head of department in talking of the pressure to maintain a high research profile asserted that heads of department had considerable power, and could focus the pressure on staff to ensure that research is being conducted by calling in every member of staff to ask about their individual research. This is in the context where at divisional level (combination of departments) funds are related substantially to research track record, although some resources are available for new staff and to seed new projects.

His perception of the relatively new female vice-chancellor was that she was not an active, initiating executive, that attending at meetings she 'expects others to do most of the talking and come up with ideas' and that she 'relies heavily on the registrar and pro-vice-chancellors'. This could simply be seen as a comment on an individual vice-chancellor's managerial style and clearly each vice-chancellor has his or her own characteristics which influence and sometimes dominate the organizational culture of the university. It could also be seen as referring to a less macho managerial style. Maybe it is a style which echoes on the one hand a traditional model of vice-chancellors as spokesmen [*sic*] or chairmen [*sic*] acting as first among equals, but which could also be characterized as a 'new' more feminine or even feminist approach. A managerial style which is less directive, loud and dominating and more listening, considering, consulting and facilitating.

In contrast, a central administrator at a former CAE, reflecting on the process of amalgamation prior to university designation, the need for rapid programme development and the danger of being carved up or amalgamated with an adjacent established university, advocated a strong 'executive' and 'entrepreneurial' style of management. He saw his own role as 'facilitator, pusher, sometimes bully to take things forward to develop activities appropriate to a modern university'. He stressed the need to 'start the ball rolling – others must keep the ball rolling – to act as something of a catalyst'.

The vice-chancellor of a technological university in Australia saw himself as a chief executive and he pointed out that his office led him to a corporate view of the university; one of the main tasks was to generate funds! The fund-raising aspect had become more important in the 5 years between 1986 and 1991. Another vice-chancellor at a former Australian CAE was seen by many of his staff as a dominant administrator concerned with detail, exercising strong authority and control. He characterized his own role rather more gently. He saw himself both as a figurehead and chief executive concerned with maintaining 'morality, conscience and as a standard setter for the place'. He referred to Chester Barnard's (1956) work, *The Functions of the Executive.* He said he had an 'overview of the institution' but did not intervene unless necessary on college programmes, but he did maintain an overview on staff recruitment, he would see all recommendations and sit on appointments as committee chair. Over the ten years to 1991, he had dropped his involvement in new building and financial matters but not that in academic work and personnel.

A deputy vice-chancellor at an old established Australian university asserted that as an acting and deputy vice-chancellor in a research-based university, he would characterize his own role as 'academic leader', 'administrator', 'scholar' and 'chief executive'. He stated that:

> in the 5 years to 1991, there had been some pressure to become more managerial, to cope with external pressures and rising internal tensions. However, internal tensions and reactions are also leading to a reaction against managerial model as a protest. As usual, vice-chancellors and deputy vice-chancellors walk a tightrope between the tensions.

A union representative at the same institution saw the new vice-chancellor – a woman in a conservative institution – as not having 'an overbearing style' and with strengths and weaknesses, approachable and authoritative. With the deputy vice-chancellor they constituted a 'hardman/softman' [*sic*] team, the deputy vice-chancellor being 'a financial manager with too much of an accountant's style – and while not necessarily having a public face, to his own staff being quite powerful'.

A professor of history and politics who had been a school teacher and described himself as a 'media commentator', 'administrator' and 'researcher', as well as holding elected positions, gave contrasting characterizations of three recent and current vice-chancellors in Western Australia: the first as a 'technical-administrator', the second as 'a publicist, ideas man, entrepreneur of research', and the third as 'a roving ambassador'.

If we turn to the second level of administration or management – vice-chancellors' deputies, deans and heads of departments (sometimes termed 'chairs') – we find many of the same pressures and concerns as for vice-chancellors but usually directed to more specific problems. In a western Canadian university, the chair of a social science department described his role as an 'awful administrative job – my job is to make it possible for people in the place to do their work – to facilitate research to maintain a research centre, to keep it state of the art'. In terms of attracting staff, he could not offer them anything by way of money but he could reduce their teaching loads. In terms of the departmental teaching load, he aimed to reduce the teaching of good researchers and to increase the teaching of a couple who did no research. This became an issue every year at salary and promotions time because of what he described as 'an archaic method whereby we compare with everyone else in the faculty'. This gives something of the day-to-day strategic administrative concerns of many heads of department in Canadian universities. There is a more general context, as he put it:

> I imagine things are no different here to anywhere else. As you take money out of the system the quality of education declines. It's unfortunate that it's rather difficult to get hard measures of that, to prove to government that it's hurting and that it's students that are getting screwed. A student revolt – not political – is beginning and there are signs – expecting student pressure.

There were also particular problems to do with distance and isolation similar to the situation in some Australian institutions: 'While E-Mail makes a difference there is the difficulty of making connections. There is often ignorance of departments in the next nearest institution which could be 170 miles away. Face-to-face contact costs money, maybe C$200 a day and to meet colleagues from institutions further away the cost was outrageous'. In his institution, a 'speaker exchange program had "crashed" and they had to cancel the external examiner program for Phds'.

A senior dean of arts, with 18 years experience at another western Canadian university, reflecting on his present role, saw it as 'giving policy advice, strategic planning, but administering a large faculty with 430 staff and 8000 students inevitably involved a heavy administrative load including 130 salary evaluations each year'. At this institution, he saw himself as 'part of the administrative team and, as there were relatively few deans, there was a more significant role as a team player in the institutional role as compared with others'. He thought he had more power than deans at, for example, UBC or Toronto. He had had a succession of 5 year terms and was now looking forward to going back to research. In the past at this institution as dean of an interdisciplinary faculty with fairly generous resources, he had been able 'to do interesting creative new things' and he had been involved in building a new faculty with eight or ten new programmes of an interdisciplinary nature. Since becoming the dean of faculty of arts, his role had become more traditional, concerned with personnel problems and administration.

These reflections by senior administrators, heads of department, deans and deputy vice-chancellors make the perhaps obvious point that their role varies and indeed has changed with the increased size of some of their institutions compared with the stabilization experienced in others. A real or relative cutback in resources is characteristic of all levels of administration, whether department, faculty or university over the last decade. However, the establishment in a few instances of a relatively well-resourced department or faculty as compared to the more common maintenance of an existing under-resourced structure clearly imposes a different range of constraints. It is within these parameters that the role of the academic administrator, leader or innovator is played out. On the university stage as elsewhere, as Marx put it: 'Men make their own history but not under conditions of their own choosing'.

Universities are part of the cluster of institutions which with the media, international agencies and think-tanks have formed the cultural tracks which have played their part in providing the ideas which have guided action generated by interests (Weber 1948: 280). Specialization and positivism were well established in Australian universities before the 'reforms' of the 1980s, and they provided access to the state bureaucracy by particular disciplines, in particular economies and law. Pusey (1991: 232) quoting Collins (1985: 156) explains:

> The universities, which codified and certified useful knowledge, have been mostly post-Darwinian creations. The particular scientific paradigm they have enshrined has reinforced the tendencies of utilitarianism. Empiricism has been a natural enemy of speculative thought; positivism has reigned, almost without challenge, in science, law, philosophy, history, economies, and the Social Sciences. The secular 'engineering' character of Australian tertiary education is nowhere more evident than in the professional separation from the humanities and social science adhered to by law and economics. The autonomy of law

and economics faculties has been to the detriment of each and at the cost of all, since they supply the graduates who chiefly govern the nation.

This is an interesting contrast to the radical criticism usually made in the UK of the over-reliance in recruitment to the civil service of Oxbridge classicists, historians and 'modern greats' scholars. However, the comment that Pusey makes on Australian universities in the late 1980s with respect to what he calls the 'new manipulative sciences of management, marketing and accountancy' and their position under the protective umbrella of the disciplines of economics and psychology, which imparts an instrumentalism 'that is permanently at odds with culture, tradition, critical reflection, and with most intellectual representation of the identity and collective interests of the Australian people' (Pusey 1991: 233), resonates with the similar way these subjects are taught and the way they influence administration outside and inside the university in the UK. Thus a vice-chancellor in an English technological university in the course of memos to middle management staff on vision statements, trading company models (TCM), total quality management (TQM) and service level agreements (SLA), will not only refer to simple notions of entrepreneurial and bureaucratic models of American management textbooks, but also a version of work pyschology derived from Herzberg (1959) and Maslow (1954), using their analysis to promote a particular style and structure of management.

Pusey describes changes in the bureaucracy of the Australian state which has, 'in less than ten years, generated, its own unified, self-referential and artificial language, of eco-managerial biz-speak, that is used everywhere, even in the universities, to neutralize potentially intelligent communication through "ordinary", "raw", "uncooked", or "natural" language wherever it is still to be found' (Pusey 1991: 202).

The practice and discourse of the management of universities has to be seen within a broader field of governance and societal change, whether in Australia, Canada or the UK. Hall (1993), one of the foremost analysts of the ideological power of Thatcherism, argues that the Thatcherite project was still largely in place under the premiership of John Major 3 years after Mrs Thatcher's departure from office. He asserts that 'the philosophy at the heart of the Thatcherite project involves refuting the idea that individuals should order their own interests and drives to take account of the existence of others in society' (p. 15), and that it was 'a certain distinctive set of practices, ideas and institutional reforms which constituted a very important new way of thinking about how rules and processes, norms and habits could be inculcated and regulations put in place that would alter the conduct of others' (p. 15).

Hall illustrates how this works by reference to his own experience as a professor of sociology at the Open University, an institution established under the Wilson Labour government and dedicated to open access with an egalitarian and democratic ethos. He maintains that the struggle for the development and examination of a new Thatcherite ideology involves first a struggle about conduct – hearts and minds follow later.

> The Open University is [was] filled with good social democrats. Everybody there believes in the redistribution of educational opportunities and seeks to remedy the exclusiveness of British education. And yet in the past ten years, these good social democratic souls without changing for a minute what is in their hearts and minds, have learned to speak a brand of metallic new entrepreneurialism, a new managerialism of a horrendously closed nature. They believe what they have always believed, but what they do, how they write their mission statements, how they do appraisal forms, how they talk to students, how they calculate the cost – that is what they are really interested in now. The result is that the institution has been transformed.
>
> (Hall 1993: 15)

A distinction can be drawn between the old type of bureaucracy prevalent in the public sector and the new managerialism. In the old bureaucracy, there were clear divisions between public and private. People knew their roles and duties within the organization. Hall (1993: 15) puts it this way:

> The new entrepreneurial ethos does not have any such boundaries. You have to take the whole organisation home overnight, go to bed thinking about it, wake up and ask: 'Why aren't I at work?' Now there is no bureaucratic norm – there is flexitime. You should have been there an hour before you woke up and should be leaving an hour after you should be leaving.

There is in this pervasiveness, some similarities between the new managerialism and one version of the collegial tradition, particularly that associated with collegiate organization, where boundaries between public and private, academic and pastoral, were blurred and sometimes institutionalized as in college residences and the requirements for communal eating common in many Oxbridge colleges. This contrasts with the traditional bureaucratic procedures of the big civic universities, polytechnics and technological universities in the UK and most large Canadian and Australian universities.

In so far as the new managerialism is coming to dominate the culture of universities, Hall argues 'that there is the production of a new kind of subject, who think about themselves in relation to the organisation in a different way, internalising many of the norms'. This new managerialism is prevalent in both the public and private sectors. One of the characteristics of its directly economic aspect is the emphasis on cost reduction, which can be analysed in terms of increasing exploitation of labour, both manual and mental. However, another aspect which may be more effective and insidious is through the transformation of the culture of institutions notable through the propogation of particular languages and the discourse of the market. The language in which we address ourselves is changing. We are not only producers but also salesmen and customers. We all 'mimic the market' (Hall 1993: 15). So the new managerialism in universities not only controls audits and plans, but puts in place procedures, trading company models, service level agreements and SWOT analysis, which attempts to replicate the 'realities' of the market in some idealized private sector free market, which it is assumed is more effective at meeting the needs of society and even the state. Managerialism and the market imply and support each other.

The discourse of managerialism draw predominantly on particular aspects of the broad disciplines of economics and psychology. Its products are packaged in airport lounge, business guidebooks, no less than in government reports, and they have a ubiquity in the English-speaking world which encompasses and penetrates the management of the universities of Australia, Canada and the UK.

In this chapter, there has been a review of the different types of universities with their varying traditions of governance and a consideration of a range of analytical and prescriptive models of management, set alongside a sampling of the views of academic managers of their roles and practices. A recurring theme has been the overt pressures and demands of the state combined with the more implicit needs of the economy, which together shape the structure, style and language of managerial practice in universities.

5

Case Study: Aston University

The focus of this chapter is the management of change in one university, the University of Aston in Birmingham. Aston was one of the colleges of advanced technology designated a university in the 1960s; it received its Royal Charter as a technological university in 1966. Other technological universities include Bath, Bradford, Brunel, Salford and Surrey in England and Strathclyde and Heriot-Watt in Scotland. It was also one of a group of universities most heavily hit by cutbacks in central government grants administered by the UGC in 1981. Others included Salford, Bradford, Keele and Hull, with cutbacks of between 20 and 40 per cent. Aston was not typical of English universities in the early 1980s either in origin, character or the scale of financial difficulties the university management had to deal with. That university management also emerged as being distinctive, even extreme, in its policies and style. There is a problem as to whether Aston and its management is a maverick or extreme case, but whatever the judgement about that, the problems faced and the management structure and style described can be used to illustrate more general questions.

Aston University was one of the universities selected by the UGC in 1981 to suffer fundamental change, losing one-third of its funding and one-fifth of its students. Walford (1987) has given a detailed case study account, using a sophisticated model of political decision making to chart the dynamic of management changes at Aston. This chapter draws on and extends that account, and focuses on the impact of changes in managerial practice and strategy.

There has been considerable change at Aston. Between 1980 and 1989, the university changed from an institution with four faculties (including one of humanities and social sciences) with 24 departments and groups and nearly 540 full-time academic staff, to one of three faculties (science, engineering and management and modern languages) with only nine departments and under 250 academic staff. While there was a substantial reduction in the student population, the staff–student ratio increased from 1:10.3 in 1980 to 1:12.9 in 1985–86 and 1:15 in 1988–89. As the November 1985 response from the university to the UGC's *Planning for the Late 1980s* put it: 'The restructuring that has occurred in the University over the last five years in its academic programme, staffing, student body and physical facilities is probably more profound than anywhere else in the UK university system' (Aston University 1985: 6–7).

There are several detailed accounts of how the Conservative government, committed to reducing government expenditure and faced by the demographic decline of the number of 18-year-olds by 1994 to two-thirds of the peak of 1983, imposed drastic cuts in 1981 (Kogan and Kogan 1983; Scott 1984). These cuts were implemented by the UGC consequent on the reduction in funding overall, and followed the directive from the DES to be selective and directive.

In fact, the implications the government drew from the demographic figures were wrong. Demand from students for higher education places increased instead of decreasing for several reasons. There was no appreciable fall in the birth rate in the social classes that produce the overwhelming majority of students. Academic attainment at A level increased and degree courses were seen increasingly as the necessary foundation for a successful career. The effects of recession in reducing employment possibilities for 18-year-olds probably also encourages those qualified to continue studies at university rather than enter the job market.

University administrations' responses to the cuts of the early 1980s often consisted of varieties of inaction or rhetorical resistance, particularly where initially the cuts were not too severe. At Keele and Cardiff, where the cuts were deep, vice-chancellors' strategies did not necessarily involve compliance with UGC directives; sometimes there was short-term accommodation (Samut 1986) followed by the development of expansionist strategies, particularly at Keele. In the case of University College Cardiff, there was outright defiance combined with maladministration, which resulted in an enquiry, the resignation of the vice-chancellor and a merger with the University of Wales Institute of Science and Technology (UWIST) to form the University of Wales College of Cardiff.

At Aston and Salford, both heavily hit in terms of cuts (Aston 32 per cent and Salford 43 per cent), different strategies were adopted by their then 'new' vice-chancellors, professors Frederick Crawford and John Ashworth. At Salford, the main preoccupation was the generation of new income over and above UGC sources and the strengthening and extending of links with industry. So while recurrent university income – excluding UGC grant and the home fees of students – at Aston increased from 20.1 per cent in 1980 to 26 per cent in 1985, at Salford it increased from 16 per cent in 1980 and 1981 to 39 per cent in 1985. Links with industry have not been neglected at Aston, with the establishment of a science park jointly with the city council and Lloyds Bank, and the creation of a Technology Transfer Unit with the West Midlands Enterprise Board. However, the connections with industry have been perhaps less integral than at Salford, where integrated chairs jointly funded from the university and industry were established.

The managerial strategy at Aston involved the establishment of a centralized directorate. This has also occurred to some degree in many other UK,

Australian and Canadian universities. What was most marked at Aston was the degree of control management established over a range of issues, but particularly academic staffing. Thus throughout much of the 1980s, there were staff reductions at Aston on a larger scale than elsewhere, and the comparatively late move to staff recruitment was on a smaller scale than in most equivalent universities. Furthermore, academic staff management was characterized by confrontation rather than cooperation with the academic staff union (the AUT), marked in 1989 by a major court case on the issues of redundancy, tenure and academic governance and followed by votes of no-confidence in the vice-chancellor and secretary/registrar by senate and academic staff.

At Aston, information-gathering, analysis and strategic decision making were established centrally, primarily in the vice-chancellor's hands, soon after his appointment in 1980 and the process of central control increased following the 1981 cuts. The vice-chancellor's superior information base on courses, student characteristics and staff enabled him to use one-to-one negotiations with heads of department to present to senate a package of course reductions which was difficult to resist. At the same time, the establishment of the vice-chancellor's advisory group on budget adjustment (AGBA), which was composed of the vice-chancellor as chair, the senior pro-vice-chancellor, the deans of faculty and, significantly, three administrative officers including the finance officer, provided a small, centrally placed, well-informed committee which could analyse the situation, take decisions and make recommendations to senate and council with considerable authority.

Information management has now become a major activity within universities as they struggle to present an 'appropriate' image of themselves to their various publics. These include students and staff within the university, potential future students and staff, local and national industry and commerce, politicians, and the range of funding bodies, particularly the HEFC.

The refinement and extension of management information at Aston can be seen as a product of external pressures from the government to assess and monitor value for money, efficiency and effectiveness, and from the UGC and the UFC to distribute resources more selectively. There has been a trend towards the centralization of the key decision-making process away from the official committee structure and the development of parallel centralized advisory groups and committees. To support this process, separate layers of information with different degrees of accessibility throughout the institution have emerged.

Two main tiers of information can be identified. The first tier was available to the vice-chancellor and, at most, a small number of senior managers. Examples of information with such restricted access would be personal files about each member of staff, the review of staff workloads and efficiency, staff projections, draft policy and/or resources allocation papers (e.g. the determination of academic and non-academic staff ranges for departments, documents recommending the discontinuation or closure of departments or areas). The second tier would be available through the formal committees or through heads of department and therefore indirectly to members of the university and others. Examples of information with this degree of availability would be final versions of policy and/or resources allocation papers, proposals for new courses, selected information about university performance, economy or efficiency.

In order to increase the university's status and reputation internally within the university system and to outside agencies, management sought to project a corporate identity and embarked on a process of 'image' management within a context of general information management. A key element of this process was the establishment, at the behest of the vice-chancellor, of the university external relations unit (UERU). The unit had its own director who serviced all key committees and reported directly to the vice-chancellor. The UERU encompassed the careers advisory service, schools liaison and the information office. The information office published *Aston Fortnight*, the main medium of management–staff communication, which also served as an external public relations broadsheet. Some staff referred to it as *Pravda*, and it was seen by many as being an organ for the dissemination of the vice-chancellor's views of the institution. At one time in the early 1980s, a few letters to the editor did appear, but since then despite assertions by editors that there is no censorship by the vice-chancellor, critical comment by staff on the university's management or policy has been noticeable by its absence.

The publication was, by university standards of the 1980s, quite well produced, even slick. There were two notable features. First, there was the relaying of important state initiatives on university policy by the funding bodies or education department by means of reprinting letters to the vice-chancellor or by extracts from ministerial pronouncements. These were sometimes accompanied by an explanation from the vice-chancellor. The effect of this was certainly to inform academics about government policy and make them aware of the constraints within which the university functioned, but it allowed little room for the discussion of alternative strategies. The second feature was the prominence, particularly pictorially, of the university's senior management, specifically the vice-chancellor. The staff were left in no doubt about who represented the university.

The development of a corporate image at Aston was taken seriously by the senior management. The services of a firm of international public relations/image consultants, Wolff Olins, were enlisted. The initial cost of this venture was reputed to be £50,000. The main lasting outcome appears to be the concept of the 'Aston Triangle', which encompasses the physical shape of the university campus and adjacent science park into a corporate symbol for use on all official publications and correspondence. This process had become general in the late 1980s. The redesignation and renaming of the ex-polytechnics as universities provided a field-day for corporate image-makers.

The university's image was promoted through a number of public events organized by the senior management. Well-known establishment figures opened new building ventures, including the extension education centre (Keith Joseph), new sky-lifts (Lord Young), computer and computer suite (Kenneth Baker) and vision sciences (Prince Charles). The process for attracting publicity apparent at Aston in the mid-1980s is now the norm for most universities, new and old.

University policy was presented by management as a commitment to academic excellence and strict financial probity. In practice, these general aims meant a sustained effort to improve the quality of the undergraduate entry by insisting on A level scores above the national average in each subject area, a staff recruitment policy that required in almost all cases that candidates should possess a first-class undergraduate degree as well as a Phd, and various efforts to improve research productivity and quality. The financial probity aspect translated into a plan to balance the books on a year-by-year basis – up until 1994 this has been achieved. Together with these major aims, there was attention to public relations and extensive campus improvement – tree planting, fountains and a lake, and a new entrance complete with Beaubourg-like lifts.

Management policies concerning student recruitment, staff recruitment and mobility and research had discernible causes and effects. It was assumed by many that the pattern of the 1981 UGC cuts to universities was informed by the relative strength of different departments' courses as measured by the A level grades they were able to ask of students. It was therefore hardly surprising that the strategy to respond to the cuts and improve Aston's standing in case of continuing cuts should include measures to raise A level scores for all courses. However, A level grades were not only to be improved because this was expected to lead to more favourable treatment by the UGC, but also because they could be used as a way of restructuring departments and putting pressure on some staff to leave. Even before the 1981 cuts, the vice-chancellor had gathered comparative figures on these scores, including information on overseas and non-traditional entry for each subject for all universities. Data were also collected on student drop-out rates and on degree results. The vice-chancellor persuaded senate to discontinue many of the university's courses within a week of the UGC announcement in 1981.

In 1982, senate adopted a policy to improve entry grades so that the average was to become higher than the national average in *each* subject for student entry in October 1983. This drastic shift in policy has had several implications. Admission tutors' discretion was severely limited, with 10 per cent quotas imposed for overseas and non-traditional entry, and the required A level grades (using the points system) became the determining criterion in admissions policy. If numbers of students on courses which had previously accepted low A level scores, and which were now not able to attract above-average scoring students, dropped below the minimum acceptable to the university management, the courses were speedily axed with consequent pressure on staff in those areas to retrain, move to other departments or to leave the institution. Hence decisions on A level entry were instrumental in the wider reshaping, restructuring and redeployment of staff. In areas which were popular, recruitment was allowed to expand, which brought its own pressures on staff, who were expected to teach larger groups of students. This became particularly acute in subject areas such as marketing and accountancy, where it was difficult to attract staff, particularly of the high academic standard demanded by the vice-chancellor.

There was an obvious connection between student numbers and the deployment of staff, but staff policy was equally influenced by the need to balance the budget and improve the quality of staff, staff costs being 60–70 per cent of total budget as in most universities. Management's perception seemed to be that many staff (some inherited from Aston's previous status as a college of advanced technology) were too old or mediocre to contribute to Aston's future as a 'quality-driven institution'.

Staff numbers at Aston were reduced by over 50 per cent between 1981 and 1990. The process has been centrally directed. Policy largely emanating from the vice-chancellor and the advisory committee on budget adjustment has been accepted by senate and council, except that senate has consistently refused to condone compulsory redundancy. The process has involved the setting of public targets for overall staff reduction to 350 in 1982, 300 in August 1984, 260 in 1987 and 250 in 1989 – with staff ranges being established for each department based mainly on student numbers. A variety of pressures and incentives were applied to encourage staff to transfer to other universities, retrain or just leave. The process was effective in that Aston's management reduced academic staff from 543 in 1980 to 276 in 1985. In comparison, Keele University had 291 staff in 1980 and 246 in 1985, Salford 491 staff in 1980 and 339 in 1985. Two features of staff recruitment policy at Aston are striking. New lecturing staff were only offered a three year contract in the first instance with the possibility of a second three year contract before being considered for a continuing appointment. Second, despite professorial departures, no new professors were appointed between 1981 and 1989.

At this point, it is useful to focus on four issues, which although described from the point of view of an academic at Aston, have a resonance for university management and staff in most universities in the UK, Australia and Canada. First, the impact of governmental regulatory and funding bodies attempts to control and reform the practices of particular universities. In this case, a visit by the UGC and the reactions of university management and union representatives are described. This is one example of a wide variety of interventions which influence management strategy and style. In the 1990s, the development of quality assessment and quality audits relating to teaching on a university-wide basis or to particular discipline areas have become important in the UK and Australia.

The second issue concerned staff appraisal. The introduction of appraisal became embroiled in a national salary dispute but was also contentious locally at Aston. However, the form of appraisal, its function and how it relates to the management of universities in general is an issue common to universities in Australia and Canada as well as the UK. This is also of course true of the third issue, salaries. Again at Aston there was a particular configuration of management – union relations, but the interplay of local and national factors and organizations is again of wide significance.

Fourth and finally, Aston was the scene of a fairly dramatic case of attempted compulsory redundancy. There have been other cases at Cardiff and Hull in the UK and at the University of British Columbia in Canada. While these cases are relatively rare, they do pose in extreme form the question of managerial control of staff, which is of course central to questions of power and the management of change of universities.

The University Grants Committee visit

Early in the autumn term of the1988–89 academic year, the impending visit of the UGC was one of the preoccupations of both the Aston management and the AUT branch committee. The UGC *Notes for Guidance for Visits* refers to their 'purpose of enabling universities to give the committee a direct impression of its policies, organization, aspirations and problems as centres of teaching and research' and to 'take account of any relevant staff and student associations and trade unions' (Miller 1989).

The Aston administration had chosen to organize their consultation and presentation along thematic lines and there was no provision for AUT representatives as such to meet the visiting party. Eventually, arrangements were made for the students to meet the UGC separately but not the AUT. In this situation, the union wanted to have some direct impact on the visiting party, so three pages of briefing notes on the areas of concern were prepared. These were about staffing and the rigidities governing appointments, the recruitment of students, the situation of staff on 3 year contracts and other matters. The registrar agreed to pass this document on to the visiting party, probably realizing that if he did not it would get there anyway.

The union executive were faced with a delicate task. They didn't want to be too derogatory or damaging about their own institution, but at the same time they perceived serious problems of management style and policy which were in their view damaging the interests of AUT members and making the institution much less effective, even in management terms, than it might be. They hoped the UGC report would have an effect on the university management's policy. The document from the AUT and guild of students (NUS) shared a number of points (both much briefer than the official presentation). Their points were reflected in the UGC report, eventually delivered to the vice-chancellor and council. To quote briefly three points from the UGC report:

> (3) Having reached the end of a phase in its history, in which an impressive campus and computing set up had been achieved, the University needs to shift its attention to its next set of problems. This

> meant developing a degree of flexibility: whilst in a major crisis there had to be unbending concentration on one thing. New problems needed new attitudes. It was not sensible to be in a crisis management situation year after year: Although the Jarratt report had been primarily written for larger universities than Aston, its spirit was sensible for every university, and a measure of devolved responsibility was now needed at Aston.
>
> (7) In relation to student numbers, every university would have to be concerned in future with students who had non-standard qualifications. This would be particularly true at Aston because of its subject mix . . .
>
> (8) . . . the Committee was concerned about the large number of vacant professorships. Whilst it was not easy at present to fill chairs, the university had said that it would be making renewed efforts in this direction. The Committee's impression was that Aston was pitching standards too high. It should be aiming at the best results possible, not the best possible results. It was not in Aston's interests to aim at standards so high that chairs remained vacant which could otherwise be filled. The UFC would be keeping a watchful eye on progress in this matter, which was seen as Aston's single most important task in the next few years.
>
> (UGC 1988: 3)

The AUT welcomed the external pressure the report placed on the university administration to change its policies.

Appraisal

Appraisal generally has multiple facets. There are two main features on which management and unions often agree. The first is performance review, which allows academic managers and appraisees to identify possibilities for improvement in the current work. The second is potential review, which identifies types and levels of work which might be possible and to consider ways of preparing for this. Typically, targets may be agreed in conjunction with measures to provide training or improve facilities for teaching or research. The difficulty arises when these two purposes become confused with a third – the use of appraisal as a basis for rewards or punishments, promotions or demotions, or extra payments in the guise of performance-related pay. One of the problems in UK universities is that the implementation of appraisal systems has come about under pressure from government. Procedures were agreed in outline by vice-chancellors and the AUT but the proposals coincided with the imposition of discretionary awards by the Department of Education on the national pay negotiations. Some university managements have appeared to want to use appraisal schemes not only for performance review and potential review but also as a mechanism for reward, promotion and control. This has provoked resistance and suspicion from individual academics and their union. It is also likely to lead to a situation where none of the functions of appraisal are performed well (Storey and Sissons 1993: 149).

In the 23rd report of Committee A (the main negotiating committee of the university employers and the AUT) issued on 6 February 1987, all UK universities were required to make arrangements for the introduction of an appraisal system for all academic and academic-related staff. Nationally, employers and the union sought out examples of 'best practice' in appraisal schemes to be offered to organizations as a model. However, it was understood from the start that schemes would be determined locally, according to the special needs and resources available in different institutions.

On 6 June 1988, Aston's 'Draft Procedures for the Appraisal and Promotion of Academic and Related Staff' was published in *Aston Fortnight*. The deadline for comments was given as Friday 17 June, just 11 days! The AUT committee had already submitted proposals of appraisal, based on its own research and help from the AUT regional official. Aston management's proposals differed radically in several respects from the type of scheme acceptable to the local union representatives.

The first of four objectives of the Aston scheme was 'To assist the university in achieving its overall goal and objectives through the more effective and efficient participation of staff.' The union preferred the ordering of the sentiments of the Edinburgh University scheme, which said: 'To promote the full potential of the individual and thereby to benefit the university'. The union also had serious objections to the section headed 'Link with other Management Functions'. The proposed Aston scheme read as follows:

> Although the retention of the appraisal record will be limited to the head of department and the member of staff, it may sometimes be necessary for other university officers, committees or formally constituted boards, to have access to the appraisal record. Examples would include:
>
> 1. Committees dealing with promotion, accelerated increments, merit awards, discretionary increments and reappointments.
> 2. Appointments boards for transfer to a different post within the university.
> 3. Senior officers or committees dealing with disciplinary proceedings concerning performance-related problems.

The AUT committee rejected the proposal that the scheme be linked to disciplinary procedures, and indeed that the appraisal should be anything other than confidential to the appraisee, unless written consent was obtained in specific instances from the appraisee. The CVCP draft document had recommended that the appraisal should be confidential between appraisee, appraiser and head of department. The third main objection concerned the absence of an appeals procedure.

The scheme was put to the council of the university on 29 June 1988, without any of the amendments suggested by the union, and was passed. At an AUT general meeting on 27 June, staff expressed their unhappiness with its contents. In September 1988, management implemented the scheme by arranging training courses for appraisers and appraisees, and the AUT recommended a total boycott of the scheme.

At the same time, anger was mounting nationally with the CVCP, who were refusing to negotiate a pay settlement for a cost of living increase relating to April 1988. (The 23rd report of Committee A had produced a salary offer in two stages. It had provided for an increase of 16.6 per cent from 1 December 1986 and 7.4 per cent from 1 March 1988 on the 1985 base.) At the time, this was not much better than the rate of inflation. Having paid for an increase on 2 March 1988, the CVCP continually stated that there were no funds available for an increase for 1988, which would normally have occurred in April. In October 1988, the AUT issued a national ballot asking members to withdraw from participating in the appraisal scheme until such time as the April 1988 pay dispute was settled. The members voted in favour of withdrawing their cooperation, and local action boycotting particular appraisal schemes became subsumed under the national dispute.

In May 1989, the pay dispute for 1988 and 1989 was finally settled, and the national ban on appraisal was lifted. By this time, many Aston academics had forgotten the objections to the local scheme, and with a more urgent agenda of coping with the threat of compulsory redundancy, the committee issued a reminder to members that they were not happy with the scheme, but did not pursue opposition at the time with any vigour.

Appraisal has been on the agenda of most conciliation and grievance committee meetings since 1988. The union constantly raised objections to the scheme, as it was implemented. In January 1990, a questionnaire was sent to all AUT members asking for comments on the appraisal scheme; over half of the members who responded thought that the scheme was confidential. The university council had agreed to the scheme subject to a review after 2 years. In practice, implementation of appraisal seems to be patchy, but the issue of confidentiality and its relation to management remains unresolved.

The national pay dispute 1988–89

September 1988 saw the beginning of a protracted pay dispute that occupied the time and attention of university managers and union representatives at both local and national level until May 1989, when it was finally resolved. The details of the dispute are complex, involving a disagreement over whether a settlement made in 1985 was for 2 or 3 years. Eventually, after balloting its members, the union took national action involving a ban on marking examination scripts. Whenever this sort of action is taken, it has implications for local union–management relations. The same pattern can be seen in the November 1993 dispute in Australia over managerial prerogative for the termination of employment. Some university managements take a hawkish line, threatening academic staff with disciplinary action and the rigorous implementation of pay deductions; others take a more relaxed stance, preferring the dispute to be resolved at national negotiations.

The Aston management in general took the line that this was essentially a national dispute exacerbated by government intervention. Nevertheless, there were what were perceived as threats by staff in one department, where the registrar sent a memo listing the actions that management had deemed appropriate, which included being sent home, summary dismissals or reduction of pay. Union members in this department were particularly solid, defied the memo and called in the regional official. No more threats were made.

Eventually, a settlement was imposed rather than negotiated which, while it gave some increases, fell far short of what most academics felt was justified. Further, part of the settlement insisted on by the Department of Education and Science was the use of 1 per cent of the salary bill to cover some promotions, accelerated increments, movements onto discretionary points at the top of existing salary scales and for an increase in pay for professors. This was significant in the UK context because it paved the way for both performance-related pay and market-related pay at the discretion of local university management. While the initial amount was not very great, this amount and the proportion of the total has been increased at subsequent pay settlements. Awards were required to be made to less than 50 per cent of any particular category of staff. The process was essentially divisive and increased managerial power.

The process was mandatory on all universities. Money would be forfeited if awards were not made. The money could be used for promotions or for discretionary awards. One of the paradoxes was that at Aston in 1989 (and this would have applied to few other UK universities), there had been so few promotions that it in effect forced management's use of discretionary awards to reward significant numbers of academic staff. This put the local union in a difficult position, because while they and the national union were opposed to discretionary awards on principle, it gave material advantage to a substantial minority of academic and academic-related staff. In practice, discretionary awards have become part of the overall reward and control system of the management! With the development of the trading company model, by 1993 control of the use of discretionary money passed to the departments, effectively in most cases to the heads of department. Further variations developed, so that in some departments one-off lump sums were awarded to staff on the basis of their performance in the previous academic year.

Compulsory redundancy and tenure

In order to understand the significance of the threat of compulsory redundancy and the Aston court case in 1988, something needs to be indicated about a similar situation at Aston in the early 1980s, and the national importance of the case, as it related to the defence of tenure in UK universities generally and the 1988 Education Reform Act.

It was generally accepted by the management and the AUT that Aston University had written into its charter and statutes one of the strongest defences of tenure among UK universities. Clauses in the charter and statues defined the limited grounds and procedures under which dismissal of academic staff could occur. These amounted to 'good cause', which can be summarized as follows:

- conviction for a criminal offence;
- physical or mental incapacity;
- immoral, scandalous or disgraceful conduct; or
- conduct judged by the authority in question as constituting failure or inability of the person concerned to perform the duties of his or her office.

The charter and statutes of the university provide that full-time, permanent staff engaged upon teaching and research described as 'teachers' could not be removed from office unless by grounds of 'good cause' as specified above, and not without being given reasonable opportunity to be heard by council and senate, sitting together in joint session (Browne-Wilkinson 1989: 6). Thus it seemed clear that staff could not be dismissed on the grounds of 'redundancy' as defined by the university management.

Following the 1981 UGC cuts of 31 per cent in its recurrent grant, the Aston administration saw the university as being in considerable financial difficulty, with the prospect of deficits of around £1 million in 1983–84 and 1984–85 budgets unless there were major expenditure reductions, which could only mean staff reductions. Considerable numbers of staff took voluntary redundancy or early retirement but apparently not enough to balance the budget. On 20 October 1982, council voted for a postal ballot of its members, which then voted in favour of the following resolution by 19 votes to 17 (with one abstention): 'Council agrees to extend the means available to bring about academic staff movement to include involuntary redundancy and to authorise the vice-chancellor to initiate steps 1 to 5 to bring that about' (Aston University 1982). These steps were as follows:

1. Declaration by council to make staff redundant.
2. Notices issued to trade unions and Department of Employment.
3. Statutory period of 40 days.
4. Consultation period with the trade union.
5. Selection of redundant staff.

Prior to this resolution, academic members of staff had received 'A' or 'B' letters indicating whether their departure was in the managerial interest. Academics in departments which were in the process of dismemberment and dissolution were being invited to leave or relocate to other departments.

Senate passed motions against compulsory redundancy. A national AUT demonstration, meeting and lobby of council was organized. Whether because of the initiation of legal action by two senior members of staff backed by the AUT, or because of continuing voluntary movement of staff, the vice-chancellor did not implement the ballot result.

This early crisis was followed in October 1984 by the vice-chancellor in an address entitled 'You and the New Aston' (Crawford 1984), seeking to reassure staff that Aston was going to survive and flourish. Significantly, there was no clear commitment to avoid introducing compulsory redundancy again. While 'buy-out' schemes still operated and there was massive restructuring and job loss, a substantial refurbishment of the campus began. Within a few years, Aston had succeeded in attracting high A level grade students and achieved about average performance in research ratings.

However, it seemed to many ordinary members of staff that the managerial style remained autocratic, rigid and centralized, and most academics felt that the vice-chancellor had an overwhelming influence on major decisions, for example on student admissions and the appointment of staff. The insistence on the above national average A level recruitment policy and the failure, noted by the UGC in their visit in November 1988, to recruit staff, formed the background when council voted once again to implement compulsory redundancy in 1989.

There were, at the time, approximately 30 academic staff vacancies, 13 of them at professorial level. In the Business School, five out of nine established chairs had been vacant for 10 years, and in one of the threatened departments – electrical engineering – Aston had failed to appoint to the British Telecom funded chair for 5 years. It was reported that of the professorial applicants rejected, 18 had obtained chairs elsewhere.

It seemed odd that the administration should consider compulsory redundancy when Aston had problems recruiting staff, and when there was already legal evidence from 1982–83 that any attempt to break the statutes and charter would be likely to fail. It could be that the Aston management was fulfilling a role of national significance in its attempt to undermine tenure and thus facilitate government as well as university management control of academic staff. At the university level, if compulsory redundancy could be imposed, it would give management increased control, which could be used to restructure and revitalize the academic staff as well as balance the budget.

By the end of March 1989, the vice-chancellor was circulating members of staff in the engineering faculty, reporting that the university's council had resolved:

1. That the vice-chancellor report to each of the next three meetings of council on the response of staff in overstaffed areas to further offers of early retirement, retraining and redeployment.
2. That at the forthcoming council meeting, decisions be taken on what action should be implemented in 1989, including the possibility of compulsory redundancy.

He asked them 'to consider possibilities of "buy out" and voluntary redeployment . . . any reductions in overstaffing must be in the managerial interests of the university, and I expect to inform individuals soon if they would definitely not be considered for "buy out" or redeployment' (Crawford 1989).

Three departments, all the product of restructuring and amalgamations of previous separate departments, as their titles indicate, were identified as being overstaffed: electronic engineering and applied physics one and a half academics overstaffed; civil engineering (which includes transport) two and a half academics overstaffed; chemical engineering and chemistry four academics overstaffed. The AUT committee sought to refute the administration's argument that the three engineering departments were overstaffed. This was important internally because it was clear that there were wide differentials in staffing.

The Business School was finding it difficult to attract or retain staff in some areas, and had high student–staff ratios. Unlike the early 1980s, the number of staff targeted as being vulnerable to compulsory redundancy was only 23, as compared to over 200 before, and they were concentrated in the engineering faculty. In this situation, it was open to management to appeal to academics in understaffed departments to support the abolition of tenure and the removal of staff in overstaffed departments so that new staff might be recruited to ease their load. This clearly presented a problem for the union if maximum solidarity and support was to be obtained across the university.

The president was able, through contact with other AUT branches, to establish up-to-date figures of staffing ratios in comparable departments (see Table 1). These figures (AUT 1989) were circulated to members, given out in press releases, and in articles for other universities and the AUT Journal. The argument was reiterated again and again that in the departments concerned, Aston was not in comparative terms overstaffed, that Aston's overall staff–student ratio was relatively high and the real and pressing problem was understaffing! The union's point was that the so-called overstaffing problem was a product of the administration's rigid student admission policies, and staff recruitment policies that were inappropriate to Aston's situation, as the UGC visiting party had reported. The union received a wide measure of support for this argument from within the university, but also from other universities and from AUT local and national officials.

The feelings and frustrations of members of staff were running high, and eventually faculties, faculty boards and departments started passing resolutions deploring the compulsory redundancy threat, but the senate was not particularly effective in displaying solid opposition to the proposals. There was an impression of disarray, with the professors and other academics failing to counter the vice-chancellor's skilled chairmanship and presentations.

The union tried to lobby council members both through pre-council meetings and written information to their homes, but union efforts could

Table 1 Comparative staff–student ratios, 1988–89

	Chemical engineering/Chemistry			*Electronic engineering/Physics*			*Civil engineering*	*University average*
Aston		9.5			14.2		13.5	15.5
Birmingham	9.5			9.5			9.5	
Loughborough	10.0		10.7	11.8		9.6	12.7	12.3
Bath	8.0			12.1		11.4	12.1	

not compare with the long-term lobbying, including pre-meeting luncheon parties, that the administration was able to organize. Union officials did hold meetings with two heads of department, the deans of faculty and the members of staff concerned. It appeared that a combination of most lay members of council and some senior academics constituted a majority for holding a secret postal ballot on compulsory redundancy. A motion to that effect was carried by 19 votes to 13. By this time, the university secretary/registrar was talking about 12 redundancies, neatly four from each of the threatened departments, yet the overstaffing identified previously was less than this, which suggested that the university was attempting to use compulsory redundancy as part of a more general policy of increasing managerial control.

It was becoming apparent that although there was considerable opposition to the moves towards compulsory redundancy within the university, it was unlikely that lobbying or solidarity action would be effective in stopping it. Pressure was building to go to the courts. The union officials nationally and locally thought they had a good case, but the law is always uncertain and expensive, so the union did not want to act prematurely. It is possible that the university administration thought the AUT was too disorganized to impose legal remedies in time to stop redundancies.

In the event, it was a close run thing. The AUT retained solicitors, who wrote to council members attempting to dissuade them from voting in favour of redundancy. Three academics were identified who were prepared to be plaintiffs in the legal action, involving an injunction restraining the council and officers of the university from breaking its own charter and statutes.

The legal action was complex. The plaintiffs and the AUT lost the first round, when its application for an injunction restraining the university was refused on 19 June, on the grounds that the dispute fell within the jurisdiction of the Visitor, Her Majesty the Queen. The AUT appealed, and on 23 June won the appeal by a two to one majority: 'although the dispute was of a kind which fell within the direction of the Visitor unless and until there was a reference to the Visitor, section 206 of the Education Reform Act 1988 gave jurisdiction to entertain the Action' (Browne-Wilkinson 1989). The university administration indicated its intention to refer the matter to the Visitor and undertook not to issue redundancy notices before 30 September.

The AUT and Aston academics were lucky to get an early hearing by the Queen's appointed representative, confusingly titled 'vice-chancellor' Sir Nicholas Browne-Wilkinson on 2 August. If the hearing had been delayed and the university administration had been able to make staff redundant, while damages might have been obtained, tenure would have been broken at Aston and elsewhere. The Visitor found for the AUT and the plaintiffs, and restrained the university from breaking its charter and statutes. He indicated that the sanctions he could apply in the event of non-compliance included the removal of the council from office or the revocation of the charter of the university. Costs of £90,000 were paid by the university.

The court ruled that the council had to abide by the university's charter and statutes and could not dismiss tenured academic staff except for 'good cause'. The issue at stake, although presented by the university administration's lawyers as about financial exigency and the need for redundancy, went deeper than that, to the core issues of managerial power and authority. The registrar at Aston was quoted in the *Birmingham Post*: 'the judgement appeared to remove Aston's right to manage, with implications for universities across the country' (Morris 1989). The issue of procedures for the removal of academic staff and attempts by vice-chancellors to increase their powers became a major issue in Australia in 1993 and provoked a 24 hour strike by the union (Maslen 1993b: 16).

After the court case, which effectively protected tenure not only at Aston but also at other UK universities, there were implications for management–academic relations. At Aston for a brief period, there was the possibility that management might collapse. There were votes of no-confidence by academic staff by ballot and at the senate. However, these votes were not backed by any consistent attempts to force the resignation of the vice-chancellor, or registrar – and they were not inclined to relinquish their position. Management accepted the legal decision and for a time took up a more conciliatory stance towards personnel issues. The union attempted to democratize procedures within the university. Certainly for a time the balance of power on important committees – the senate included – did change. The professoriat began meeting and as a group were able to increase their own influence over policy decisions taken at senate.

One effect of the Aston decision on tenure was to reinforce a division between academics who had been appointed before the 1988 Education Reform Act, who appeared to be protected against dismissal except for good cause, and those appointed or promoted after the passing of the Act, who came under different jurisdiction and which allowed dismissal on the grounds of redundancy. Although the Act was amended in the Lords to protect academic freedom, there have been fears in many universities that dissenting or unpopular staff might be dismissed by defining their area of work as redundant in terms of some existing or future academic plan. Certainly, while the union victory in the Aston case was important, its effect was somewhat diminished by another case involving a member of academic staff, a philosopher called Edgar Page at Hull University. The union was not able to obtain his re-employment when he was made redundant. This was despite protracted legal action and political pressure, involving a boycott of appointments, examinations and conferences. Also, as has been noted, the protection the Aston case gave was limited to pre-1988 Education Act appointees and, over time, they have become a smaller proportion of the total staff.

Aston in the 1990s

By the early 1990s, it appeared that central management had recovered from the shock and challenge to its authority, symbolized by the court case.

Although the advocacy of total quality management (TQM) and the establishment of a Trading Company Model (TCM) was presented as a move to a less centralized and directed system of academic management, both these initiatives originated from the centre and remained largely influenced by it. In practice, they maintained and even increased control over crucial decisions on resources and staffing. The central principles of strategy and policy, emphasis on quality of student entrants and academic appointments, investment in the estate and infrastructure, reluctance to take measures to allow or promote rapid expansion, and adherence to balancing the budget on a yearly basis remained. While the 1991–92 and 1992–93 academic plan did allow for some expansion in student numbers and some new appointments were made, the adequacy of this strategy in the light of changing external conditions relating to funding, the establishment of a unified system after 1992 and changes in government policy suggested that Aston's change of strategy had been 'too little and too late'.

With hindsight, it is possible to see strategic errors on the part of Aston's management. Aston was facing government cuts imposed by the UGC, a body dominated by traditional academics using traditional academic criteria. These criteria apparently included not only research excellence, but also the use of A level grades as an indicator of the popularity and quality of undergraduate programmes and by implication the quality of the institution. While Aston had in the 1970s quite a wide range of courses and research activities, A level grade requirements were quite low, with many students entering courses through clearing house procedures after they had not secured a university place at a more favoured institution. In some of the engineering courses, there were high drop-out rates. In this context, it was reasonable for the new vice-chancellor to implement a policy which emphasized 'quality' in traditional (high A level) terms. The effect of rigid selectivity of staff and students was certainly to improve 'quality', but initially it reduced quantity; and even in the late 1980s and early 1990s, when again there was a degree of expansion in student numbers, it was at a pace rather less than that of many competing institutions and not sufficient to attract substantial additional funding. Little attempt was made to recruit substantial numbers of overseas undergraduates or postgraduate students, unlike many other universities.

In the early 1990s, many of the features of management style and policy had developed consequent on the appointment of a new vice-chancellor and the massive cuts of the early 1980s. This was due in no small part to the power, influence, persuasiveness and forceful personality of the vice-chancellor, as well as the absence of a strong collegial tradition or powerful professional schools such as medicine or law which are present in most large universities. There were, however, some new features at Aston, notably the emphasis on TQM and the introduction of a TCM, which are not untypical of developments in the managerial structure and culture of many universities in the UK, Canada and Australia.

The emphasis on recruiting high-quality faculty and on professors with an international reputation was only slightly modified in the 1990s. After almost a decade in which there were no professorial appointments, a number were appointed from 1989, not least in an attempt to attract staff with good publication records and actual or potential research grants to improve Aston's competitive position in the research/rating exercise of 1992, which had a more significant impact on funding than previous exercises in 1986 and 1989.

It was still largely the case that lecturers were offered, initially, 3 year contracts with the possibility of renewal for a further 3 years and maybe continuing status at the end of this process. This was a longer and more stringent 'probationary' period than in most UK universities, and not surprisingly many young staff after the initial 3 year period, when still being offered only a temporary contract of 1, 2 or 3 years, sought and obtained posts at other universities which offered continuing appointments, often in departments highly rated for research.

It is difficult to quantify comparable rates of movement, but the impact on morale of this sort of turnover of new staff in a small institution where there had been massive staff cuts in the early and mid-1980s, followed by a period of limited growth in overall academic staff numbers, has been considerable and negative for the staff that remain. This is not only because of the loss of valued colleagues, many of whom were developing research potential, but also because departures placed additional burdens on existing staff to cover teaching commitments. It was rare that another full-time member of staff could be appointed immediately, so often recourse had to be made to part-time staff, who while they might fulfil teaching duties could rarely take on the administrative or pastoral roles that most full-time members of academic staff undertake.

In general, the importance of research and publication records and the capacity to attract research grants has increasingly been emphasized in the 1980s and 1990s in most UK, Australian and Canadian universities. Funding mechanisms which separate teaching and research make the rewards for competitive performance in research performance clear and significant.

Research selectivity

At Aston, from the establishment of the university research committee and faculty research committees in 1983, there has been an attempt to identify key researchers and research strengths within the university and channel resources into these areas. Of course, given limited resources, this inevitably means a reduction in resources to less-favoured areas and to those staff not undertaking research. The university management developed an allocation of resources for research policy which rewarded strong and flourishing areas and removed resources from weaker areas, while allowing a degree of discretion at university and faculty level, largely vested in the deans and research committees for extra awards.

The pressures on all academics to enhance their research performance has increased. A points system in the Aston Business School, giving scores for different types of publications and for student load and administrative duties, was established in the 1980s. The scores of individual members of staff have been recorded, ranked, published and divided in quartiles. While it was initially claimed that this was not being used to allocate duties, clearly such a public expression of monitored work performance lays individual academics open to peer as well as management pressure in terms of their workload. The publication of this points monitoring system epitomized how management action on student recruitment, class size, research policy and staff control comes together in at least symbolic pressure on the individual academic. In the 1990s, with increased selectivity and funding being more closely tied to research output and review, the pressure on academic staff to publish has increased. In the Business School, there are direct monetary rewards for publication of articles in refereed journals, and a system of internal fellowship has been established which provides resources for relief from teaching to staff who promise a research output.

Research selectivity exercises had started in 1986. They had involved the rating of cost centres (roughly equivalent to departments based on disciplines) primarily in terms of the quality of their research output. This had been rated by committees of academic experts appointed by the UGC and subsequently the funding councils which gave ratings on a scale of 1–5. This was then used in combination with other factors to form the basis for differential allocation of research funding by the granting/funding bodies. In the exercises of 1986 and 1989, the main multiplier of the funding level had been the number of students allotted to a cost centre. In 1992, this was changed to the number of active research staff whose work had been submitted to the research assessment exercise. Also, the proportion of research funds allotted on the basis of the research exercise increased from 10 per cent in 1986 to 30 per cent in 1989 and to 100 per cent in 1992.

The impact of these changes was painfully obvious after the 1992 research exercise. The change in the formula for calculating the award of funds revealed the weakness of the managerial strategy adopted at Aston. In 1992, instead of funding being related to the number of students in each cost centre adjusted by the level of peer ranged performance, the 1–5 rating was multiplied by the number of active research staff. Thus while the departments at Aston in all but one case either improved or retained their research rating, because fewer staff compared with other institutions from the old university sector were participating in research, the total amount of funds distributed was low and substantially lower in some departments (notably the Business School) than in the previous exercise in 1989. Even some of the ex-polytechnics, while in general not scoring such high research ratings as the old universities, compared favourably with Aston, with significant numbers of active research staff earning funds. While there had been some growth in student numbers from the mid-1980s, staff numbers had lagged behind, and while this did not matter too much in the first two research exercises, by 1992 it had become a serious weakness. By then, Aston was one of the smallest universities.

One of the consequences of its small size, together with a policy of investment in material infrastructure rather than the appointment of new staff, was that the ratio of central service and administrative costs to academic staff was comparatively high. As management pointed out, it is extremely difficult to make accurate comparisons between universities as to central administrative costs when compared with direct departmental academic costs. Different universities are not only organized differently in terms of administrative structure but also in terms of accounting procedures. Thus a member of staff who might appear in one university as a member of the academic-related staff in a certain department, in another he or she might appear as part of central administrative services. Nevertheless, it did appear that because of the combination of small size, slow rate of growth, investment policy, as well as administrative structure, that Aston in reality (as well as in university statistics) had a high ratio of central administrative costs as compared to departmental costs. As it was, the academics who could earn funds through research, consultancy or increased student numbers were limited in number and this presented a serious problem for the future financial and academic viability of the university.

Trading company models

The development of more transparent accounting procedures consequent on the implementation of the Trading Company Model (TCM) made the balance of what appeared as direct and indirect costs clearer. The introduction of the TCM initially in a shadow form in August 1991 at Aston, had been preceded by similar moves at other UK universities and there are similar systems in most Canadian and Australian universities.

In essence, the TCM sets up academic departments and administrative departments (like the library, estates and registry) as cost centres. All departments supplying services are made responsible for budgeting income and expenditure to meet their academic or administrative targets. In its early stages, it is a sort of pseudo-managed market. However, some decisions and criteria with university-wide implications remain the responsibility of central university management; for example, at Aston, student entry criteria, staff appointments, the total budget and the requirement to balance it each year. As the system develops, service level agreements between academic and administrative service departments relating the price, quality and quantity of service provision are instituted. Even in the early stages, the indirect costs attributed to departments as payments for central administrative service (e.g. registry, estates, library and central computing facilities) become apparent. This is important because it makes costs more transparent, but it can also apparently tend to place responsibility at the departmental level, thus undermining the power of university-wide constitutional, collegial bodies like the senate to shape strategy.

This is the background to the efforts by the university management – both central and departmental – to deal with projected deficits largely consequent on the results of the research funding outcome of 1992. Aston's relatively poor performance in attracting UFC funds for research and teaching, compared both with its immediate past performance and a range of other institutions, put it into immediate financial jeopardy in 1993. This situation was alleviated by the granting of a support fund of £1.4 million by HEFCE. The negotiation of this support could be seen as a tribute to the vice-chancellor's continuing ability to convince the funding councils of Aston's capacity for regeneration. Initially, it was understood that this funding would be phased out over a 3 year period up to the projected next funding exercise, but in the summer of 1993 it was announced that it would cease after 2 years. This shortened time period may have been a response to other universities, who saw their own funding being capped to bail out Aston and a few other universities, but it certainly sharpened the pressure on Aston.

The way in which proposals to reduce expenditure were formulated, the process of implementation and the degree of legitimation, acceptance and commitment illustrate the interaction of a number of features of the Aston management structure, style and culture which, while they may be more marked and perhaps a little idiosyncratic, are nevertheless present in most universities in the UK and with different forms and nomenclature in Australia and Canada. These features include:

1. The university's central executive directorate: the vice-chancellor, chief administrative officers and some senior academics.
2. The formal constitutional structures: senate and council, faculty boards, deans, etc.
3. The informal administrative structures, often initially *ad hoc* but often becoming permanent and acquiring status and acceptance (if not legitimacy) at Aston.

The latter has included the Advisory Group on Budget Adjustment (AGBA), which consists of a core group of administrators as well as pro-vice-chancellors and deans. This was extended to Big AGBA, which included heads of departments. The heads of department, consequent on the TCM and in view of the budget crisis, were also meeting as the 'Academic Heads Budget Review Group' to collate and coordinate proposals for senate, finance committee and council. The teams implementing TQM were another set of *ad hoc* bodies, but did not seem to be particularly effective in influencing constitutional bodies or affecting the decisions being made about resources and staff.

The main formal structures have not been central to the formulation of policy, or even its discussion. Departmental heads did present their proposals for dealing with the deficit to an extended meeting of senate on 20 October 1993. However, the vice-chancellor made it very clear in the course of an exchange with a member of senate protesting at the lack of financial information available to allow senate to make financial and academic decisions, that he saw the exercise at senate as being essentially an information exercise where academic staff were encouraged to express their views. By implication, policy would be made elsewhere. That certainly seems to be the case, although where precisely the decisions are made is less clear.

The academic planning committee (APC), a sub-committee of senate and small enough to be engaged in pro-active policy proposals, does not work in that way. It receives reports from other committees and debates and decides on specific proposals, for example the franchising of a course to a local further education college, or special arrangements for the admission of more A level students to undergraduate courses. However, the APC has not been involved in the formulation of a university-wide policy on franchising or the admission of non-A level students to courses in general. The important element of Aston's policy relating to the insistence on high A level grades for entry to undergraduate courses is reviewed annually by a further sub-group, which reports to the APC but which seems to have a high degree of power and autonomy.

Quality and TQM

Concern for 'quality' and quality circles at Aston and elsewhere had become part of universities' managerial, if not institutional, culture by the late 1980s. TQM can be seen as an intensification of management's efforts to exercise control over academics' work by attempting to elicit an involvement in a number of groups addressing particular 'quality' issues. The development of TQM at Aston, and probably elsewhere, is characterized by an uneasy relationship with the established constitutional bodies of the university, for example the senate or faculty boards. TQM activities are reported periodically to senate and implicitly endorsed, in that they appear as part of institutional academic plans submitted by the university to the UFC after admittedly late and brief consideration by senate. However, senate did not initiate TQM committees, and while key senior academic and administrative staff are dominant members of both TQM groups and key sub-committees of senate, the relationship of proposals and procedures proposed and propagated by TQM groups with established institutional committees like the first degrees committee, higher degrees committee or academic planning committee is unclear.

TQM has been rigorously promoted by the vice-chancellor and the director of staff development has TQM prominent in her remit. Indeed, the vice-chancellor has become prominent in the advocacy of TQM throughout UK universities and has provided a guide for the CVCP and is chair of their working group on quality.

Nevertheless, TQM at Aston has been met by a degree of scepticism and even cynicism by ordinary academics. There are a number of reasons for this, including the perception that it is a management ploy to increase control and extract more work. There is also suspicion of its American/Japanese origins, and there are doubts about the applicability of a system perceived as devised with privately owned, profit-seeking manufacturing industry in mind. As Storey and Sissons (1993: 50) point out:

> ... a great deal of Human Resource Management discourse is cursorily decontextualised from the real world. All the talk of 'winning commitment', encouraging flexible working and gaining trust can appear glib in economies where unemployment is high (around 10 per cent in the UK, Australia and Canada in 1992 and 93); where workforce reductions are announced virtually daily; and where pressure from the Treasury results in reductions in public-fund training budgets.

While Storey and Sissons are referring to the national personnel management and industrial scene in the UK, much the same could be argued for Australia and Canada and even more so when applied at the level of a university. Management may have a rhetoric of TQM, quality caring and commitment; however, the reality is that in a situation of financial constraints and crises where a high proportion of staff are on short-term contracts with very little security of employment, substantial 'voluntary' redundancies are implemented and TQM takes a lower profile.

The TCM – as I have described it at Aston – involved the development of a quasi-market and it increased the transparency of accounting and resourcing procedures within the university. It also apparently devolved responsibility to the departments, in effect largely to heads of department, for budgeting and setting targets in relation to academic work. In practice, while the devolution of responsibility was extensive, power to modify the overall plan was limited. In its working, the TCM tended to emphasize the competitive elements between academic departments and service departments, while diverting attention from the broader issues affecting the strategic plan for the university as a whole, for example, whether it should attempt rapid expansion, deficit financing or consider merger with another institution.

By the end of August 1994, it was by no means clear that Aston's management, even using TQM and TCM, would be able to develop a strategy and ensure the commitment of academic staff that would not only balance the budget but also put the institution's research effort in a strong enough position to improve its competitive performance for the 1996 research selectivity exercise. Though some departments might be able to improve their research ratings, it is possible that Aston will be squeezed. There are parallels for some universities in Australia.

However the feature that made Aston's situation particularly acute in 1992 and seems likely to continue into the mid-1990s is its comparatively small size. By 1992, it was the third smallest English university. This led to increasing discussion within the institution as to whether Aston can remain a viable independent university. This was raised at a union meeting and at the university council in November 1993. Mergers in the UK have been much less common consequent on the establishment of a unified system than in Australia. The Department for Education has not developed a strong case for mergers and has specified a much lower minimum size for the attainment of university status (i.e. 2000 students) than in Australia, where 8000 has been specified for full university status and funding. Indeed in the UK case, ministers have emphasized the virtue of diversity.

However, the possibility of merger at Aston started to take on some credibility at the end of 1993. There was a perception by some staff that the management had failed in its strategy and that a continuation of the same policies and management style would not improve the situation. From a business perspective, Aston had substantial assets – a well-developed central site with a good infrastructure, a balanced budget with no debts looming, and substantial unused capacities. There were distinctive departments of pharmaceutical and vision sciences, clusters of good researchers and a limited range of courses recruiting students at above the national average A level score. All these features might make it an attractive package to the management of another university. A further contingent factor was that the vice-chancellor is to retire in 1996. When a chief executive leaves his or her post, it is often easier for such a fundamental change to take place.

The situation at Aston illustrates the more general point that can be made about university management. The general message that may be derived from a particular case study is that while there are strong patterns of constraint from both the state and the economy, and through the history and culture of particular universities, there remains room for the development of differing managerial styles and structures, even where the competitive stance of one university to another paradoxically induces a degree of conformity.

In the final chapter, emphasis is placed on analysing the common patterns affecting academics in universities in all three countries. But this case study should have established that while the degree of variation of experience consequent on different institutional histories and positions is important, so is the effectiveness or otherwise of academic managers (pre-eminently vice-chancellors) in implementing successful strategies for change.

6

Management and Academic Work

This final chapter draws together some of the themes that have emerged in the preceding discussions which analysed the relation of universities and their management to the state and economy. University managements are adopting some of the practices and language of private corporations and the market, and this is affecting the day-to-day activity and consciousness of the ordinary academic. Some of this has already been illustrated by quotations from a range of academics. The management of change in higher education can be seen not only from the point of view of the managers – whether of the university, state or economy – but also from the point of view of the managed. Broad parameters affecting academics as an occupation or profession shape and are shaped by the management strategies for managing academics individually and collectively.

By focusing on the 'labour process debate' and 'proletarianization thesis' as applied to academics, something of the structure and culture of academic work and its management in universities in Australia, Canada and the UK can be analysed. This provides a basis for speculations on future trends. There are political choices facing academics, their managers, politicians, students, corporations and citizens. The purposes and modes of university management and governance and the degree of access and type of accountability appropriate for the closing years of the twentieth century are not predetermined.

Proletarianization and the academic labour process

It is necessary to make some comments on what is meant by the academic labour process and how it relates to professionalism and proletarianization, the state and economy. A.H. Halsey (1992: 13), in his *Decline of Donnish Dominion,* characterizes it as a process which entails:

> The gradual proletarianisation of the academic professions – an erosion of their relative class and status advantages as the system of higher education is propelled towards a wider admission of those who survive

> beyond compulsory schooling. Managerialism gradually comes to dominate collegiate cooperation in the organisation of both teaching and research. Explicit vocationalism displaces implicit vocational preparation, as degree courses are adapted to the changing division of labour in the graduate market. Research endeavours are increasingly applied to the requirements of government or industrial demands. The don becomes increasingly a salaried or even a piece-work labourer in the service of an expanding middle class of administrators and technologists.

Halsey's analysis is founded on a careful historical account and the results of three surveys of academics, their situations and attitudes (in 1964, 1976 and 1989). It has been argued that similar processes with different speeds and political contexts are underway in Australia and Canada.

Trow, the American joint author with Halsey of a 1971 study of British academics, presented an analysis at a Times Higher Education Conference on Quality in September 1993 not dissimilar to Halsey's in *The Decline of Donnish Dominion.* He presented a theory that 'the government has, over the past ten years, revolutionised higher education, wasting away university autonomy and imposing its own ideals of "hard managerialism" on academics as a substitute for trust in their professionalism' (Brooksman 1993: 7). The government, in attempting to establish assessments of teaching quality through the Higher Education Council has, Trow argued, instituted a process that 'has required the deprofessionalisation of the academic workforce and their transformation into middle managers or skilled craftsmen, interested in promotion and better pay as rewards for better performance as determined by external assessors against yardsticks supplied by government agencies' (Brooksman 1993: 7). Universities' best defence, Trow advised, would be 'for the universities to wrest back control through "soft managerialism", administrative leadership from within the universities which sees managerial effectiveness as an important element in the provision of higher education of high quality'.

Burton Clark (1983), one of the foremost analysts of comparative higher education systems, identified the central elements of his analysis of the work of academics in relation to the broader social system. His work is concerned with the academic labour process. Like Weber, he focuses on power and politics in his analysis of education systems and their relation to society. He also argues that the distinctive processes of academic work, teaching and research (but particularly research) form the most important features of the academic profession and that each education system will have distinctive features related to the history and politics of the society in which it exists.

Trow (1983), in focusing on the finance of higher education, identified in Clark's work four analytically, if not practically, distinct ways or modes, which organize and decide the size, shape, character and funding of higher education systems. These ways of organizing and managing the institutions of higher education are characterized as follows:

1. A professional guild system where academic norms and values are defined and applied by more or less eminent members of the academy through their contact or colonization of high administrative office.
2. The political system, whether it be by minister, cabinet, legislature, president or junta, may decisively control and shape higher education.
3. The bureaucracy and its rules and regulations and civil servants can be crucial in determining what happens in, and to, higher education.
4. The influence of the market, where the decisions of many actors (students, teachers or graduates) competing for goods, money or power influence the shape, structure and processes of higher education.

These formulations have been useful in analysing particular cases, but the analysis can be placed in the broader context of the influence of economic and production relations. This emphasis, present in the labour process theory, needs to be retained, and in turn to be related to the role of the state as it responds to and regulates both the economy and higher education.

The OPEC oil price rise of 1973 marked a period of prolonged crisis and restructuring among western economies. There were restrictions on the availability of public funds for higher education and pressure to bend the purpose of the universities to improving the competitiveness of corporations. The conditions of academic labour in general began to deteriorate. At the same time, Braverman's (1974) book, *Labor and Monopoly Capitalism*, renewed the labour process debate and argued that with the development of scientific management in twentieth-century capitalism, labour was increasingly controlled and deskilled. Although Braverman's analysis was focused on the degradation and deskilling of male skilled manual workers in private productive industry, it did involve a more general analysis of the development of managerial control through the separation and appropriation of the mental planning of work. Smith and Willmott (1991) argue that with a broader Marxist framework, which analyses the mutual contributions that different sorts of workers make to the collective enterprise of the production of goods and services for the state and society as well as private capital, it is possible to extend a labour process analysis to such white-collar workers in the public sector as academics (Miller 1991a).

Thompson (1983: 4), commenting on the labour process debate, wrote: 'A labour process perspective locates the basic activity of transforming raw materials into products through human labour within a given technology, within the specific dynamics of a mode of production and antagonistic class relations'. Braverman's argument focused centrally on the 'transformation of raw materials'. A wide analysis of the dynamics of a capitalist or indeed socialist system of production can include the relation of academic work to that process of transforming nature into products with a market and/or use value.

Thompson (1983) argued that the question of 'how do workers control themselves in the context of practices deeply embedded in the capitalist labour process' is important, and that 'this means taking up issues of ideology and culture and how they influence the relations between consent, control and resistance at work'. Questions of ideology and culture are central to understanding the work and situation of academics in universities. The management of changes in universities' work needs not only to be considered from perspectives concerned with the process of reproduction of labour and labour power and the needs of capital, but also the legitimation of state and the social order.

Littler and Salaman (1982), in their critique of Braverman and discussion of theories of the labour process, identify the way in which Braverman's *Labor and Monopoly Capitalism* (1974):

1. Rejuvenated the sociological study of the workplace and the labour process, by reassessing the inherently class-based nature of work organization.
2. Advanced class theory and work analysis by insisting on the connection between the two.
3. Served to restore the sociology of the labour process to its central place within sociological debate and theorizing.

They show some of the weaknesses of Braverman's analysis in terms of the restrictions of his theory of class conflict, relating this to what they see as an inadequate conception of control in the labour process. They note the extensions and revisions of Braverman's work by authors such as Offe (1976), Burawoy (1978) and Edwards (1979), particularly in the emphasis they place on the importance of dependence in employment relationships and the variety of modes of managerial control, but they conclude:

> . . . a more useful theory of labour processes cannot be restricted to the specification of work activities at the point of production itself but must take account of the control implications of decisions taken elsewhere in the organization and, indeed, outside it. The subordination of labour, real or otherwise, cannot be understood at the level of the labour process.
>
> (Littler and Salaman 1982: 266)

There is utility in raising these questions for an analysis of the work situation of academics in terms of its relation to the general dynamics of class forces. The debates have become increasingly sophisticated in terms of identifying different forms of control, but a labour process analysis which starts and focuses on industrial labour within the private sector of a capitalist society is not easily extended to deal with the public sector, or specifically higher education. It may be that links can be made if the analysis encompasses ideologies of collegiality, professionalism and service. Certainly forms of control connect with the appropriation, planning and organizing of work by the higher reaches of academic management. Conventional non-Marxist accounts of academic work and institutions seem to miss crucial dimensions of the ways in which crises within the economy and polity translate themselves into the problems facing universities. Labour process theory can be located within a broader political economy approach, which pays attention to the specifics of work and work organization within universities and yet relates these to the pressures from state and economy.

Changing academic labour

The main pressures on universities have been discussed. These are perceived by senior academics to come primarily from the state in so far as they affect the management of their own institutions. It was argued in Chapters 2 and 3 that the state is instrumental in shaping the finance, governance and demands for courses and research. However, the nature of the demands arises in large measure from the role of the state in attempting to improve the competitiveness of corporate capital. How do pressures from economy and state affect the changing conditions of academic work? Some of the pressures have already been established: reduced resources, rising student numbers and higher expectations of research productivity. A sketch of the main material and cultural factors affecting the day-to-day life of the ordinary academic, drawing predominantly on the UK experience, may show how far as a result of these pressures there is a 'degrading and deskilling' process consistent with the proletarianization thesis put forward by Halsey (1992) and Braverman (1974).

In 1970–71, the university staff–student ratio in the UK was 1:8.5; by 1980–81 it had risen to 1:9.5, in 1988–89 it was nearly 1:11.5 and in 1990–91 it was 1:12.3 (AUT 1990). The polytechnic and college average was 1:15 in 1990–91, having increased from 1:13.5 in 1986. The rise in the university staff–student ratio has been exponential, being nearly 11 per cent in the first half of the 1980s and 19 per cent in the second half and continuing at these rates in the 1990s.

The higher rate of increase in staff–student ratios in the 1980s in the polytechnics and colleges was partly due to the different subject mix in the two sectors. The 30 medical schools with low staff–student ratios were all within the old university sector. In the early 1980s, when faced with government cutbacks, the UGC attempted to protect the unit of resource by limiting student intake and cutting staff, whereas the polytechnics expanded their student numbers. Expansion in student numbers in the early 1990s has proceeded apace in both the traditional universities and the former polytechnics. In the 1991–92 academic year, for example, there were 30,000 more students in the old universities compared with the previous year, equivalent to the creation of three new fair-sized universities of the 1980s. In terms of teaching productivity, there have been substantial increases in throughput concomitant with increased class size.

If we turn to the other main aspect of academic work, research, one measure of productivity is the number of publications per member of staff. Halsey's (1992) surveys show that the mean number of papers, articles or books published in the previous 2 years increased from 3.5 in 1976 to 6.6 in 1989 in the universities and from 0.9 to 2.0 in the polytechnics. The percentage of staff who had not published at all declined from 23 per cent in the universities and 68 per cent in the polytechnics in 1976 to 9 per cent and 46 per cent, respectively, in 1989. Some commentators assume that institutional funding changes promoting research selectivity is producing a division between staff engaged in research and those who solely teach. That may happen in the future, but the evidence so far suggests increased competition has produced effective pressures on more academic staff in both the old and new universities to publish. More research is being done with the same or scarcely increased resources. It is difficult to assess if quality is being maintained.

Halsey's respondents reported that in 1989, 13 per cent of those in universities felt they were under a lot of pressure to do research and 23 per cent a little pressure; in the polytechnics, the figures were 7 and 27 per cent, respectively. The main obstacle to research was identified as time spent in teaching and other commitments. Most academic staff in UK universities (and the same would apply to academics in Australia and Canada) are torn by three-way pressures – teaching, administration and research. It is hardly surprising that Carroll and Cross (1990) reported that just over 77 per cent of their UK 'old' university sample had become more stressed in recent years, with less than 4 per cent less so; 62 per cent expected their posts to become even more stressful in the future and only 3 per cent expected to experience any reduction in job-related stress. In terms of job satisfaction, 33 per cent reported it to be less and 15 per cent much less in recent years, with only 24 per cent experiencing increased job satisfaction. Important sources of job dissatisfaction included an inadequate salary (74 per cent), inadequate resources (73 per cent), conflicting and increased job demands (65 per cent), no prospect of promotion (60 per cent), no public recognition of worth (55 per cent), job insecurity (47 per cent), lack of autonomy and control (44 per cent) and isolation from colleagues (28 per cent).

One of the features of the demands of administration is its density and complexity. There is an overlay of different structures and pressures which co-exist and compete. First, there is a departmental and faculty administrative system which focuses on the heads of departments and deans, but with its own plethora of committees. Second, there is a more or less powerful collegial system of academic assemblies, senates and councils with associated committees, minutes and papers. Third, there is a developing central management system with increasingly powerful vice-chancellors and administrators; and, in many universities, appointed deans and *ad hoc* working parties, whose role only partly articulates with older administrative and collegial structures. There is evidence to suggest that, increasingly, strategic decisions – particularly financial ones – are being concentrated in a central management team. Indeed, the Jarrat Report (1985) and government papers (Dawkins 1987b, 1988a) in Australia explicitly advocate this.

However, that does not mean that junior staff are freed from administrative responsibilities and are left to get on with teaching and research, much as many of them might like it. There are three pressures that exacerbate the situation. First, the increasing pressures from the state in terms of acccountability, planning and competition between institutions, means that there are increasing demands on all staff to be involved at least at the level of providing data and consent in the processes of planning courses, ensuring quality, devising research strategies and raising money. Second, the central management of an institution may be keen to devolve certain responsibilities, often financial, to the departmental level, thus relieving itself of having to face difficult political choices. This is epitomized by the development of corporate trading models, as discussed in Chapter 5, or similar systems which devolve financial responsibility to department, school or faculty. Yeatman (1990: 172), commenting on this process in Australia, relates it to the discursive practice of policy makers at the state and institutional level:

> With regard to highly empowered discursive producers as in the case of the professional educators within . . . the higher education system, the state . . . has embarked on subtle strategies of containment of the claims generated by these masters of discursive production. The general thrust has been in the direction of corporate management whereby, in the current general environment of declining public resources and services, and as legitimised by the discourse of decentralisation (letting the managers manage, etc.) the management of reduced budgets is given over to the units closest to the coal face. The Commonwealth Government [devolve authority] to individual institutions of higher education; and, within the latter the central administration devolves the management of reduced budget to faculties. This means that claims and claimants are brokered much lower down the line, and it becomes all the more difficult for their advocates to elaborate them into generalised and generally visible discursive maps and claims.

Academic staff do attempt to maintain general claims about resources, the direction of curricula or research, and the right through collegial processes to be involved in crucial decisions about, for example, reductions in staff. Sometimes this is done through the defence of established collegial structures and processes, sometimes through increased union activity, and often through a combination of both. There are costs when trusted union representatives are elected to senates or councils, for this means the increased pressures of meetings, minutes and newsletters, petitions, lobbies and delegations. Conscientious and collegially minded academics are sometimes forced out through sheer exhaustion (Miller and Wheeler 1989).

These processes relate to an important aspect of the Braverman labour process theory: the concentration of intellectual planning functions in the hands of managers and their removal from the control of the practitioners. There have been largely successful attempts by the state with the (sometimes willing, sometimes unwilling) compliance of senior academics in universities to institute corporate executive styles of planning and management.

Yet academics have by no means totally lost control of the organization of their work of teaching and research. It may be increasingly constrained, monitored and documented, but there are peculiar features of the academic labour process which make the forms of control, alienation and exploitation ones which often involve the individual academic in the construction of his or her own fate. There is often a curious collusion between management and academics, whereby degrees of at least apparent control are retained by the individual on the implicit understanding that the targets of increased student numbers, more articles or more form filling are met.

Wilson (1991: 259) draws on his experience as a union researcher to characterize the situation of some university academics:

> For them the absence of fixed laws of attendance requirements can be seen as an unspoken bargain. The price of the autonomy is, say, the pressure to produce a book every two years. Even though ten years ago books were perhaps required only every four years the bargain may still be worthwhile for both management and academics. Control is gained not by engineering responsible autonomy but by conceding it.

In all three countries and in all three areas of work – teaching, research and administration – there seems to be an intensification of effort. But does this amount to a process of degradation and deskilling, as in Braverman's labour process thesis?

In teaching, if the analogy with industrial production is pursued, the movement is perhaps best understood as craft workers moving from small-batch to large-batch production, as lectures, seminars, laboratory classes and tutorials have all increased in size. There are certainly processes of the commodification and compartmentalization of knowledge underway, often through the development of module or credit systems. And although technology – the overhead projector, tape–slide sequence or Xerox copier, the use of TV programmes or computer-assisted learning of various sorts – can be used to supplement or supplant direct staff–student interaction, overall it would be an exaggeration to assert that higher education has moved to assembly-line, mass production methods. Thus, while there may have been some degradation and deskilling in the teaching situation, particularly the opportunities to engage in small group teaching, some staff at least have acquired both old and new skills, such as performing before large audiences, or the accomplished use of word-processing and computer equipment. Thus there may be a process of degradation and intensification but not necessarily wholesale deskilling.

Academics as workers, intellectuals and professionals

Academics in the UK, Canada and Australia share some of the characteristics of a broader group of lecturers and teachers working throughout the education system. The great majority are state employees, although there are a few academics working in small private universities like Buckingham in the UK or Bond in Australia. Among teachers, by contrast, there is a much bigger and more significant group working in independent schools in the three countries. Most academics are primarily dependent on wages in the form of a monthly salary, usually on scales with incremental points. Some are able to supplement this income from consultancy fees and others with royalties from books and earnings from journalism in various media.

In common with other cultural workers, the position of academics can be analysed in terms of their labour process and their broad class position, but also through their location and categorization within the discourses of professionalism and the intellectual.

Through classic debates in the work of Marx (1976), Gramsci (1971) and Mannheim (1956) and, more recently in the UK, in the work of Anderson (1990), Williams (1979) and Hickox (1986), there has been ongoing attention to the relationship of intellectuals to class structure and action. Debray (1981) formulates a wide-ranging and comparative analysis of intellectuals which seeks to relate them to different bases, institutions and sets of productive cultural relations. Thus the education system, publishing and modern electronic media, although interlinked are different bases from within which different types of intellectuals, teachers, writers and celebrities work. He distinguishes between the different political and cultural traditions and their associated institutions, and the different cultural apparatuses which distinguish, for example, France, the UK and the USA.

Mulhern (1981) argues that in the USA, the development of mass markets through the applications of research and development occurred earlier than in the UK or France, so that, for example, in the 1930s the French educational elite was roughly half the size of that in the UK, and the USA had more institutions of higher education than France did academic personnel.

Differences in configuration are also important. Thus in France, there is significant centralization in Paris of intellectual life, academic publishing, media and political institutions. In the UK, there is a dominant Oxford–Cambridge–London nexus and in the USA, New York, Boston and Washington still form somewhat separate but linked centres of control. The eastern triangles of Toronto, Ottawa and Montreal in Canada or Sydney, Canberra and Melbourne in Australia exercise similar degrees of dominance, not least because these cities have a high proportion of the total population and the federal seats of government. In the USA and UK, the Ivy League colleges and Oxford and Cambridge may still retain a degree of intellectual dominance, despite the fact that expansion of higher education from the late nineteenth century has occurred largely in provincial institutions like the huge state and private universities in America or the UK civic universities and polytechnics.

The different relations between state, politics and universities have already been alluded to in the work of Clark (1983). In the French case, there has been close association between the political and intellectual establishment since at least the Third Republic. One could argue that from the revolution to the Fifth Republic, the intellectual and political scene in France has been in the main at least formally meritocratic and universalistic, so that intellectuals (including academics) are seen to comprise a distinct stratum or milieu, not simply a network of family connections dependent on a dominant class. This description might apply more easily to the English scene. The question of the existence, never mind the nature, of English intellectuals remains in dispute, so Hickox's (1986) article was entitled 'Has there been a British intelligentsia?' It may be too much to deny its existence, but clearly intellectuals do have a specific, almost residual character within the British social scene. Many, including academics who in other cultures would describe themselves as intellectual, refuse to do so.

The notion of the 'professional' seems to sit more easily on English (and on most Australian and Canadian) academics than that of the 'intellectual'. Fores and Glover (1981) and Child (1983) see it as a peculiarly Anglo-Saxon phenomenon, and Lawn and Ozga (1981), Larson (1977), Ginsberg *et al.* (1980) and Meiskins (1985) have all recognized the deeply ideological (yet nevertheless still potent) nature of professionalism, which limits the possibilities of alliance with sections of the working class. The consciousness of status in professionalism is expressed by Meiskins (1985: 115):

> a powerful sense of distinctiveness, of entitlement to special privilege and respect and its success may also rest on its ability to provide at least temporary protection from the worst effects of wage-labour by legitimising the profession's 'right' to autonomy and high social reward although 'deprofessionalisation' remains a constant danger.

This seems opposite to the situation of academics threatened with (among other things) the abolition of 'tenure'. In the vocabulary of academics and teachers, 'profession' is mentioned as often as 'union' (Ginsberg *et al.* 1980).

Larson (1977) points out differences in the ways in which professionalism has been formed and is articulated in the USA and the UK, because of the different roles of, and relations between, the universities, ruling elites and professions. Canada and Australia could be seen to lie somewhere between the US and UK cases. Within universities, the different professional cultures of law, medicine, engineering and accounting all have their impact on the self-image, power and prospects of academics working within these institutions, who may often see themselves as members of two overlapping professional groups. The formation of academics and intellectuals in Australia and Canada has been different from that in the UK, reflecting in both countries their colonial status in the nineteenth century and the influence of university and academic cultures and personnel from England, Scotland and the USA.

Pusey (1991) describes some features of class, culture, state and education in Australia more sharply than an English commentator might dare to. He argues that Australia has a history where from the time of the squatters and the wool kings, 'the wealthy classes have never provided leaders or shown the community any guidance in political matters' (Eggleton 1953: 11), and that in the time of Australian settlement in the nineteenth century:

> . . . there was none of the (completely untransplantable) civic republicanism of those old American New Englanders who were driven to public duty, and to learning by the fear of God. The 'poor quality of leading Australians' (Stretton 1987: 197) on the contrary is the continuing moral and cultural failure of an elite that is not very interested in Australian identity and which has always sent its sons and daughters abroad only so that they could return with some advantage over their compatriots whom they for the most part despise. That is certainly still the way in which expectations, careers and orientations to university are formed in the 'best' Australian private schools from which a disproportionate number of our top public servants have come.
>
> (Pusey 1991: 233–4)

In Canada, the different histories of Anglophone and Francophone universities and elites reflects the different relations to state, religion and education still marked by the history of colonialism and conquest in the eighteenth and nineteenth centuries.

Academic labour process

Let us now turn to the core labour processes of the 'typical' academic, keeping in mind the variations in culture, professional history and institutional setting. It is possible to identify, analytically at least, the major components of academic work, while recognizing variations established by discipline and market situation. The central dynamic is the impact of various forms of control emanating from university management, which itself mediates state and market pressures.

In the UK, most academics other than professors, readers and those with a specific research label, carry the title 'lecturer'. In Australia to an increasing extent and in Canada almost totally, the nomenclature is professor, associate professor and assistant professor. Whatever the appellation, lecturing and other forms of teaching constitute the main part of academic work for most of the profession. The teaching includes the formal lecture, the seminar, class or laboratory session and individual or small group supervision. The range, social relations, hours and intensity of work can be very varied. Typically, the activity is solitary and not directly supervised, but there are laboratory classes which involve work with and supervision of technicians, and more rarely team teaching. Usually, the teaching is part of some larger course or degree programme, which has specified syllabi and established patterns of teaching, assessment and examination. Thus, while in the immediate context of teaching the lecturer could be seen as similar to a lone craftsperson, in the wider context he or she works as part of a team. He or she may be both leader and led and certainly works within constraints. The lecturer is subject to a degree of collegial control and adapts to pressure from the university, the market, a professional body or state agencies on course content, mode of teaching, or even the very existence of the course itself.

It has been argued that for most academics the managerial and market pressures are stronger than before, but much of the core activity remains the same. There is lecturing to students in ever larger numbers, trying to stimulate seminar discussion, attention to the problems and possibilities of individual students, and the routines of setting, invigilating and marking examinations. The plant and technology remain largely the same – the lecture hall, seminar room and office. The overhead projector, Xerox handout and the use of video and computer interactive programmes have become more widespread over the last decade, but it is difficult to see the increasing uses of technology as having yet fundamentally changed the teaching relationship.

More significant is the steady massification of the student–lecturer relation. As the staff–student ratio worsens, the quality of lecturer–student relations is changing. There is a difference in experience between teaching 40 and 140 students, and the students feel that as well. And a further consequence of the reduction in economic resources from the state has been increased pressure on student counselling services in universities (Wheeler and Birtle 1993).

Administration itself, of courses, resources or research contracts, involves many academics in a supervisory relationship with secretaries, technicians and administrative assistants. Besides those who are part of the formal university management structure, there is a substantial group of people who, depending on their seniority and the size of research resources at their disposal, have managerial control of several people and substantial amounts of money and equipment. However, for most academics, the interaction with other universities or college employees is limited to a small group and even here the managerial control exercised by the academic is often not clear, as secretarial and administrative staff are subject to administrative as well as academic staff control. Nevertheless, can all academics be regarded as managers of people and resources, as well as particular forms of symbolic expression? A federal labor board ruling in the USA prevented academics in private universities and colleges being represented by labor unions on the grounds that they are effectively managers of their institutions. Certainly, if one takes the students as being a part of the institutional workforce, practically all academics could be seen as, in a sense, managers directing their efforts. However, as we have seen, partly through pressures from state and economy, management within the university has become increasingly concentrated in the hands of a central directorate.

If the form of teaching varies by discipline, even more so does the research enterprise. Despite variations between subjects and old and new universities, involvement in research is often taken to be the distinctive feature of the university academic in Australia, Canada and the UK. While many university managements emphasize the importance of teaching, it is research productivity and quality which is taken as the hallmark of the successful academic, department or university.

From the early 1980s, it has been shown that state institutions have not only sought to direct the research enterprise more closely towards the needs of industry, but have rewarded financially those universities and departments active and excellent in their research efforts. The UGC seemed to use, if clumsily and ambiguously, criteria relating to research productivity and quality (placing particular emphasis on research supported by the research councils) in implementing the 1981 government cuts. The Economic and Social Research Council penalized institutions with low PhD completion rates, and the Science and Engineering Research Council in 1987 disciplined 41 departments with low submission rates by removing studentships from their quota. The process of increasingly selective support for universities and departments with strong research records has proceeded through successive research exercises and funding allocations by the UGC and subsequent funding councils.

Monitoring and selective support of PhD students in particular institutions or departments is part of a more general move at the national and even international level to closer scrutiny of research productivity and relevance. There is an increasing tendency to concentrate resources in those areas deemed already to be strong.

This process can be seen as a result of three forces. First, there is the increasing power and cost of research, particularly scientific, technological and medical, which is well above general levels of inflation. Lyotard (1984: 44) puts this in a general and historical context when he writes:

> The need for proof becomes increasingly strong as the pragmatics of scientific knowledge replaces traditional knowledge or knowledge based on revelation. By the end of the Discourse on Method Descartes is already asking for laboratory funds. A new problem appears: devices that optimise the performance of the human body for the purpose of producing proof require additional expenditures – no money, no proof – and that means no verification of statements and no truth. The games of scientific language become the games of the rich, in which whoever is wealthiest has the best chance of being right. An equation between wealth, efficiency and truth is thus established.

Second, the state is driven by a programme to reduce public expenditure (except perhaps immediately before an election). This is masked by a free market rhetoric, and is accompanied by increased attempts to direct and control research. Lyotard catches something of the complexity of the forces deriving from the dominance of private corporate management which affect research activity and its funding:

> The prevailing corporate norms of work management spread to the applied science laboratory; hierarchy, centralised decision making, teamwork, calculation of individual and collective returns, the development of saleable programmes, market research and so on. Centres dedicated to 'pure' research suffer from this less but also receive less funding. (Lyotard 1984: 45)

The shaping of research and knowledge production by those exercising state or corporate power through their control of research can be stated quite sharply:

> Research funds are allocated by states, corporations and nationalised companies in accordance with this logic of power growth. Research sectors that are unable to argue that they contribute even indirectly to the optimization of the system's performance are abandoned by the flow of capital and doomed to senescence. The criterion of performance is explicitly invoked by the authorities to justify their refusal to sustain certain research centres. (Lyotard 1984: 47)

The conditions of academic work

When looking at the factors which affect academics in general – salaries, promotion, tenure provision, working conditions and managerial control – it must always be remembered that different disciplines and departments (and even apparently similar ones) have their own ideologies, discourses and sets of social relations among staff and students. So, for example, Thomas (1990) has shown that there are not only obvious differences between physics and English in terms of discipline and attractiveness to male and female students, but also significant differences between physics and physical science and English and communications studies taught in 'old' or 'new' universities. These differences extend to the conception of the discipline, the varying practices of teaching and research and, at a fundamental level, the different market situations of academics as lecturers, consultants and researchers, as well as the differing career prospects of the students they teach. Thus in a management school, it may be very difficult to attract lecturers at current university salaries in areas like law, accountancy or marketing, where much more can be earned outside the university. This of course affects the power position and bargaining strength of academics in these areas.

In the UK, a 1986 report by the PA international management and consulting group, commissioned jointly by the CVCP and AUT on behalf of Committee A (dealing with salary negotiations) to examine factors affecting the recruitment and retention of staff, shows some of these differences, but it also revealed remarkable uniformity in the expectation held by most staff interviewed of worsening conditions of salary, promotion opportunities, job security and tenure, overall workload, status, administrative work, working conditions and environment, and teaching duties and research facilities. Only opportunities for consultancy were seen to be improving.

In the 1989 UK salary award, we can see the pressures of state and market and how they reinforced managerial authority. One-seventh of the pay award was made at the discretion of local management for market reasons and to reward exceptional performance, but to qualify for funding a university had to commit itself to the introduction of selective payments in each of the professor and lecturer grades. While management may consult with the union, the ultimate decision about these discretionary rewards – whose distribution can be seen as divisive and controlling – rests with management. Subsequent salary negotiations have continued the pattern of discretionary rewards, direct state intervention and awards at or below the level of inflation, and a failure to reward increases in productivity.

If we turn now to contractual relations and tenure, we see developments which parallel the changes in the market situation of academics, but which also signal a perhaps more fundamental change in their position. The introduction of ever larger numbers of short-term contracts for lecturing as well as for research staff affects not only the staff so employed, but also the relationship with tenured staff and the overall cohesiveness of the academic body. Moves towards more flexible short-term contracts and a weakening of tenure bring universities and their workers more into line with current industrial and commercial practice. Contracts of employment and work conditions have become less distinctive in precisely those aspects most valued by academics and which attracted them to the work in the first place – that is, in the freedom to pursue research and excellence in conditions of security (PA Personnel Services 1986).

One could argue, as Lyotard does, that the temporary contract has become part of a very general development in social interactions well beyond the bounds of the work contract, extending to the professional, emotional, sexual, cultural, familial and political domains. Certainly, the 'temporary contract is favoured by the system due to its greater flexibility, lower costs, and the creative turmoil of its accompanying motivation, all these factors contribute to increased operability' (Lyotard 1984: 50).

In the case of academics, this means that universities are able to employ younger people at the bottom end of the lecturer scale, and the renewal of one's contract or the offer of a tenured position is dependent on proven performance, particularly in the research area, and unless one's performance is outstanding this could mean being replaced by a younger and cheaper academic labourer. There may of course be costs, as the emphasis on short-term research productivity may inhibit long-term scholarship and certainly pressurizes time-consuming commitments such as teaching, administration and pastoral duties. This is one of the areas which may cause conflict between tenured and non-tenured staff, thus enhancing managerial control.

The question of managerial control – or, as it has often been put recently, 'the right to manage' – is clearly at the centre of the state's moves to limit tenure, but this also can be related to a more general move within the commercial–industrial sphere, of which examples might include the strategies pursued by Michael Edwardes at British Leyland or Rupert Murdoch at the News International plant at Wapping. In university work, this has become a particular issue due to the highly labour-intensive nature of academic work and the pressure of government cuts from the early 1980s onward, which has meant that because of financial exigency and the need to rationalize teaching, managements in universities have been compelled (more or less willingly) to attempt to break existing tenure arrangements in order to dismiss staff for reasons other than 'good cause'. This meant that in the UK, at least some university managements welcomed proposals in July 1987, prior to the 1988 Education Reform Act, which threatened to 'ensure that [universities] have the power to terminate the appointments of their academic and academic-related staff for reasons of redundancy or financial exigency', thus limiting tenure arrangements. The DES also intended 'to add inefficiency to the category of "good cause" for dismissal' and to appoint commissioners to review and change relevant statutes of universities. It was proposed that existing procedures for dismissal (which usually are the prerogative of councils, or even, on appeal, of the senate and council acting together) would be replaced by a procedure whereby 'the vice chancellor or principal would decide on the dismissal or other penalty to be imposed on the member of staff'. There would be a right of appeal to a small board, chaired by a lawyer and consisting of persons appointed by council and persons nominated by representative staff. There would be no internal appeals procedure beyond this. These proposals substantially weakened tenure conditions for staff. They also strengthened managerial prerogative by including 'inefficiency' as a ground for dismissal. They increased the chief executive's power over dismissal and reduced the collective collegial authority of councils and senates as final appeal bodies.

These proposals and their enactment in the 1988 Education Reform Act produced considerable debate and criticism. The 1988 Act preserved existing arrangements for tenure for academic staff appointed before November 1987. This was, as described in Chapter 5, tested in a case at Aston University, when the Visitor ruled that the council of the university could not breach its own statutes and charter, and that the implied but unwritten power which the university's lawyers argued applied to make staff redundant at a time of financial need in terms of managerial interest did not apply. Although the position of existing, tenured unpromoted staff has been protected, university managements are increasingly appointing staff on short-term contracts whose position is not protected. University commissioners, appointed as a result of the 1988 Reform Act, have used their powers to change university charters so that any academic staff appointed or promoted after November 1987 may be dismissed on the ground of redundancy. Lord Justice Dillon, in a judgement in the Aston case, noted one aspect of the change in attitude towards academics' security of employment. Referring to the statute protecting academic tenure established at Aston in 1968, he said:

> These adopted the then view of academic independence. It was easy then to remember how academic staff had been treated in Nazi Germany . . . in the changed political climate and the changed financial policy towards the funding of the Universities, the fashionable watch cries now are economy and the managerial interest.
>
> (Pearce *et al.* 1989)

To return to Halsey and the condition of academics in the UK, one can set his account in a more political economy framework, which pays attention to the deep dynamics affecting the labour process of academics. However, his summary of the 'short term and real meaning to be attached to the decline of donnish dominion since the middle of the twentieth century', has been supported by a range of statistical sources and by the comments of academics on their situation not only in the UK but also in Australia and Canada:

> We have sadly portrayed deteriorating conditions of intellectual work. The autonomy of institutions has declined, salaries have fallen, chances of promotion have decreased. The dignity of academic people and their universities and polytechnics has been assailed from without by government and within by the corrosion of bureaucracy.
>
> Dons themselves have largely ceased to recommend the academic succession to their own students. They see themselves as an occupational group losing its long established privileges of tenure and self-government, pressed to dilute its tutorial methods, hampered in the control of syllabuses, and restricted with research ambitions by chronic shortage of funds – they are unloved by their political masters.
>
> (Halsey 1992: 268)

The question remains, why are they unloved by their political masters? As Wakeford and Wakeford pointed out with regard to state/university relations as long ago as 1974, 'The degree of integration of the contemporary university remains problematic and constantly subject to re-negotiation' (p. 184).

Australia, Canada and the UK, despite different political complexions of government, have all been affected by continuing economic difficulties in contrast to the relatively secure growth experienced in the 20–25 years after the end of the Second World War. This has had multiple interacting effects, but chief among them has been the pressure on the one hand to reduce public expenditure and on the other to improve the economic performance and competitiveness of business. This we have seen has had its effects on university finances, on mechanisms for control and accountability, and attempts to influence the direction of research and the provision of courses.

Just as important in the management of change both on and in the universities has been the shift in economic ideology to the celebration of the market and competition. Again this has not been simple, and while some factors support and amplify each other in their effects, others remain ambiguous, paradoxical or even contradictory. Thus at the same time as we have shown that there has been an increase in central direction and planning both from the state and in the university, there has been a greater ideological commitment to the operation of the market and to the virtues of competition. The institutional arrangements reflected and are framed by a changed language and discourse where references to managers, executives, quality, market and customers have come to dominate over language, which refers to knowledge, scholarship, teachers and students.

In conclusion, while the differences in economy, history, culture, and the forms of the state and politics between Australia, Canada and the UK remain important in themselves and shape the culture of universities in these countries, there are a number of common features which bear on academics and the management of universities. Two of the features that are common are embodied in the title 'Management and Change'. While it is not always clear that university managements are effectively managing change, the explicit reference to 'managers' in universities is a relatively new phenomenon, which has developed at a different pace in different institutions in the 1980s. That is not to say that universities have not always in some sense been managed, but the notion of a separate managerial function, the dilution of collegial authority and the explicit need to develop policy strategy and tactics to husband resources is relatively recent. This in part arises from two other common and interlinked features which have been explored here: first, the increased intervention of the state in the governance, control and even management of universities; and, second, the perceived increasing importance to the economy of the activities of the university in the provision of an educated and skilled workforce and the undertaking of useful and profitable research. These two features are linked by the assumption by the state, its politicians and functionaries, that they have a role in bending the purposes of the university to meet the needs of competitive capitalist enterprise.

This produces some paradoxes. In the UK, *laissez-faire*, market-oriented monetarists, in principle committed to the reduction of the powers of the state, find themselves involved in ever more intrusive expansions of state power into the domain of civil society in the name of improving the competitiveness of British industry. Then, on the other side of the world, an Australian Labor government coming from a social democratic, welfare state tradition is adopting an 'economic rationalist' policy and practice which celebrates market and economy. Indeed, one of the striking common features of the governance and management of higher education and universities has been the degree of parallel developments. In Australia and the UK, a binary system has been replaced by a unified system and a period of quite rapid expansion in the late 1980s and early 1990s has been subject to attempts by the state to reduce the pace of expansion on the twin grounds of public economy of resources and a questioning of the utility of the expansion for the private economy of competitive enterprise. Underlying these common features of structure and similarities of political programme lie yet more basic if unresolved questions of what *should* be the relationship of the universities to state and economy. These questions are reflected in the continuing debates within the university about the nature and purposes of teaching and research. This is related to the question of how the university should be governed. Should it be managed by a directorate along the lines of corporate enterprise? Are apparently archaic forms of collegial control in fact quite appropriate for an institution, where academics as professionals have to take responsibility not only for their own teaching and research but for providing an environment where these activities can flourish? And not only in the forms approved by the state, corporations or even students and citizens, but also in the awkward, critical and even subversive forms which remain true to the pursuit of truth for its own sake.

Appendix

Questions for vice-chancellors and senior administrators in Australia: Changes in higher education 1991

1. How has the development of a unitary system of higher education rather than a binary one affected your own institution?
2. Which other developments in the last 5 years do you think have been particularly significant for your own institution?
3. What are the specific pressures from the commonwealth?
4. What are the pressures from the state?
5. What are the pressures from industry and commerce?
6. In view of separation of teaching and research funding, how do you see your own institution competing?
7. What steps are you taking to encourage research productivity, e.g. reducing teaching hours for productive researchers?
8. Is there a significantly changing mix of teaching and research? How easy is it to move resources and staff to meet that?
9. Are you concerned about an ageing staff profile?
10. If so, what measures could be taken to remedy it? Are there funds for early retirement, enhanced mobility payments, funds for new staff?
11. How would you characterize your own role, e.g. academic leader, administrator, scholar, chief executive?
12. Do you feel that your role has changed in the last 5 years?

Questions for academic and senior administrators in Canadian universities: Economy and education – images and administration

1. What developments in the last 5 years do you think have been particularly significant for your own institution?
2. What are the specific pressures from the federal government?
3. What are the specific pressures from the provincial government?
4. What are the pressures from industry and commerce?
5. What strategies has the university/faculty undertaken to gain/maintain funding?
6. Are there any specific strategies relating to corporations and the market?
7. How important are they? Do they affect the pattern of teaching and research?

8. Are you concerned about an ageing staff profile? Are there measures being taken to remedy this?
9. How would you characterize your own role, e.g. academic leader, administrator, scholar, executive?
10. Do you feel that your role has changed in the last 5 years?
11. Do you feel that there is a clear pecking order in Canada/province? Where would you place your own institution?
12. How would you characterize competition and cooperation at an institutional level?

Questions for academics and senior administrators in UK universities and polytechnics: Management and change in higher education

1. What developments in the last 5 years do you think have been particularly significant for your own institution? (a) student numbers; (b) resources; (c) research.
2. What do you think will be the effect of the White Paper *Higher Education: A New Framework* published in May 1991 and resulting legislation?
3. What do you see as the main pressures coming from the UK government?
4. Are there any specific pressures from government or elsewhere relating to your situation in Scotland, Wales, Northern Ireland, England?
5. What are the pressures from industry and commerce?
6. Has the institution developed strategies relating to corporations and the market?
7. How important are they? Do they affect the pattern of teaching and research?
8. What strategies has the institution/faculty/school/department undertaken to gain/maintain funding?
9. Are you concerned about the effects of an ageing staff profile? Are there measures being taken relating to this?
10. How would you characterize your own role, e.g. academic leader, administrator, scholar, executive?
11. Do you feel your role has changed in the last 5 years?
12. Do you feel there is a clear pecking order of institutions in the UK/Scotland, Wales, Northern Ireland, England? Where would you place your own institution?
13. How would you characterize competition and cooperation at an institutional level?

References

Althusser, L. (1972). Ideology and ideological state apparatuses. In Cosin, B. (ed.), *Education, Structure and Society.* Harmondsworth: Penguin.

Alumni News (1991). *Planning in Higher Education.* Coleraine: University of Ulster.

Anderson, P. (1990). A culture in contraflow. *New Left Review,* 180: 41–80.

Association of University Teachers, Aston Branch (1989). *Staff–Student Ratios.* Circular. Birmingham: Aston AUT.

Association of University Teachers (1990). *Goodwill Under Stress: Morale in UK Universities.* London: AUT.

Aston University (1982). *Minutes of Aston University Council,* 20 October. Birmingham: Aston University.

Aston University (1985). *Planning for the Late 1980s.* Birmingham: Aston University.

Australian Confederation of Trades Unions/Trades Unions Development Council (1987). *Australia Reconstructed: A Report by the Mission Members to the ACTU and TDC.* Canberra: Australian Government Publishing Service.

Bachrach, P. and Baratz, M.S. (1962). The two faces of power. *American Political Science Review,* 56: 947–52.

Bagley, E. (1910). *The Borough Polytechnic Institute: Its Origins and Development* (with an introduction by Sidney Webb). London: Elliot Stock.

Baldridge, J. (1971). *Power and Conflict in the University.* New York: John Wiley.

Baldridge, J., Curtis, D., Ecker, G. and Riley, G. (1978). *Policy Making and Effective Leadership.* San Francisco, CA: Jossey-Bass.

Barnard, C.(1956). *The Functions of the Executive.* Cambridge, MA: Harvard University Press.

Bartlett, R. (1993). *The Making of Europe.* Harmondsworth: Penguin.

Becher, T. and Kogan, M. (1992). *Process and Structure in Higher Education.* London: Routledge.

Becher, T. *et al.* (1977). *Systems of Higher Education: United Kingdom.* London: International Council for Educational Development.

Becker, H. (1961). *The Outsiders.* New York: Free Press.

Bertramsen, R., Thomson, J. and Torfing, J. (1991). *State, Economy and Society.* London: Unwin Hyman.

Blumer, H. (1969). *Symbolic Interaction: Perspectives and Method.* Englewood Cliffs, NJ: Prentice-Hall.

Bowe, R., Gerwitz, S. and Ball, S. (1992). *Captured by the Discourse? Issues and Concerns in Researching 'Parental Choice'.* Centre for Educational Studies Working Paper, Kings College, London.

Bowles, S. and Gintis, H. (1976). *Schooling in Capitalist America: Educational Reform and the Contradictions of Economic Life.* New York: Basic Books.

Braverman, H. (1974). *Labor and Monopoly Capitalism.* New York: Monthly Review Press.

Brittain, S. (1988). *Economic Consequences of Democracy.* Aldershot: Wildewood House.

Brooksman, J. (1993). Breaking the shackles will free quality control. *Times Higher Education Supplement,* 1 October, p. 7.

Brown, D., Cozales, P. and Jasmin, G. (eds) (1992). *Higher Education in Federal Systems.* Kingston, Ontario: Institute of Intergovernmental Relations.

Browne-Wilkinson, N. (1989). *In the Matter of the University of Aston in Birmingham.* London: Royal Courts of Justice.

Brunsson, N. (1982). The irrationality of action and action rationality: Decisions, ideologies and organizational actions. *Journal of Management Studies,* 19(1): 29–44.

Buckbinder, H. and Newson, J. (1988). *The University Means Business.* Toronto: Garamond Press.

Burawoy, M. (1978). *Manufacturing Consent.* Chicago, IL: University of Chicago Press.

Cameron, D. (1992). Higher education in federal systems in Canada. In Brown, D., Cozales, P. and Jasmin, G. (eds), *Higher Education in Federal Systems.* Kingston, Ontario: Institute of Intergovernmental Relations.

Carroll, D. and Cross, G. (1990). *University Stress Survey.* Research Report, School of Psychology, University of Birmingham.

Carspecken, P. (1991). *Community Schooling and the Nature of Power: The Battle for Croxteth Comprehensive.* London: Routledge.

Castells, M. (1978). *City Class and Power.* London: Macmillan.

Cawson, A. (1986). *Corporatism and Political Theory.* Oxford: Basil Blackwell.

Child, J. (1983). A price to pay: Professionalism and work organisation. *Sociology,* 17(1): 63–78.

Churchill, D. (1993). M.B.A.s: The brave new world. *The Observer,* 25 April, p. 39.

Clark, B. (1983). *The Higher Education System.* Berkeley, CA: University of California Press.

Cockburn, C. (1977). *The Local State.* London: Pluto.

Cohen, M. and March, J. (1974). *Leadership and Ambiguity.* New York: McGraw Hill.

Cohen, M., March, J. and Olsen, J. (1972). A garbage can model of organizational choice. *Adminstrative Science Quarterly,* 17(1): 1–25.

Collins, H. (1985). Political ideology in Australia: The distinctiveness of a Benthamite society. In Graubord, S.K. (ed.), *Australia: The Daedalus Symposium.* Sydney: Angus and Robertson.

Coopers and Lybrand (1993). *Research Accountability.* Bristol: Higher Education Funding Council.

Crawford, F. (1984). 'You and the new Aston'. Address to staff, Aston University, Birmingham.

Crawford, F. (1989). 'Aston University Council decisions'. Memo to Staff, Aston University, Birmingham.

Crawford, F. (1992). 'Vision and mission statement'. Memo to staff, Aston University, Birmingham.

Cuthbert, R. (1984). *The Management Process.* Block 3, Part 2 E324. Milton Keynes: Open University Press.

Dahl, R. (1961). *Who Governs? Demographic Power in an American City.* London: Yale University Press.

Dawkins, J. (1987a). The challenges for higher education in Australia. *Ministerial Statement,* 22 September, Canberra, AGPS.
Dawkins, J. (1987b). Higher education: A policy discussion paper. *The Green Paper,* December, Canberra, AGPS.
Dawkins, J. (1988a). Higher education: A policy statement. *The White Paper,* July, Canberra, AGPS.
Dawkins, J. (1988b). *A New Committment to Higher Education.* Canberra: AGPS.
Dawkins, J. (1988c). *Higher Education Funding for the 1989–91 Triennium.* Canberra: AGPS.
Debray, R. (1981). *Teachers, Writers, Celebrities.* London: Verso.
Department of Education (1987). *Higher Education: Meeting the Challenge.* London: HMSO.
Department of Education (1991). *Education and Training for the 21st Century.* Cmnd. 1536. London: HMSO.
Department for Education (1993a). *The Charter for Higher Education.* London: HMSO.
Department for Education (1993b). *Realising Our Potential: A Strategy for Science, Engineering and Technology.* Cmnd. 2250. London: HMSO.
Department of Employment, Education and Training: Higher Education Division (1993). *National Report on Australia's Higher Education Sector.* Canberra: AGPS.
Drucker, P. (1959). Long-range planning: Challenge to management science. *Management Science,* 5(3): 238–49.
Durkheim, E. (1933). *The Division of Labour in Society.* Glencoe, IL: Free Press.
Edwards, R. (1979). *Contested Terrain.* New York: Basic Books.
Eggleston, F. (1953). The Australian nation. In Caiger, G. (ed.), *The Australian Way of Life.* London: Heineman.
Enderud, H. (1977). *Four Faces of Leadership in an Academic Organization.* Copenhagen: Nyt Nordisk, Forlag Arnold Busck.
Fayol, H. (1949). *General and Industrial Management.* London: Pitman Press.
Fielden, J. and Lockwood, G. (1973). *Planning and Management in Universities: A Study of British Universities.* London: Chatto and Windus.
Flowers, L. (1993a). *The Review of the Academic Year: Interim Report.* Committee of Enquiry into the Organisation of the Academic Year. Bristol: Higher Education Funding Council.
Flowers, L. (1993b). *The Review of the Academic Year: Final Report.* Committee of Enquiry into the Organisation of the Academic Year. Bristol: Higher Education Funding Council.
Fores, M. and Glover, I. (1981). The British disease: Professionalism. *Times Higher Education Supplement,* 24 February.
Friedman, M. (1962). *Capitalism and Freedom.* Chicago, IL: University of Chicago Press.
Galbraith, J. (1974). *The New Industrial State.* Harmondsworth: Penguin.
Gavin, D. (1992) Student Flows, Personal Communication. Londonderry: University of Ulster.
Gerth, H. and Mills, C. (1947). *Essays from Max Weber.* London: Routledge and Kegan Paul.
Giddens, A. (1985). *The Nation State and Violence.* Cambridge: Polity Press.
Giddens, A. (1990). *The Consequences of Modernity.* Stanford, CA: Stanford University Press.
Ginsberg, M. *et al.* (1980). Teachers' conception of professionalism and trades unionism: An ideological analysis. In Woods, P. (ed.), *Teachers' Strategies: Explorations in the Sociology of the School.* London: Croom Helm.

Grace, G. (1991). Welfare labourism and the New Right: The struggle in New Zealand's education policy. Paper presented to the *Education Reform Act (1988) Network,* Warwick, November.

Gramsci, A. (1971). *Selections from the Prison Notebooks.* London: Lawrence and Wishart.

Gray, R. (1992). History, Marxism and theory. In Kay, H.J. and McLelland, K. (eds), *E.P. Thompson: Critical Perspectives.* Cambridge: Polity Press.

Gregor, A.D. (1991). *The Universities of Canada Commonwealth Universities Yearbook.* 1013–26 London: Association of Commonwealth Universities.

Grosz, E. (1990). Contemporary theories of power and subjectivity. In Gunew, S. (ed.), *Feminist Knowledge: Critique and Construct.* London: Routledge.

Habermas, J. (1975). *Legitimation Crisis.* New York: Beacon Press.

Hall, S. (1993). Thatcherism today. *New Statesman,* 20 December.

Halsey, A. (1992). *The Decline of Donnish Dominion.* Oxford: Clarendon Press.

Harrison, M. (1991). Crisis deepens on British campuses. *The Observer,* 10 November.

Harvey, C. (1988). *Retrenchment Strategies in Two Canadian Universities: A Political Analysis.* Research Paper 88–08, Montreal, McGill University.

Hayek, F.A. (1949). *Individualism and Economic Order.* London: Routledge and Kegan Paul.

Hayek, F.A. (1976). *The Constitution of Liberty.* London: Routledge and Kegan Paul.

Hayek, F.A. (1979). *Law, Legislation and Liberty, Vol. 3: The Political Order of a Free People.* London: Routledge and Kegan Paul.

Held, D. (1984). Power and legitimacy in contemporary Britain. In McLennan, G., Held, D. and Hall, S., *State and Society in Contemporary Britain.* Cambridge: Polity Press.

Herzberg, F. (1959). *The Motivation to Work.* New York: John Wiley.

Hickox, M.F. (1986). Has there been a British intelligentsia? *British Journal of Sociology,* XXXVII(2): 260–8.

Higher Education Funding Council/Coopers and Lybrand (1993). *Research Accountability.* Bristol: HEFC.

Holton, R.J. (1992). *Economy and Society.* London: Routledge.

Hudson, H. *et al.* (1986). *Review of Efficiency and Effectiveness in Higher Education.* Canberra: Commonwealth Tertiary Education Commission.

Ignatieff, M. (1992). Collision course with democracy. *The Observer,* 20 October, p. 21.

Jackson, R. (1993). Personal view. *Times Higher Education Supplement,* 10 December, p. 13.

Jarrat, A. (1985). *Report of the Steering Committee for Efficiency Studies in Universities.* London: Committee of Vice-Chancellors and Principals.

Jessop, B. (1985). *Nios Poulantzas: Marxist Theory and Political Strategy.* London: Macmillan.

Karmel, P. (1988). The role of central government in Higher Education. *Higher Education Quarterly,* 42(2): 121–33.

Kennedy, P.M. (1989). *The Rise and Fall of the Great Powers.* London: Unwin Hyman.

Kennedy, P.M. (1993). *Preparing for the Twentieth Century.* London: Harper/Collins.

Kerr, C. (1966). *The Uses of the University.* Cambridge, MA: Harvard University Press.

Kogan, M. and Kogan, D. (1983). *The Attack on Higher Education.* London: Kogan Page.

Laclau, E. and Mouffe, C. (1985). *Hegemony and Socialist Strategy.* London: Verso.

Landman, M. and Ozga, J. (1992). Democracy and participation in mass higher education: A case of equal opportunities? Paper presented to the *British Educational Research Association Conference,* Stirling University, September.

Larson, M. (1977). *The Rise of Professionalism.* Berkeley, CA: University of California Press.

Laurens, R. (1990). University management: Tensions in a changing environment. *Journal of Tertiary Educational Administration,* 12(1): 25–42.

Lawn, M. and Ozga, J. (1981). *Teachers, Professionalism and Class.* Lewes: Falmer Press.

Littler, C. and Salaman, G. (1982). Braverman and beyond: Recent theories of the labour process. *Sociology,* 16(2): 251–69.

Lockwood, G. and Davies, J. (1985). *Universities: The Management Challenge.* Windsor: SRHE/NFER Nelson.

Lodge, D. (1975). *Changing Places.* Harmondsworth: Penguin.

Lodge, D. (1984). *Small World.* Harmondsworth: Penguin.

Lodge, D. (1988). *Nice Work.* Harmondsworth: Penguin.

Lukes, S. (1974). *Power: A Radical View.* London: Macmillan.

Lukes, S. (1979). Power and authority. In Bottomore, T. and Nisbet, R. (eds), *A History of Sociological Analysis.* London: Heinemann.

Lyotard, J.F. (1984). *The Post-modern Condition: A Report on Knowledge.* Manchester: Manchester University Press.

Mannheim, K. (1956). *Essays on the Sociology of Culture.* London: Routledge and Kegan Paul.

March, J. and Simon, H. (1985). *Organizations.* New York: John Wiley.

Marcuse, H. (1968). *One-Dimensional Man.* London: Routledge and Kegan Paul.

Marginson, S. (1990). Privatisation and commercialisation of Australian education. Paper presented to the *Australian Association for Research in Education Annual Conference,* Sydney, December.

Marginson, S. (1993). *Education and Public Policy in Australia.* Melbourne: Cambridge University Press.

Marshall, C. and Marshall, N. (1992). *Federalism and Public Policy.* Canberra: Canberra Australian National University.

Marx, K. (1976). *Capital.* Harmondsworth: Penguin.

Maslen, G. (1993a). Cash switch helps Australian urban regeneration. *Times Higher Education Supplement,* 15 January, p. 1.

Maslen, G. (1993b). Strike stand against more power to sack. *Times Higher Education Supplement,* 15 October, p. 9.

Maslen, G. (1994). Universities hit technical hitch. *Times Higher Education Supplement,* 14 January, p. 6.

Maslow, A. (1954). *Motivation and Personality.* New York: Harper.

Mead, G. (1934). *Mind, Self and Society.* Chicago, IL: University of Chicago Press.

Meiksins, R. (1985). Beyond the boundary question. *New Left Review,* 157: 101–20.

Middlemas, K. (1986). *Power, Competition and the State, Vol. 1: Britain in Search of Balance.* Basingstoke: Macmillan.

Middlemas, K. (1990). *Power, Competition and the State, Vol. 2: Threats to the Post-War Settlement.* Basingstoke: Macmillan.

Miller, H. (1985). The local state and teachers. In Barton, L. and Walker, S. (eds), *Education and Social Change.* Beckenham: Croom Helm.

Miller, H. (1989). Memo to AUT members re: UGC visit. AUT, Aston University, Birmingham.

Miller, H. (1991a). The academic labour process. In Smith, C. and Willmott, H. (eds), *White Collar Work: The Non-manual Labour Process.* Basingstoke: Macmillan.

Miller, H. (1991b). Corporate managerialism in higher education. Paper presented to the *Australian Sociological Association Annual Conference,* Perth, December.

Miller, H. (1993). The state of the academic profession. *The Australian Universities' Review*, 35(2): 25–32.

Miller, H. and Wheeler, S. (1989). Changing patterns of power in higher education: A case study. Paper presented to the *Ethnography and Educational Reform Conference*, Warwick, September.

Milliband, R. (1969). *The State in Capitalist Society*. London: Quartet.

Morris, N. (1989). Union claims victory on Aston staff cuts. *Birmingham Post*, 3 August, p. 6.

Mulhern, F. (1981). Introduction. In Debray, R., *Teachers, Writers, Celebrities*. London: Verso.

Murphy, J. (1993). A degree of waste: The economic benefits of educational expansion. *Oxford Review of Education*, 19(1): 9–31.

Newman, J. (1910). *The Idea of a University*. London: Longman.

O'Connor, J. (1974). *The Fiscal Crisis of the State*. Oxford: Basil Blackwell.

O'Connor, J. (1987). *The Meaning of Crisis: A Theoretical Introduction*. Oxford: Basil Blackwell.

Offe, C. (1976). The theory of the capitalist state and the problem of policy formulation. In Lindberg, L., Alford, R., Crouch, C. and Offe, C. (eds), *Stress and Contradiction in Modern Capitalism*. New York: Heath.

Palfreyman, D. (1988). The Warwick way: A case study of innovation and entrepreneurship within a university context. MBA dissertation, University of Aston, Birmingham.

Parsons, T. (1951). *The Social System*. London: Routledge and Kegan Paul.

Parsons, T. and Smelser, N. (1956). *Economy and Society*. London: Routledge and Kegan Paul.

Patel, K. (1993). European framework research budgets. *Times Higher Education Supplement*, 3 December.

Pearce, G. *et al.* (1989). Aston University Court of Appeal, 23 June, London.

PA Personnel Services (1986). *Report on Factors Affecting Recruitment and Retention of Non-clinical Academic Staff*. London: University Academic Salary Committee A.

Pedersen, K. (1991). University autonomy (a Canadian perspective). Paper presented to the *Conference of Executive Heads: The Association of Commonwealth Universities*, New Delhi, January.

Polanyi, K. (1977). *The Livelihood of Man*. New York: Academic Press.

Porteous, J. (1990). *Landscapes of the Mind: Worlds of Sense and Metaphor*. Toronto: University of Toronto Press.

Poulantzas, N. (1969). The problem of the capitalist state. *New Left Review*, 58: 67–78.

Poulantzas, N. (1973). *Political Power and Social Classes*. London: New Left Books.

Pusey, M. (1991). *Economic Rationalism in Canberra: A Nation-building State Changes its Mind*. Cambridge: Cambridge University Press.

Richmond, M. (1993). Mission in the market place. *Times Higher Education Supplement*, 2 July, p. 9.

Rex, J. (1961). *Key Problems in Sociological Theory*. London: Routledge and Kegan Paul.

Robbins Report (1963). *Report of the Committee on Higher Education*. Cmnd. 2154. London: HMSO.

Robertson, S. and Woock, R. (1989). Towards a social analysis of Australian education. Paper presented to the *17th World Congress of Comparative Education*, Montreal, June.

Robinson, E. (1968). *The New Polytechnics: The People's Universities.* Harmondsworth: Penguin.

Rosecrance, R. (1964). The radical culture of Australia. In Hartz, L. (ed.), *The Founding of New Societies.* New York: Harcourt Brace.

Rothblatt, S. (1993). Science Policy. *Times Higher Education Supplement,* 14 October, p. 14.

Russell, C. (1993). *Academic Freedom.* London: Routledge.

Samut, R. (1986). The management of universities in a period of rapid change: Comparative case studies. MPhil dissertation, University of Aston, Birmingham.

Scott, P. (1984). *The Crisis of the Universities.* London: Croom Helm.

Scott, P. (1990). *Knowledge and Nation.* Edinburgh: Edinburgh University Press.

Sheffield, G. (1990). A comparative case study of innovation entrepreneurship and the management of change in two West Midland universities. MBA dissertation, University of Aston, Birmingham.

Simon, B. (1991). *Education and the Social Order.* London: Lawrence and Wishart.

Skidelsky, R. (1983). *John Maynard Keynes,* Vol. 1. London: Macmillan.

Skidelsky, R. (1992). *John Maynard Keynes,* Vol. 2. London: Macmillan.

Smart, D. (1989). The Dawkins 'reconstruction' of higher education in Australia. Paper presented to the *American Education Research Association Annual Meeting,* San Francisco, CA, March.

Smith, A. (1976). *An Enquiry into the Nature and Causes of the Wealth of Nations.* Oxford: Oxford University Press.

Smith, C. and Willmott, H. (1991). The new middle class and the labour process. In Smith, C. and Willmott, H. (eds), *White Collar Work: The Non-manual Labour Process.* Basingstoke: Macmillan.

Smith, D. (1990). *Capitalist Democracy on Trial: The Transatlantic Debate from Tocqueville to the Present.* London: Routledge.

Smyth, J. (1991). Theories of the state and recent policy reforms in Australian higher education. *Discourse,* 11(2): 48–69.

Storey, J. and Sissons, K. (1993). *Managing Human Resources and Industrial Relations.* Buckingham: Open University Press.

Stretton, H. (1987). *Political Essays.* Melbourne: Georgian House.

Tapper, T. and Salter, B. (1992). *Oxford, Cambridge and the Changing Idea of the University: The Challenge to Donnish Domination.* Buckingham: Open University Press.

Teacher, D.C.B. (1990). Trans-binary amalgamations in Australia: A college perspective. *Higher Education Review,* 23(1): 40–52.

Thomas, K. (1990). *Gender and Subject.* Buckingham: Open University Press.

Thompson, D. (1983). *The Nature of Work.* London: Macmillan.

Thompson, E.P. (ed.) (1970). *Warwick University Ltd: Industry, Management and the Universities.* Harmondsworth: Penguin.

Thompson, E.P. (1993). *Customs in Common.* London: Routledge and Kegan Paul.

Thompson, G.I. (1984). Rolling back the state? Economic intervention 1975–82. In McLennnan, G., Held, D. and Hall, S. (eds), *State and Society in Contemporary Britain,* Cambridge: Polity Press.

Touche Ross (1992). *A Happy Marriage.* London: Deloitte Touche Tohmatsu International.

Toyne, P. (1991). Appropriate Structures for Higher Education Institutions. Paper presented to *International Seminar on Management in Universities*: British Council, Brighton, July.

Trow, M. (1983). Defining the issues in university–government relations. *Studies in Higher Education*, 8(2): 115–28.

Trow, M. (1993). The business of learning. *The Times Higher*, 8 October, pp. 20–1.

Trow, M. and Halsey, A. (1971). *The British Academic.* Cambridge, MA: Harvard University Press.

University Grants Committee (1988). *Report of the Visiting Party to Aston University Council.* London: UGC.

Waldegrave Report (1993). *Realising Our Potential: A Strategy for Science, Engineering and Technology.* Cmnd. 2250. London: HMSO.

Walford, G. (1987). *Restructuring Universities: Politics and Power in the Management of Change.* Beckenham: Croom Helm.

Wakeford, F. and Wakeford, J. (1974). Universities and the study of elites. In Giddens, A. and Stanworth, P. (eds), *Elites and Power in British Society.* Cambridge: Cambridge University Press.

Wallerstein, I. (1974). *The Modern World System.* New York: Academic Press.

Wallerstein, I. (1979). *The Capitalist World Economy.* Cambridge: Cambridge University Press.

Weber, M. (1947). *The Theory of Social and Economic Organizations.* New York: Free Press.

Weber, M. (1948). Science as a vocation. In Gerth, H. and Mills, C.W. (eds), *From Max Weber: Essays In Sociology.* London: Routledge and Kegan Paul.

Weber, M. (1978). *Economy and Society*, 2 vols. Berkeley, CA: University of California Press.

Wheeler, S. and Birtle, J. (1993). *A Handbook for Personal Tutors.* Buckingham: Open University Press.

Williams, G. (1992). *Changing Patterns of Finance in Higher Education.* Buckingham: Open University Press/SRHE.

Williams, R. (1979). *Politics and Letters: Interviews with New Left Review.* London: Verso.

Williams, R. (1985). *Towards 2000.* Harmondsworth: Penguin.

Woods, D. (1983). *Sociology and the School.* London: Routledge and Kegan Paul.

Woods, P. (1980). *Teachers' Strategies: Explorations in the Sociology of the School.* London: Croom Helm.

Wilson, T. (1991). The proletarianisation of academic labour. *Industrial Relations Journal*, 22(4): 250–62.

Yeatman, A. (1990). *Bureaucrats, Technocrats, Femocrats: Essays on the Contemporary Australian State.* Sydney: Allen and Unwin.

Index

The Society for Research into Higher Education

The Society for Research into Higher Education exists to stimulate and co-ordinate research into all aspects of higher education. It aims to improve the quality of higher education through the encouragement of debate and publication on issues of policy, on the organization and management of higher education institutions, and on the curriculum and teaching methods.

The Society's income is derived from subscriptions, sales of its books and journals, conference fees and grants. It receives no subsidies, and is wholly independent. Its individual members include teachers, researchers, managers and students. Its corporate members are institutions of higher education, research institutes, professional, industrial and governmental bodies. Members are not only from the UK, but from elsewhere in Europe, from America, Canada and Australasia, and it regards its international work as amongst its most important activities.

Under the imprint *SRHE & Open University Press*, the Society is a specialist publisher of research, having some 45 titles in print. The Editorial Board of the Society's Imprint seeks authoritative research or study in the above fields. It offers competitive royalties, a highly recognizable format in both hardback and paperback and the world-wide reputation of the Open University Press.

The Society also publishes *Studies in Higher Education* (three times a year), which is mainly concerned with academic issues, *Higher Education Quarterly* (formerly *Universities Quarterly*), mainly concerned with policy issues, *Research into Higher Education Abstracts* (three times a year), and *SRHE News* (four times a year).

The Society holds a major annual conference in December, jointly with an institution of higher education. In 1991, the topic was 'Research and Higher Education in Europe', with the University of Leicester. In 1992, it was 'Learning to Effect' with Nottingham Trent University, and in 1993, 'Governments and the Higher Education Curriculum: Evolving Partnerships' at the University of Sussex in Brighton. Future conferences include in 1994, 'The Student Experience' at the University of York.

The Society's committees, study groups and branches are run by the members. The groups at present include:

Teacher Education Study Group
Continuing Education Group
Staff Development Group
Excellence in Teaching and Learning

Benefits to members

Individual

Individual members receive:

- *SRHE News*, the Society's publications list, conference details and other material included in mailings.
- Greatly reduced rates for *Studies in Higher Education* and *Higher Education Quarterly.*
- A 35% discount on all Open University Press & SRHE publications.
- Free copies of the Precedings – commissioned papers on the theme of the Annual Conference.
- Free copies of *Research into Higher Education Abstracts.*
- Reduced rates for conferences.
- Extensive contacts and scope for facilitating initiatives.
- Reduced reciprocal memberships.

Corporate

Corporate members receive:

- All benefits of individual members, plus
- Free copies of *Studies in Higher Education.*
- Unlimited copies of the Society's publications at reduced rates.
- Special rates for its members, e.g. to the Annual Conference.

Membership details: SRHE, 334–354 Gray's Inn Road, London, WCIX 8BP, UK, Tel: 071 837 7880
Catalogue: SRHE & Open University Press, Celtic Court, 22 Ballmoor, Buckingham MK 18 IXW Tel: (0280) 823388